MW01200593

THE SAVILE ROW SUIT

THE ART OF BESPOKE TAILORING

PATRICK GRANT

gestalten

For all the bangers, clappers and codgers
I've had the privilege of working with
these past two decades.

CONTENTS

FOREWORD

THE LAST, and only definitive, bespoke tailoring manual was *The Modern Tailor, Outfitter and Clothier* by AS Bridgland, published in 1928 by *Tailor & Cutter* magazine, the trade bible of the tailoring industry. It was updated on a number of occasions, its fourth and final edition published in 1949. In its three hardback volumes it outlined the processes of both bespoke tailoring and cutting and included an overview of all aspects of the trade, from how to cut Inverness capes to how to build a wholesale business. In the 75 years since it was last published very little has changed in the methods used by bespoke tailors, but the instructions in *The Modern Tailor* are scant at best and require a high degree of existing knowledge for them to be in any way useful. Making trousers was covered in just 12 small pages. It was certainly not a comprehensive record of the art of bespoke tailoring, nor a usable manual for the non-professional.

I am often asked to recommend a book on bespoke, but today complete copies of *The Modern Tailor* are as rare as hen's teeth, and there is no other manual in existence that details the unique processes employed by tailors working on Savile Row. I think such a book is important, both as a detailed historical record of a craft that is globally revered and as a means of allowing those outside our small community to make tailored clothes to the standards practised by London's bespoke makers.

In this book I have sought, with the help of my very learned collaborators, to set out a definitive text detailing the method of production for the three main tailored garments produced on Savile Row: the coat, waistcoat, and trousers, following the methods used by three Savile Row bespoke tailors with whom I have had the pleasure of working for almost 50 years combined. I have also detailed the method for producing a handmade shirt, following the method of one of the best shirt makers on Jermyn Street – and indeed the world. We document their specific personal methods, not a universal method, because none such exists. We have attempted to include every single detail of their process and to illustrate each step where necessary, because an unambiguous account of their skilled practice is essential for the historical record. I know many people with some knowledge of sewing who will take pleasure in following the steps and making clothes for themselves in the Savile Row or Jermyn Street method. I hope that for the reader who has no interest in sewing, this book will clearly demonstrate, through its painstaking detail, why a Savile Row garment is as good, and as expensive, as it is. I also wish, by celebrating a few, to celebrate all of the craftsmen and women who work there.

I love the world that sits behind the curtains of Savile Row – the people and the workrooms, the practices and idiosyncrasies, that make the street so special. I have attempted to paint a picture of this facet of Savile Row, which is so seldom written about in any great detail and certainly features very sparsely in the many wonderful books written about the street in recent years. I have also attempted to describe the fascinating broader community of cloth makers and merchants without whom the tailoring community would not exist. All are wonderful and unique.

I have to extend the biggest thank you to Riki Brockman, who has written the technical instructions for the trousers, waistcoat and coat tailoring sections in this book. I am confident no one has ever created a better or more comprehensive Savile Row methodology, and knowing the difficulty, I would recommend no one attempt to do so ever again. Riki is a very fine cutter;

during his time with Gieves & Hawkes he won the prestigious Golden Shears award, the Oscars of the Savile Row apprentice world, and was once described by *GQ* as 'the future of Savile Row'. But more than his skill it is his infectious positivity that sets Riki apart. He is one of those rare characters within the Savile Row community that no one has ever had a bad word for. He now runs his own bespoke tailoring house, Solomon Browne, from a studio in Margate that he shares with Rachel Alice Smith whose bespoke coat-making method is documented later. He also transcribed the methods used by trouser maker Chris Ktori, and waistcoat maker Felicity Hamacher. All three have made both for Norton & Sons and for me personally over many years. I thank them for giving their time and for their help reading and correcting the texts. I must also thank Lizzie Willett, Jacquie Grant, Kath Muir and Sam Wakely of Emma Willis for patiently showing me their shirt-making method, and to Emma for generously letting me invade her beautiful workroom.

Savile Row is a very special place. It has been one of my life's great privileges to have had a small part to play in its long and fascinating history. •

A LIFE IN CLOTHES

A personal reminiscence on suits, bespoke tailoring
on Savile Row and Norton & Sons

Even as a very young child I had strongly held opinions about what I would and would not wear. By the time I reached my teens, I had grown tall enough to wear my father's suits, tailored in the 1960s by an Edinburgh firm called Thompson. They were sharply cut, with slim trousers and lapels, and they felt different to the other clothes I was wearing at the time. Back then, I didn't know enough to understand why, but today I know very well the pleasure of wearing hand-tailored clothes made from cloth of exceptional quality.

My first new suit was from Marks & Spencer; I was 14 and needed a dark formal outfit to wear to chapel on Sundays. The cloth was a pure wool, charcoal herringbone with a blue over-stripe; it was cut as a two-show-three double-breasted and its label proudly declared that it was made in Britain. I wore it at least once a week for four years and it looked as good when I finished school as the day it was bought.

I'm not sure at what age I first became aware of Savile Row, but I can't remember a time when I wasn't. For any young man growing up in Britain, a Savile Row suit was, and still is, the Holy Grail of men's clothing. These were the suits worn by film stars, rock stars, and fictional

heroes – by the most stylish, most famous, most notorious men. It has a legendary, almost mythical status. But as a regular young man from a middle-class family, owning even one Savile Row suit, unless it was second-hand, was not something I ever imagined for myself.

When I first started earning money of my own, I spent it all on clothes. My first designer suit was a navy single-breasted two-button from Paul Smith. I added suits from Gucci during the Tom Ford era – a grey sharkskin and a navy plain weave. I had a slim-cut, dark navy, three-button from Prada; a beige sateen double-breasted from Jil Sander; and a heavy black barathea number from Helmut Lang. I loved these suits and felt special when I wore them. I couldn't imagine for a moment how other clothes could be any better than these. And then, at age 33, I had my first suit made on Savile Row, and I couldn't wear any of my designer ones ever again.

Norton & Sons, at number 16 Savile Row, was established in 1821. During its long history it has tailored to emperors, kings, and presidents, but in 2005 the firm found itself 'on its uppers'. It was through a series of chance events that I came to know it was for sale, and through a lot of hard work, a certain amount of persuasiveness, and some small amount of risk, I became the youngest 'guvnor' on Savile Row.

I could not represent this almost two-centuries-old bespoke tailor in off-the-peg Prada, so with the help of our Head Cutter, John, I selected the cloth and decided on the style and details of my first bespoke suit. It felt like a moment of great significance, and I recall vividly the excitement and pleasure I felt throughout the process. With the greatest consideration, I selected a 12 oz charcoal herringbone worsted from Smith & Co (number 83201) and a dark burgundy ermazine-taffeta lining from Bernstein & Banleys. John cut it in a two-button single-breasted style, with straight jetted pockets and flaps, and flat-fronted trousers with an 18-inch bottom.

This first bespoke suit felt otherworldly, and my formerly beloved designer suits now felt like poor facsimiles – lifeless, shapeless, clumsy. But it wasn't just how this suit looked that made it special: it felt special because of the people and process that created it.

On Savile Row we make coats and overcoats, not jackets and coats, and these are made by coat makers. Wally Pattenden had been a coat maker at Norton & Sons since the mid-seventies, commuting in from Essex on a very early train each day. He had served his apprenticeship at H Huntsman & Sons under the great Colin Hammick before joining Norton. He worked for the firm at their previous address around the corner in two large buildings on Conduit Street, where he served under the highly regarded but somewhat tyrannical Head Cutter, John Granger, who had bought the firm from the Norton family in the sixties. Wally worked in our small workroom behind the shop at 16 Savile Row, where I spent much of my time during my early years performing the duties of undercutter, trotter, trimmer, and tea boy. Wally liked his tea so strong you could almost stand a spoon up in it, and as a result, his mug was tar black inside. Once, in a moment of overzealous cleanliness, I took the bleach to it, and Wally got the hump with me until his mug had regained its original oily patina.

I gazed in awe as Wally constructed my coat. I had seen several made in the Norton workshop but had never studied the process so closely. I watched transfixed as he canvassed the foreparts and the collar, steaming and moulding the pieces into human form over his ancient tailor's ham (the tightly stuffed pillow that is used as a curved mould for pressing curved parts of clothing). He sewed the main seams on our beloved 1960s Brother sewing machine, its throaty rattle providing the backing track to the making process. Later Wally taught me to sew a coat following his method – the only method I ever learned.

The trousers for my first suit were tailored by Chris Ktori. Chris was and remains to this day our most prolific and finest trouser maker. I would go back and forth every day to his small workshop at the top of a very steep flight of stairs behind an unprepossessing door on Kingly Street in Soho (between Regent Street and Carnaby Street), dropping off and picking up jobs. Apart from a six-week spell in the summer when he'd disappear to Cyprus to sit on the beach and swim in the sea, there was never a time when he was not in his workroom – where, incidentally, no one can enter without being offered an orange, kept in a small fridge below his tailoring board. I always take one if offered. Who doesn't like an orange?

Bespoke trousers are not just sewn, they are shaped, just as coats are, to make them fit the bumps and hollows of the human lower half. To watch Chris effortlessly manipulate his heavy iron to shrink or stretch the cloth is mesmerising, and he later taught me how to sew a pair of trousers.

The beauty of a Savile Row suit derives in equal parts from its exquisite hand sewing, its elegant cutting, and its immaculate fitting – the latter two stages being the cutter's responsibility. My first bespoke suit was cut and fitted by the legendary John Kent, who combined the role of Head Cutter at Norton & Sons with that of being the Royal Warrant Holder and long-time tailor to HRH Prince Philip, Duke of Edinburgh.

John started out in a tailor's shop in Bethnal Green in East London, and through hard work and force of character worked his way up to become tailor to royalty. His career in the West End began with 16 years as a cutter under the tutelage of legendary guvnor, Teddy Watson. Watson had left school at 13 and, after serving under the great Frederick Scholte, joined the firm of Hawes & Curtis (not to be confused with the current incarnation of the same name). There, Lord Mountbatten noticed Watson's talent and dispatched him to India to organise the wartime tailoring effort. On his return to London, Watson bought his alma mater and set about transforming its fortunes. He was introduced by Mountbatten to the young Prince Philip, and would go on to build a royal clientele that would later include Prince Charles, now King Charles III. John loved Teddy Watson and his famous irascibility – it was Watson who infamously turned away a young Fred Astaire for daring to ask for the same waistcoat as the then-Prince of Wales – and Watson clearly saw something of himself in John, because on his retirement it was his wish that John should succeed him as Royal Tailor.

John was a whirlwind. Single-handedly, he cut and fitted both the Norton & Sons suits and the significantly larger quantity of suits he continued to make for his own private clients – a combined total that exceeded 20 suits most weeks, a number that would make most contemporary cutters quail. He cut all of his patterns on a Monday, then saw customers virtually back-to-back through the rest of the week, finishing at lunchtime on Friday, when he would manage his logs and run around the workshops paying his tailors and listening to their various and usually significant moans.

Under John I learned my way around the cutting board. He took me into the fitting room and taught me to measure and fit. I learned my way around a bespoke pattern: I did the striking (marking around the patterns and cutting out the fabric pieces), the trimming, and trotting on every Norton & Sons job. I got pretty handy with a pair of shears.

John liked to teach because he really liked to talk. He would tell stories all day and was a master at the legendary Savile Row workroom game, 'Whistle and Bar'. He loved the gossip of the trade, and the stories collected from his famous and infamous clients. One favourite was that of the well-known and revered boss of a famous jewellery business, whose wife quietly cut off the left sleeve (the one facing the back of the wardrobe) of every one of his considerable collection of hand-tailored suits after discovering him with one of his many mistresses. John had chutzpah. If he forgot to do the alterations on a job, he would quickly brush out the chalk marks, slip it on the customer, and then with great ceremony, tell the customer that perhaps he had altered it too much. If on the rare occasion he had completely forgotten to prepare a customer's fitting, he would hide in the cupboard and leave the wonderfully dry and laconic Stephen Lachter, shirt maker to Frank Sinatra, amongst others, and John's long-time business partner, to invent an excuse for his absence.

Our workshop was always filled with great characters who liked to talk: John; Steve; Wally; Dennis Cooper (another legendary Savile Row coat maker who had worked at Norton when it bought E Tautz & Sons in the seventies and following a couple of decades down the street at Huntsman, returned to work at Norton until his retirement); Stevie Venn and Dave Hayes, coat makers at both Norton and Huntsman; Nick Hammond, who apprenticed as a Cutter with us and cut the best trousers I ever wore; Johnny Maggio, who could sew a coat in a day and claimed to have started sewing aged six in his native Italy; Rachel Alice Smith, who began her apprenticeship at Dege & Skinner but completed it at Norton; and the many other fantastic tailors and cutters who passed through the workroom, either temporarily or more permanently. Everyone would share stories and gossip while they sewed. They were my personal Savile Row university. I spent many happy years in that workshop in the company of incredible individuals whose encyclopaedic knowledge of the ins and outs of Savile Row in the last quarter of the 20th century was unrivalled.

The coat from that first charcoal herringbone suit – a two-button single-breasted, with Wally's elegantly curved notched lapel, a natural shoulder with a subtle roping at the sleeve head, a natural chest, and a slight suppression to the waist – became the archetype for the Norton style during my time there. I wore this suit at least twice a week, often more, for a decade. I wear it less frequently now, but it still makes an occasional appearance. I have worn it with great pride at least one thousand times. The only repair it has ever required was a resewing of the lining around the arm holes. It is better now than when it was made; its canvases and cloth have, over the years and many wears, eased and moulded themselves perfectly to my form.

> # My connection with fine tailoring dates back almost two decades, but my connection with the finest British cloth is more than double that.

Even more than its beautiful appearance, it is my connection to the craftsmen who made it that makes it special to me. When I wear it, I can picture Wally at his board, mug of mahogany-brown tea by his side; John, chattering and whistling as he cuts and marks; and Chris, shaping cloth beside the framed photographs of his beloved daughter. Between them, they have tailored for rock royalty, Hollywood royalty, actual royalty, and a roll call of the most famous and infamous men on the planet during their careers, with more than 160 years of experience between them. All of that is in my suit, which is filled with their spirit.

My connection with fine tailoring dates back almost two decades, but my connection with the finest British cloth is more than double that. I'm sure that as a young child I wore lots of clothes made with British fabric, but I don't recall any specifically. The first to lodge itself firmly in my consciousness was the pale-green Harris Tweed jacket I wore as a pupil at the Edinburgh Academy. I remember the orb marque, as large as a tennis ball, on the inside-left pocket, and I remember the smell of it, like wet dog, sitting on the top deck of the number 23 bus on days when it rained. We wore them year-round, even in the full heat of the Scottish summer when they would be used daily as goal posts and occasionally as picnic blankets. My own jacket, purchased from the school exchange, had had at least one owner before me, and already had patches at the elbow. After our time together it went back into circulation to make friends with another lucky owner.

> **Great artefacts have an intangible quality that is hard to define; they possess life – the life given by the maker, the life imparted by the owner, and the stories that are collected along the way.**

My grandparents lived in the Scottish Borders, the heart of the Scottish textile industry, where the mighty River Tweed gives the great cloth its name. On our summer trips around the border mill towns of Galashiels, Selkirk, Jedburgh, Hawick and others, we would pass dozens of grand woollen mills. My grandpa had worked in the textile industry and later worked for the Borders council trying to rebuild local industry as textile weaving moved offshore. When I was young, my family holidayed in the Highlands and Western Isles, another area with a rich textile heritage. I continue to holiday in the Hebrides to this day, and it was on one such trip in my mid-twenties that I drove down the narrow single-track lane to Luskentyre Beach, passing a little hand-painted sign fixed to the outside of a weather-beaten shed declaring 'Harris Tweed For Sale'. I knocked on the door but no one was at home. Around 10 years later I returned, this time on a mission to source unique and beautiful cloth to offer the customers of Norton & Sons. Naturally I called first at that same hand-painted sign on the rutted track to Luskentyre. This time, clacking away at a pedal loom in his old tin weaving shed on the edge of the beach, sat Donald John Mackay, his dog Ben by his side. Donald John is everything you could want in a weaver; skilful, subtly artistic, committed, proud and deeply connected to the landscape in which he works. From his seat at the loom he looks out across the grassy

plain – the *machair* – the white sand, and turquoise sea to the heathered Isle of Taransay. The colours of his country can be seen in the tweeds he weaves. I have returned many times to this most beautiful of places, and on one occasion took a BBC crew to film a documentary about this most iconic cloth.

Harris Tweed, like many other handcrafted cloths, is special because of its connection to the people who weave it and the place from which it comes. It is made from wool sourced from sheep that graze naturally on the surrounding hillsides and often dyed with natural pigment scraped from the rocks on the seashore outside their workshops. The designs vividly reflect the colours and textures of the land. The tweed is literally created by human energy, which turns the pedals that drive the loom.

The same connection exists with the cloth spinners and weavers of the Scottish Borders, Yorkshire, and South West England, and many of the cloths they create arrive on the cutting boards of Savile Row. In many cases their makers have centuries of hard-earned experience, knowledge, and skill. They use only the very finest quality wool, sourced from growers with whom they have long-standing and highly valued relationships. Everything is connected, every part tells a story.

Great artefacts have an intangible quality that is sometimes hard to define; they possess life – the life given by the maker, the life imparted over many years of use by the owner, and the stories that are collected along the way. Suit and owner create a history together; the owner will cherish and repair it, and all in good time may pass it on so that someone new can write a new story for it.

We could all live well with fewer but better possessions in our lives, buying only objects whose use brings us endless satisfaction and joy. Our most valuable possessions are not those with the greatest monetary value (although our suits are of course expensive, and justifiably so), but those that we have the greatest personal connection to.

More than ever, the principle of craftsmanship over mass manufacture is of vital importance. Craftsmanship is the ability to create useful and beautiful items that enrich our lives by transforming the natural materials around us through knowledge and skills that respect nature and the environment. This is the gift that the bespoke tailors of Savile Row, the cloth weavers of Britain, and the other artisans that supply and support their craft, give to the world. •

13

MAKING TROUSERS

A step-by-step guide to making trousers by hand,
following the method of Chris Ktori

A PAIR OF BESPOKE TROUSERS from Savile Row is un-like any other. They are not merely cut and sewn; they are hewn, sculpted, moulded. Each pair embodies a multitude of unique attributes that set it apart from mass-produced versions. Each stitch – carefully applied at a precise tension and in a precise direction by the hands of the tailor – bears testament to a lifetime of dedication to learning to use one's hands and to mastering the tools of the tailor's art: chalk, shears, needle, thimble, and iron. Every aspect is considered. Every step has its reason. This commitment to excellence ensures a garment that to the eye of the connoisseur is both beautiful and practical, elegant but durable. And, above all, timeless.

Making bespoke trousers is typically divided into three distinct parts: cutting out, setting and finishing.

The *cutting out* stage involves the preparation of your chosen cloth and cutting it out. A paper pattern is laid on the fabric following a 'lay play' to ensure no fabric is wasted; then pattern pieces are chalked round; inlays (additional fabric to allow for adjustments during fitting, and letting-out over time) are added; and pieces are carefully cut. Additionally, all required trimmings are assembled, and correct quantities cut out and bundled with the fabric. Precision in cutting is essential to ensure accurate sizing, proper drape, and optimal use of fabric. Careful attention is paid to matching patterns, aligning grainlines, and cutting around tricky curves and angles. This step sets the foundation for the trouser construction, providing the maker with the necessary fabric pieces to assemble and shape the garment accurately.

The *setting* stage involves the initial construction of the trousers, when various components are machine-sewn together. This includes stitching the seams, attaching the waistband, inserting pockets, and assembling the general structure of the trousers. Setting focuses on machine sewing to ensure proper alignment of each piece and durability. Once the setting stage is complete, the trousers move on to the finishing phase.

Finishing is characterised by meticulous hand sewing, which adds beautiful details and fine levels of craftsmanship. This includes hand stitching the waistband lining; attaching buttons; hand sewing the hems; and creating delicate flourishes that elevate the trousers to the pinnacle of bespoke tailoring. The combination of machine sewing during the setting stage and hand sewing during the finishing stage results in an immaculately crafted and superbly functional garment that showcases the artistry, attention to detail, and exceptional quality that define this age-old tradition. •

Required trimmings: *1 metre of cotton silesia on the double; ½ metre ermazine trouser lining on the double; 1 length of waistband lining, 2 ½" wide-cut across the piece on the double; 1 length of waistband curtain lining, 6" wide-cut across the piece on the double; 1 length of waistband canvas, the same length as the waist plus 16"; 30 cm linen holland cut across the piece on the double; 30 cm mid-weight fusible interlining; 1 curved zip at least 10" long, to match the fabric colour; 2 oxidised 2-piece hook and bars; 2 ¾" side-adjuster buckles; 1 × 23L imitation smoked-pearl bearer button; 6 brace buttons.*

CUTTING OUT THE JOB

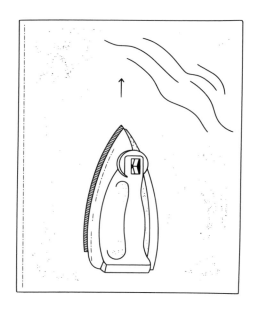

FIG. 1.1

FIG. 1.3

1   PREPARING THE CLOTH

(1.1) The cloth should be laid out folded in half, with the right sides together and the selvedge running parallel to the edge of the table. To ensure the cloth isn't twisted or warped, match the letters woven into the selvedge on either side. If the cloth has a check or stripe, ensure they match on both sides. (1.2) Concertina the cloth up and take it to the pressing board. Using only the weight of the iron, lightly steam the cloth on one side and then the other, making sure the selvedge (and check or stripe) is still aligned. The heat and steam will reset any twisted yarn, helping the cloth to settle back into its natural place. (1.3) This is a good time to look for damages or imperfections in the cloth. Many cloth suppliers will identify a damage before retailing the fabric. They are marked with a string tagged to the selvedge, directly in line with the damage. Extra cloth is given to allow for adjusting the lay and cutting around. If an unstrung damage is found, mark it clearly with chalk and avoid laying the pattern pieces over it when it is time to strike out (chalk around the pattern). (1.4) Lay the cloth back on the table as per step one and smooth it out ready to place the pattern pieces. •

2   THE TROUSER LAY

The lay refers to the order in which the pattern pieces are arranged on the cloth. This is particularly important because it allows the maker to minimise the amount of cloth needed for each garment. The tighter the pieces slot together, the less cloth required, the more money saved.

(2.1) The first consideration should be whether the cloth has a nap or not. This will dictate whether the pieces are laid in one direction (one-way cloth) or opposite directions (two-way cloth). If the cloth does have a nap, the fibres are long and brushed in one direction (corduroy and velvet) and the trousers must be cut one way. The colours can differ depending on what direction they are cut, given the way the light hits the nap. If the rough runs down the piece, the colour appears darker. If the smooth runs down the piece, the colour appears lighter. If the trouser legs are cut in opposite directions, the shading created by the nap would make the trousers appear to be two different colours. Most cloths without a nap are fine to be cut two-way, but it is a good idea to check by looking down the piece of cloth from both directions and seeing if the colour changes. If there is a noticeable difference, it is best to presume the cloth is one-way. If there is no change, the cloth is two-way. (2.2) The second consideration should be the grainline. Always lay the pattern pieces with the grainline running parallel to the selvedge (warp). This is particularly important on stripes and checks, to ensure the trousers don't appear twisted on the wearer. (2.3) It is also important to consider the space around the pieces and ensure that there is sufficient room for the inlays and fit-up, before striking out. Inlays are the extra cloth added to the seams (not seam allowance) for letting out in the future. On the topside (front trouser piece) they measure: ¾" along the waistband seam, 3" at the hem flared out to turn under for plain bottoms and 6" for PTU (permanent turn up or cuff). On the underside (back trouser piece): 1" along the waistband seam, 2¼" at the centre back to ⅜" around the curve and top of the fork, 1½" at the fork to 1" at the knee and hem through the inseam. 1" down the side seam and 3" at the hem for plain bottoms, and 6" at the hem for PTU. The fit-up is the cloth left over after the main pattern pieces have been cut out. This cloth is used for making the extra pieces within the trousers, for example the waistband, fly, pocket facings, jets and side adjusters. It is important to keep as large pieces of extra fabric as possible. •

3   STRIKING OUT THE TROUSERS

*Striking out is the act of chalking around the pattern pieces onto the fabric,
and adding the inlays (extra allowance that is hidden inside the garment for future alterations).*

(3.1) Ensuring the grainline of the pattern pieces run parallel to the selvedge, use weights to hold the pattern pieces in place. (3.2) Sharpen a piece of chalk using a chalk sharpener or, failing that, a sharp blade. (3.3) Chalk around the pattern pieces firmly, but not enough to drag or pucker the fabric. Think of the chalk as a speedboat. Push with the back edge, lifting the front as it gathers speed. (3.4) Extend the chalk marks out beyond the pattern to ensure the finish points are clearly defined. Mark the darts and notches clearly. (3.5) Remove the paper patterns from the cloth and chalk in the inlays and waistband. The waistband should measure 2½" wide by half the finished waist measure, plus 9". •

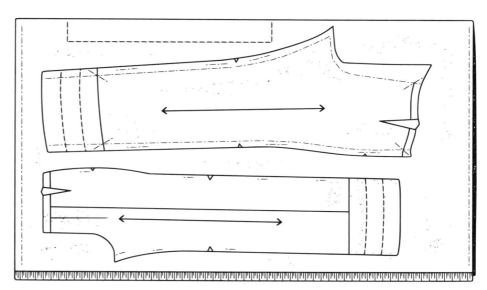

FIG. 2 & 3

4   CHOPPING OUT

*Chopping out is the act of cutting the pieces out of the fabric. It is important here to be accurate,
especially on the pieces that are cut net (without inlay).*

(4.1) The bottom edge of most tailors' shears is flat on the blade and the bottom of the handle. As the cloth is cut, use the flat edge of the shears to keep contact with the board. This will help to maintain balance and control. (4.2) Let the cloth drape over each side of the blade and use the weight of the shears to guide the pressure. Use the entire length of the blade, making long, confident cuts. (4.3) Think of the shears like a race car. Go fast down the straights and slowly around the corners. At this stage, accuracy is much more important than speed. (4.4) Start from the selvedge and cut out the topside first. Then cut out the underside. Cut neatly around the outer edge of the chalk lines and avoid cutting across any large pieces of the remaining fabric, as these odd bits of leftover fabric will become the fit-up. This will be needed later on in the making process. (4.5) Roll the trouser pieces, fit-up and trimmings into a bundle and tie them up with an offcut of selvedge. •

SETTING THE TROUSERS

1   MARK STITCHING

*Mark stitching (also referred to as 'thread marking' or 'tailor tacks')
is the process of sewing threads through two layers of fabric
to transfer important pattern markings and details to each layer.*

(1.1) Working with the right sides together, ensure both pieces
align perfectly, matching any stripes or checks. Snip small
notches into the seam allowance and inlays, through both layers of cloth at the knee, hip and the top of the darts and pleats.
(1.2) On the topside, mark stitch along the waistband seam, along
the finished hem line and the top 3" of the pleats. Make two
small mark stitches ¾" in from the notches at the knee and
hip, and at the three points of the dart. (1.3) On the underside,
mark stitch along the chalk lines around the whole piece. Start
with the side seam, along the hem line, up the inseam, around
the under-fork and seat seam, and finally across the waistband
seam. As in step 2, make two small mark stitches ¾" in from
the notches at the knee and hip, and at the three points of the
back dart. •

2   SEWING OUT THE DARTS

(2.1) With the right sides of the cloth together, fold the dart in
half vertically, matching the mark stitches at the top and tapering into the point. (2.2) Machine stitch a line on the wrong
side of the cloth from mark stitch to mark stitch, extending
past the finish point slightly. (2.3) Trim the threads leaving 2"
at the bottom of the dart, and tie a knot. (2.4) Press the darts
evenly through the middle, rather than to one side. This opens
the seam, allowing them to lie flat on the right side. (2.5) Repeat
steps 1–4 on all darts. •

3   PREPPING THE TOPSIDE

(3.1) The pocket opening measures 7". With chalk, mark the top of
the pocket opening 2" down from the waistband seam. Measure
down 7" and mark the bottom of the pocket opening. Cut 2
pieces of iron-on fusible interfacing (fusing), approximately 1½"
by ¾". Fuse over the pocket markings on the wrong side of the
cloth. (3.2) On both topside pieces, make a ¼" snip into the edge
of the fly, just as it begins to curve. (3.3) On the LEFT SIDE ONLY,
cut a piece of fusing 3" wide following the shape of the fly, finishing 1" below the snip, and fuse it onto the wrong side of the
fabric. The idea here is to make the front strong and clean, as
this will be hand stitched later. (3.4) On the RIGHT SIDE ONLY,
cut a small piece of fusing 1½" by ¾", place over the snip from
step 2 and fuse. Re-snip. Cutting into the cloth creates weak-
ness. The fusing adds strength. •

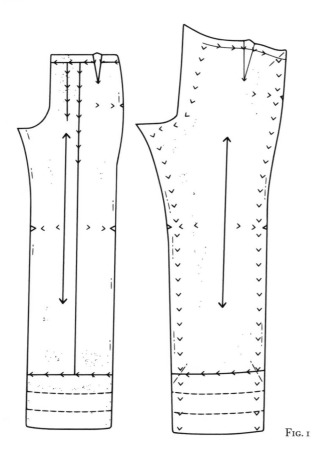

FIG. 1

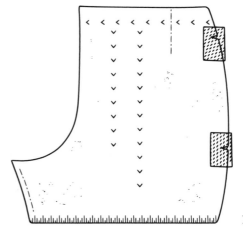

FIG. 3.1

(4.1) Cut the lining fabric in half along the folded edge. Mark the wrong side with an 'X'. (4.2) Lay the topside trouser piece onto the square of lining with the wrong sides together, leaving at least 1½" of extra lining around the top and sides. The lining's selvedge will act as the finished edge. This should finish at least 2" below the knee. (4.3) Using the topside as a guide, mark the position of the dart onto the lining (¾" by 4") and press into place. Do not sew the dart into the lining, as it requires the freedom of movement. (4.4) Pin the topside to the lining along the side seam. Mark the knee position onto the lining with chalk, on both seams, using the notch as a guide. Trim away the extra lining along the side seam, leaving around ⅜" overhanging the edge of the trouser piece. This will be trimmed away by the overlocker. (4.5) Overlock the side seam from the top to the bottom, sandwiching the fabric and

lining together. Match the notch to the knee mark made in step 4 to ensure the tension is correct and the lining remains square. (4.6) Remove the pins and flip the trouser piece over, so the lining is on top and cloth is on the bottom. (4.7) Starting at the bottom and working up, ease the lining across the width of the trouser piece towards the side seam, until there is around ⅜" of extra lining material gathered alongside the overlocking. Pin the lining in place about 1" from the side seam as you go, to hold the ease in place. (4.8) Using the notch and knee mark as a guide and ensuring the lining is square, pin the lining up the inseam and around the edge of the fly. Trim away the excess lining, leaving ⅜" overhang as per step 4. (4.9) Overlock the hem, then the inseam and edge of the fly. Remove the pins. (4.10) Pin the lining in place around 1" below the waistband seam, across the trouser piece. Flip the piece so

the lining is facing down and the cloth is facing up. Machine stitch across the mark stitches, fixing the lining in place and creating a guide for the waistband. Trim away the excess lining from across the top edge, leaving it net with the inlay. From the right side, fold the pleat into position. Pin it into place and stitch it down, sewing along the line created earlier in this step. (4.11) Lay the topside piece flat with the cloth facing down and the lining facing up. Fold in half vertically with the lined sides facing each other. Match the outside to the inside seams and create a centre crease running through the middle of the piece and rolling into the pleat. Press the crease into place, firmly, but without pulling or misshaping the pleat. (4.12) Repeat steps 1–11 on the other topside piece. (4.13) Overlock around both underside pieces, leaving the top edge raw. This may need to be trimmed back later. •

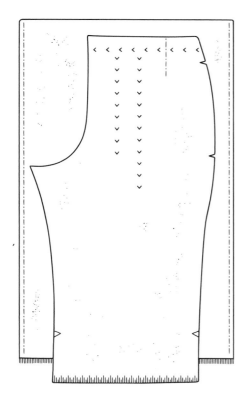

FIG. 4.2

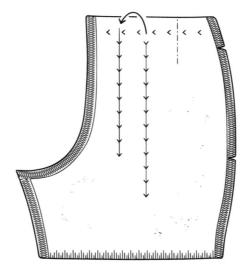

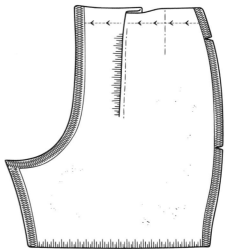

FIGS. 4.10–4.12

(5.1) At this stage the pocket bags can be drafted and prepared, but will not be required until the side seams have been sewn together. (5.2) Cut the pocketing 13½" wide by 14½" long, on a double layer of fabric. Fold the pieces in half lengthways. From the top corner of the raw edge, chalk a 9" diagonal line, starting 1½" in and running back towards the edge. At 9" snip back towards the folded edge ⅜" and run a curved line around the bottom corner, finishing at the crease. Cut along the lines through all layers. (5.3) Separate the pocketing and fold each one with the wrong sides facing each other. (5.4) Machine a ¼" seam from the folded edge around the curve, finishing at the 9" point. Bag out the pocket back and stitch the same line around the outside, trapping the seam inside. This is called a French seam. (5.5) The pocket edges, from the top to the point at 9", must be turned in and pressed in the following way: fold the top layer towards the right side of the fabric, which will be sewn to the underside of the trousers, and fold the bottom layer towards the wrong side of the fabric, which will be sewn to the topside of the trousers. •

(6.1) For the front pocket facing, cut two pieces of cloth 3" wide by 9¼" long. Cut two strips of linen interlining 1½" wide by 8½" long. (6.2) Place the topside of the trousers with the right side facing up. Lay the linen underneath the topside, extending past the side seam around ¼" and extending past the top and bottom of the pocket mouth notches 1" either side. (6.3) Lay the facing piece, with the wrong side facing up (right sides together) on top of the topside. Extending past the side seam around ¼" and extending past the pocket mouth notches, 1" at the top and 1¾" at the bottom. (6.4) The order of layers from the bottom to the top is linen, topside trouser piece and then pocket facing piece. Working between the notches only, baste all the layers together with a ⅜" seam allowance. Snip into the layers ⅜" at the notches. (6.5) Press open the seam and turn all layers back towards the wrong side of the trouser piece, so the right side of the facing piece is showing. Turn back the top and bottom seam allowances of the facing piece above and below the notches around ½". This is to avoid catching the pocket facing when the side seams are stitched. Press all layers flat. (6.6) For the back pocket facing, cut two pieces of cloth 4½" wide by 9½" long. Turn back one short edge and one long edge towards the wrong side ½". Top stitch around the two turned edges ⅛", fixing them into place. (6.7) Place the topside trouser piece with the wrong side facing up. Lay the back pocket facing piece, also with the wrong side facing up, on top of the front facing piece (the facing pieces are right sides together). The raw edge of the back facing piece should lay along the side seam and the waistband end of the topside, approximately 1½" up from the bottom of the front facing piece. Pin in place. (6.8) Flip the topside around and fix the back facing piece in place by machine stitching into the top and bottom corners of the pocket mouth. Trim the top edge of the back pocket facing in line with the top edge of the front pocket facing, around 1" below the waistband seam. (6.9) Repeat steps 1–8 for other leg. •

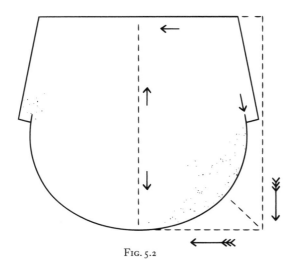

Fig. 5.2

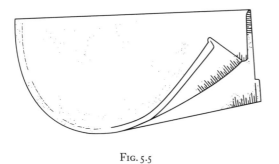

Fig. 5.5

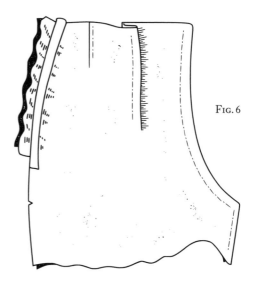

Fig. 6

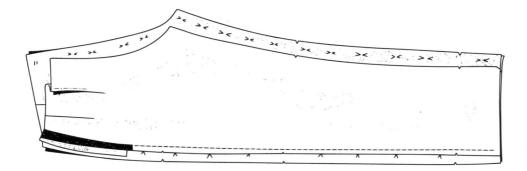

FIG. 7.3

7   SEWING THE SIDE SEAMS

(7.1) Place the underside on a flat surface with the right side facing up. Place the topside on top of the underside with the right side facing down (right sides together). Align the edge of the topside along the mark stitches of the underside, matching the notches at the hip and knee. (7.2) Pin the pieces in place, making sure the front facing piece is clear of the seam allowance. (7.3) Starting from the waistband seam, machine stitch the length of the side seam ⅜" inside the mark stitches. Be sure to catch the back facing piece and the corners of the pocket mouth at exactly ⅜" so the pocket mouth sits flush with the side seam. (7.4) Press the seam open. (7.5) Repeat steps 1–3 for the other leg. •

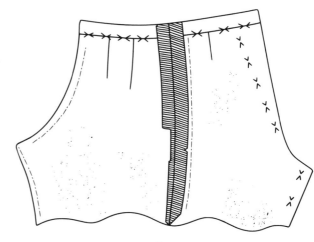

FIG. 7.4

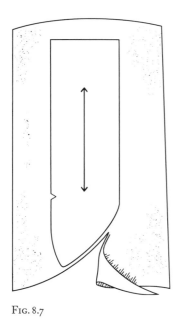

FIG. 8.7

MAKING THE LEFT FLY FACING   8

(8.1) Measure the length between the waistband seam and the notch on the fly edge. Cut a square of cloth 4" wide and at least 2" longer than the distance measured above, on a single layer of cloth. (8.2) Cut a piece of linen to match the dimensions in step 1. (8.3) Lay the fly cloth piece with the wrong side facing up. Place the fly edge of the left trouser piece, with the right side facing up (wrong sides together), around ¾" from the right edge of the cloth piece, and level with the inlay at the top. (8.4) Use the shape of the fly edge to chalk the seam line of the left fly piece, stopping 1" below the notch.

Mark the notch. (8.5) Working on the fly cloth only, draw a parallel line that is 2½" away from the first chalk mark. Extend this line along the length of the cloth, curving back into the first line 1" below the notch. (8.6) Lay the cloth piece onto the strip of linen and pin in place. Machine stitch from the top edge, down the second chalk mark and around the curve. Trim away the excess cloth and linen, leaving a ¼" seam. (8.7) Trim away the excess cloth on the front fly edge, cutting on the first chalk mark. Press the back seam open. Bag out the pieces so the right sides are facing out. Press into place. •

(9.1) Place the left trouser piece with the right side facing up. Lay the fly facing, linen side facing up (right sides together), so that the raw edge of the fly facing aligns with the fly edge of the trouser piece. Match the notches. (9.2) Baste ⅜" inside the edge from the top to the bottom. (9.3) Machine stitch a ¼" seam down the front edge, from the waistband seam to the notch above the fork. Remove the basting stitches, and then press the seam open. (9.4) Turn the attached fly facing back so the wrong sides are now together. Press flat and baste down the front edge to fix in place. •

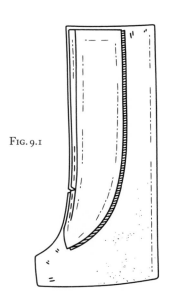

Fig. 9.1

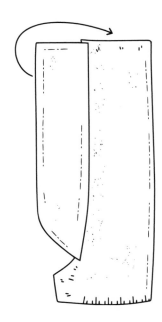

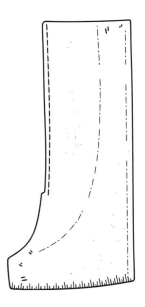

Figs. 9.4

(10.1) Cut a piece of fabric on a single layer 6" wide and around 1½" longer than the finished left fly facing. Cut a piece of silesia the same dimensions as the fabric, and a piece of linen the same length, but 3" wide. (10.2) Place the right trouser piece with the right side facing up. Lay the zip, with the right side down, against the fly edge of the trouser piece. Then lay the fly guard fabric on top of the zip, right side down, against the fly edge. Lay the linen on top of the fly guard fabric, also against the fly edge. (10.3) Baste a seam through all layers ⅜" from the edge, trapping the zip and the fly guard fabric in between the right trouser piece and the linen. (10.4) Machine stitch a ¼" seam down the fly edge, catching all layers, from the waistband seam to the notch. (10.5) Remove the baste and press the seam back towards the side seam, so the pieces lay forward of the fly edge. (10.6) Draw out the shape of the fly guard. From the fly edge seam, chalk along the mark stitches along the waistband edge. At 3¾" square down 1". Curve a hollow line back in towards the zip and straighten off at 2½" down and 2" out. Run the line parallel at 2" down the fly and curve back in towards the zip (the same shape as the left fly facing) 1" below the notch. (10.7) Trim away the excess cloth, leaving ½" of inlay around the edge to turn in. (10.8) Place the right trouser piece with the wrong side facing up. Tuck the cloth, linen and zip under the trouser piece towards the side seam, leaving the front edge seam exposed. (10.9) Lay the long edge of the silesia along the fly edge seam of the trouser piece, with the wrong side facing up and 1½" extended past the inlay at the top edge. (10.10) Machine stitch the silesia to the fly edge seam, ⅛" from the edge. Start ⅜" below the waistband seam and sew down to the notch. (10.11) Turn the cloth, linen and zip back from under the trouser piece. Turn the silesia over so the right side is facing up. Press the fold ½" back from the seam to cover the seam stitching. (10.12) Trim the silesia. Leave 2½" of extra fabric across the top edge from the waistband seam, 1" around the shape of the front edge of the fly guard, and 3" at the bottom. Make ¼" snips in the curved edge. The front edge seam is closed in the finishing process. •

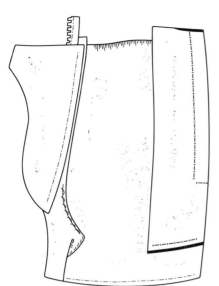

FIG. 10.3

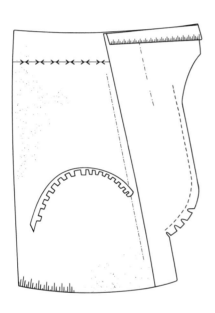

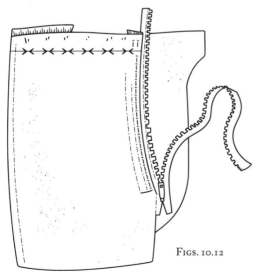

FIGS. 10.12

(11.1) Separate the waistband pieces (marked during the striking out stage) from the fit-up and trim the waistband canvas to match. (11.2) Place the waistband pieces with the wrong side facing up. Lay the unbound edge of the waistband canvas, right side facing up, over the edge of the waistband piece around ½" and pin it in place. (11.3) Machine stitch the length of the waistband ⅜" inside the edge of the waistband canvas. (11.4) Fold the fabric around the waistband canvas so the right side is now showing, and press it into place. Trim the excess fabric back so it is aligned with the bound edge. (11.5) Separate the waistbands into left and right. The RIGHT waistband is good to go. On the LEFT waistband, with the wrong side facing up, trim away 1" of canvas on the right-hand side. The uncanvassed fabric will be turned back later to create the finished edge of the extension band. (11.6) From the front edge of the waistband canvas, measure back 2¾" (extension band), and make a mark on the wrong side with chalk. (11.7) Cut 2 lengths of stay tape 6" long. Loop it around the trouser hook and tie a knot, leaving a 2" tail. (11.8) Place the first hook in the centre of the waistband, ¼" back from the edge of the canvas. Unfold the waistband fabric to avoid catching it when sewing, and machine stitch the stay tape. Place the second hook in line with the chalk mark made in step 6 and machine stitch the stay tape. Fold and press the waistband fabric back into position. •

FIG. 11.3

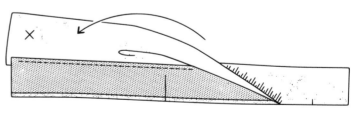

FIG. 11.4

(12.1) Place the right trouser leg right-side up. Lay the bound edge of the right waistband piece, with the right side facing down, along the bottom of the waistband seam mark stitches. (12.2) Starting at the centre back, machine stitch in the channel between the binding and the waistband canvas, always keeping the bound edge in line with the mark stitches. Ensure the side seam and darts remain flat when stitching across them. (12.3) Unfasten the zip and trap the side that is stitched down to the fly guard. Trim away any zip tape that extends past the seam allowance. (12.4) Press the waistband seam open, with the bound edge facing up, and the inlay facing down. (12.5) Trim the top edge of the waistband canvas down ½" from the front of the fly guard to nothing at the fly seam. Baste the fabric back into place. Trim the front edge of the waistband back, leaving ½" of excess cloth to turn back. (12.6) Trim the waistband canvas in line with the front edge of the fly guard. Turn back the edge of the waistband cloth towards the wrong side, and baste in place. (12.7) Place the LEFT trouser leg with the right side facing up. Position the extension band mark (see: step 6 of MAKING THE WAISTBAND) ⅜" back from the edge of the fly. Lay the bound edge of the LEFT waistband piece, with the right side facing down, along the bottom of the waistband seam mark stitches. (12.8) This time, starting at the centre front, repeat steps 2, 4 and 6. (12.9) Trim away any excess waistband in line with the centre back inlay. •

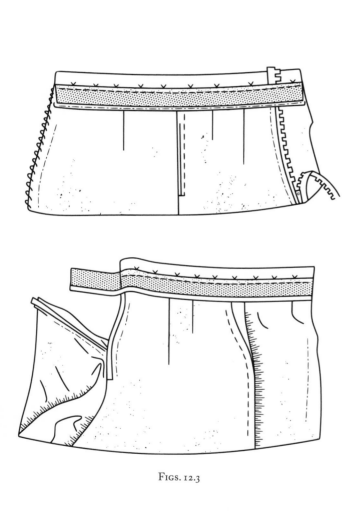

FIGS. 12.3

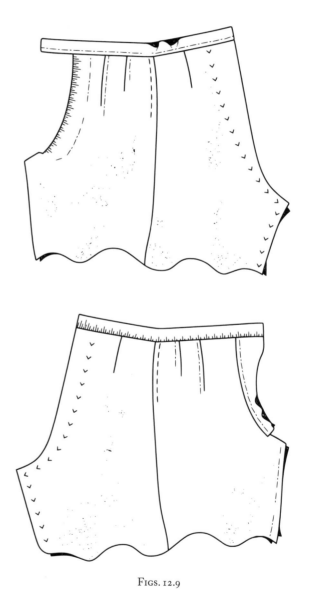

FIGS. 12.9

(13.1) It is necessary to hide the inlay at the front of the topsides, between the folded edge of the pocket bags and the fly facings. Do this with a small, pleated silesia curtain. (13.2) Cut two pieces of silesia 8" by 4". Fold the pieces in half horizontally, making a strip 8" by 2" and press into place. (13.3) On each topside piece, lay the raw, long edge of the curtain against the top edge of the waistband seam. Tuck one end underneath the fly piece and the other end underneath the pocket bag, with a 1" pleat in the middle facing the fly. (13.4) Baste the curtain in place along the waistband seam. •

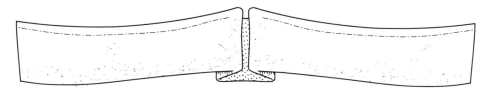

Fig. 13

(14.1) Fold the two trouser legs in half, right sides together, so the topside is laid over the underside. Place the edge of the topside along the mark stitches of the underside, matching the notches at the knee. The topside fork should extend past the underside fork ⅜", as it includes seam allowance and the underside does not. (14.2) Pin the pieces in place and machine stitch the length of the inseam ⅜" inside the mark stitches. (14.3) Press the seam open. (14.4) Repeat steps 1–3 for the other leg. •

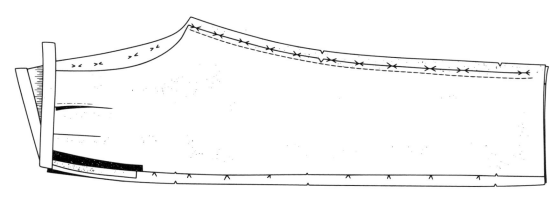

Fig. 14

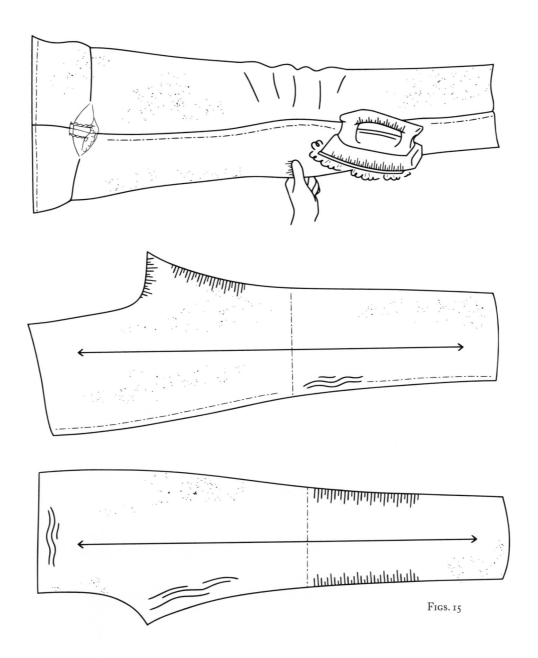

FIGS. 15

(15.1) Turn the trouser legs right-side out. (15.2) Lay one of the legs flat on a pressing board with the side seam facing down and the inseam facing up. Adjust the cloth so that the two seams are stacked on top of one another. Smooth out any twists or creases until the pieces lie flat. (15.3) Using a steam iron, start around the knee and re-press the length of the front crease. Then, stretch the calf outwards and kick the bottom inwards to create around ⅜" of fullness at the knee. Press in the back crease, creating a slight curve through the calf. Using heat and steam, shrink away the fullness at the knee. The trouser leg should look slightly banana shaped. (15.4) Repeat steps 1–3 for the other leg. •

(16.1) Turn the trouser leg inside out and place it with the side seam and pocket facings facing up. (16.2) Turn the back facing piece away from the side seam to access the front facing piece underneath. Lay the bottom layer of the pocket bag along the front facing piece ½" forward of side seam. Place the 9" point, where the French seam stops, ½" up from the bottom of the facing piece. Pin the pocket bag to the front facing. (16.3) Swing the trouser out from underneath the pocket bag, leaving only the front facing and the pocket bag lying flat, facing up. The linen should also be tucked away so it isn't caught by the machine stitch. (16.4) Machine stitch ⅛" in along the turned-back edge of the pocket bag, finishing in the corner of the French seam. (16.5) Place the trousers flat, still inside out, with the top layer of the pocket bag facing up, as if in its finished position. Peel back the loose end of the top layer to reveal the back facing piece. Swing the trouser out from underneath the pocket bag, leaving the back facing piece and pocket bag lying flat, facing up. Machine stitch the top edge of the back facing to the bottom layer of the pocket bag ⅛" in. (16.6) Close the top layer of the pocket bag. Baste ½" in, along the edge of the facing piece, through the pocket bag, only catching the two layers. (16.7) Baste the turned-back edge of the top layer to the underside inlay, covering the seam. •

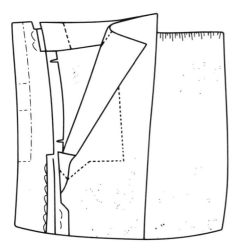

Fig. 16.2

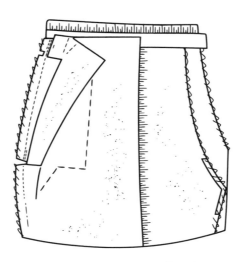

Fig. 16.3

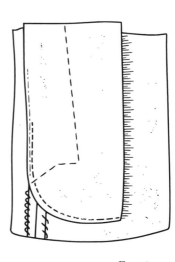

Fig. 16.7

Figs. 16.7

(17.1) Place the RIGHT trouser leg, right-side out, over a sleeve board or surface, so the fly guard is facing up and lying flat. Ensure the zip is fastened all the way up. (17.2) Lay the edge of the fly of the LEFT trouser leg over the right, as if the trousers were closed up. The fly edge should extend past the zip and onto the right fly edge, ¼" at the top and middle and ⅛" at the bottom as it begins to curve. Pin the left fly in place, right on the edge of the seam, so the pieces are held together but the facings can still be folded. (17.3) Flip

both pieces around so the fly fronts are now facing down. Fold back the fly guard on the right-hand side and baste the zip into position on the left-hand fly facing (this will be hand stitched later). Flip the pieces back around and remove the pins. Check that the left fly edge is still covering the zip fully when the pieces are laid flat. (17.4) Turn the RIGHT trouser leg inside out and place inside the LEFT leg creating a tube, aligning the waistband, seat seams and fork. (17.5) Baste along the mark stitches at the centre back, through the seat curve

and front fork, and finish at the bottom of the zip. (17.6) Turn the trouser legs back out onto the right side. Lay the trousers flat and close them up. Measure across the waistband. The finished measure should be equal to half of the total waist size. If there is any discrepancy, take in or let out the centre back waist accordingly and re-baste the seat seam. (17.7) Repeat step 4. Starting from the centre back, machine stitch alongside the basted stitch through the seat and fork, and finish at the bottom of the zip. (17.8) Press open the seam. •

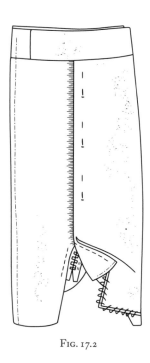

Fig. 17.2

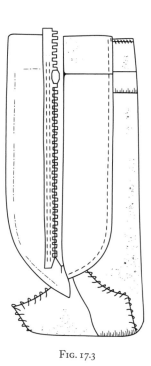

Fig. 17.3

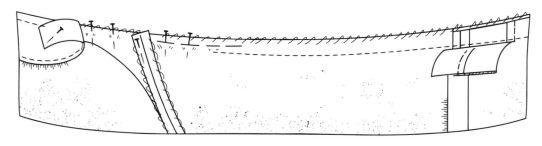

Fig. 17.5

(18.1) Place the trousers on a flat surface so the side seam of the LEFT leg is facing down. Fold back the RIGHT trouser leg towards the waistband exposing the inseam of the left leg. (18.2) Apply the inside leg seam measurement from the crotch seam intersection along the inseam and mark it on the right side of the cloth. Chalk a horizontal line across the width of the leg to define the finished length. (18.3) Measure down the preferred width of the turn-up, usually 1½"–1¾", and chalk a second line parallel to the first. (18.4) Chalk a third line the same distance below the second line. (18.5) There should be between 2" and 3" of inlay left between the third line and the trouser hem. If the distance is greater, trim back to 3" and overlock. (18.6) Flip the trouser over so that the side seam is facing up, and finish the three lines in chalk. (18.7) Turn and fold the hem inside the trouser leg along the second line. Baste ⅜" above the fold to hold it in place. Then baste along the first line, catching the inlay inside. (18.8) Turn the cuff back along the first line and baste it in place 1" above the fold. (18.9) Press into place ensuring that the seams of the cuff run parallel with the seams of the trouser leg. Repeat on the other leg. •

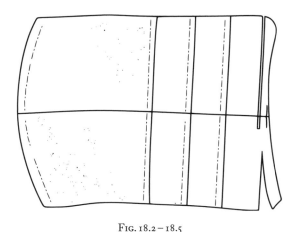

FIG. 18.2 – 18.5

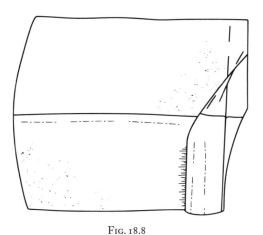

FIG. 18.8

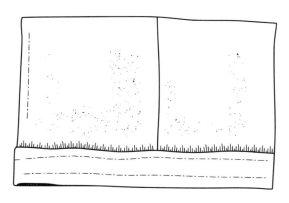

FIG. 18.9

(19.1) For the long strap part (back side adjuster), fold a small piece of cloth in half, right sides together, so each side is at least 2" deep and 9" wide. Side adjusters are generally cut from pieces of cloth that run down the length of fabric (warp), rather than across (weft). (19.2) Towards the folded edge of the cloth, chalk a tapered line 7½" long, starting 1¼" wide at one end and finishing ¾" wide at the other. Square up at each end. Machine stitch along the long side leaving both ends open. (19.3) Cut the strap out, leaving a ¼" seam allowance around the three chalked sides. (19.4) Press the seam open so it is running through the centre of the strap and then machine stitch along the narrow end, trapping the seam open. Cut a piece of interfacing around 2" long and fuse it at the narrow end, trapping the seam open. (19.5) Bag out the strap so the right sides of the cloth are facing out. Cut out a ¾" square from the open end of the strap, on the seam side only. Fold the edges back towards the cut-out to create a triangle shape and press into place. The strap should finish around 7" long. (19.6) Repeat

steps 1–5 for the second long strap. (19.7) For the short buckle part (front side adjuster), fold a piece of cloth in half, right sides together, so each side is at least 2" deep and 6" wide. (19.8) Towards the folded edge of the cloth, chalk a tapered line 4½" long, starting 1⅛" wide at one end and finishing ¾" wide at the other. Square up at each end. Machine stitch along the long side, leaving both ends open. (19.9) Cut the straps out, leaving a ¼" seam allowance around the three chalked sides and press the seam open so it is running through the centre of the strap. (19.10) Bag out the strap so the right sides of the cloth are facing out. Cut out a ½" square from the seam side of the strap, at the wide end. Fold the edges back towards the cut to create a triangle shape and press into place. The strap should finish around 4" long. (19.11) Fold the narrow part of the strap, with the seam on the inside, around the fixed end of the buckle and baste in place. The strap should be 2" long with a triangle shape at one end and the buckle attached at the other. (19.12) Repeat steps 7–11 for the other short buckle part. •

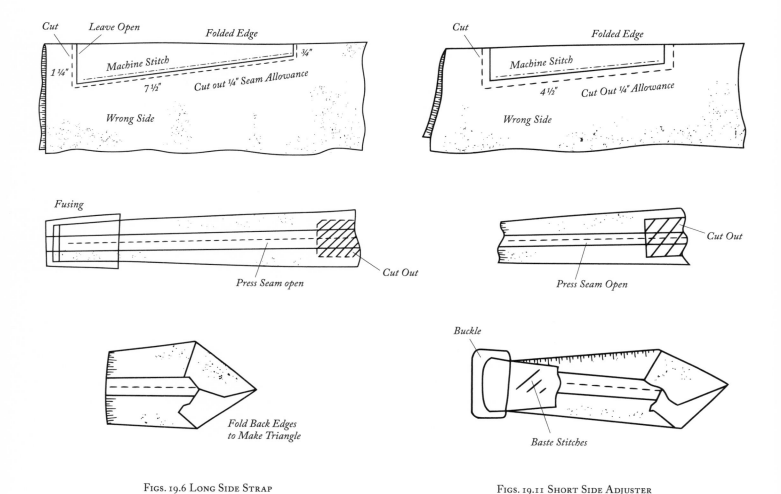

FIGS. 19.6 LONG SIDE STRAP   FIGS. 19.11 SHORT SIDE ADJUSTER

FINISHING THE TROUSERS

1   BOTTOMS

(1.1) Turn the trousers inside out. (1.2) Using a cross stitch, start at the side seam and sew towards the body. Attach the cuff to the trouser leg ⅜" below the edge of the hem. Catch only a couple of threads on the main portion of the trousers above the hem, so the stitches cannot be seen on the right side. (1.3) At the side seam and inseam, catch all but the outer layer of the cuff, to fix the PTU in place. (1.4) Stitch around the hem on both legs. •

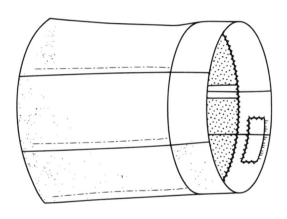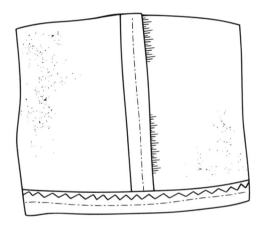

Figs. 1.4

2   SIDE POCKET MOUTH

(2.1) Mark the position of the bar tacks with a ⅜" chalk mark. Place one at the top of the pocket opening and two at the bottom. (2.2) Begin with the bottom two rows of bar tacks. With double thread, stitch four back stitches measuring ⅛" each through all layers. Start the stitch ⅛" back from the side seam on the underside and then sew ⅜" into the topside. (2.3) Do not cut the thread. Continue to prick stitch up the pocket mouth, ⅖" from the edge. (2.4) Repeat step 2 for the top bar tack. (2.5) Repeat steps 1–4 for the other pocket mouth. •

3

FRONT SIDE ADJUSTER

(3.1) Line up the triangular point of the strap with the waistband seam and place the buckle in line with the side pocket and side seam. Pin in place. (3.2) Chalk a vertical line on the strap 1½" from the tip of the triangle. Fell around the edge of the strap, starting and finishing at the chalk mark. (3.3) Double the cotton up and prick stitch across the chalk line. Sew through all layers to ensure strength. (3.4) Repeat steps 1–3 for the other side adjuster. •

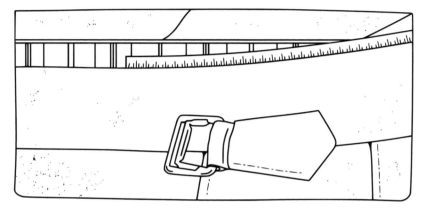

Fig. 3.1

4

BACK SIDE ADJUSTER

(4.1) Place the triangular point of the strap around 5" from the buckle. Chalk a vertical line across the strap 1½" from the triangular point. (4.2) Feed the strap through the buckle and fasten, in line with the waistband seam. Pin it in place. (4.3) Fell the edge of the strap, starting and finishing at the chalk line, leaving the front loose to allow the tightening of the side adjuster. (4.4) Double the cotton up and prick stitch across the chalk line. Sew through all layers to ensure strength. (4.5) Repeat steps 1–4 on other side adjuster. •

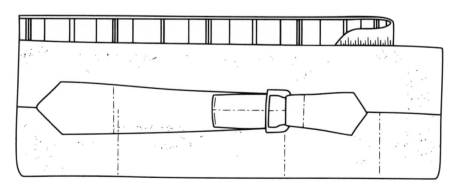

Fig. 4.2

5   SIDE POCKET FACING

(5.1) On the back of the pocket bag, feel where the edge of the pocket facing is and mark lightly with chalk. (5.2) From the inside, fold the front of the pocket bag out of the way and pin it to the trouser leg, so it does not get caught by any stitches. (5.3) Prick stitch around the edge of the pocket facing through the back of the pocket bag, catching both the bag and the facing cloth. •

6   CENTRE BACK SEAM

(6.1) It is common in bespoke tailoring to hand stitch the seat seam in addition to the machine stitching. This is to add strength. Back stitch from the bottom of the waistband, along the seat seam, through the crotch, and finish at the zip. (6.2) Double up the cotton in the last 3" to make the top fork strong. •

7   ZIP

(7.1) Starting from the bottom, prick stitch the basted side of the zip on the left fly facing ⅛" away from the teeth, catching the cloth facing and linen. Do not catch the right side of the fabric. (7.2) Continuing from the top, fell back down the edge to the fly facing. Remove basting. •

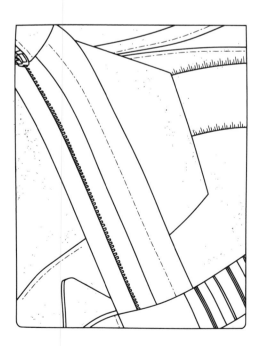

FIG. 7.2

8   FRONT HOOK

Thread up a hand-sewing needle with double thread, and sew the hook in place ¼" from the short edge of the extension in the centre. Only catch the band canvas, not the waistband fabric. •

9   LEFT FLY FACING

(9.1) Pin the fly guard to the right side of the trouser front, exposing the zip and fly facing. Starting from the top, prick stitch down the front of the left fly, ⅛" from the edge. (9.2) At the bottom of the fly opening, where the two topsides meet, sew a bar tack with double thread through all layers. (9.3) Chalk out a stitch line on the right side of the cloth, 1½" wide, from the waistband seam to the fly opening, rounding off at the bottom as it meets the bar tack. (9.4) Prick stitch back up the fly along the chalk line, through all layers, finishing at the waistband seam. This stitch fixes the fly in place, adding strength and keeping the topside from gaping open on the wearer. •

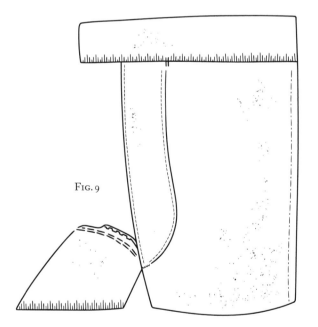

FIG. 9

(10.1) Measure off the waistband extension on the left waistband and cut a strip of silesia that's ¾" longer in length and at least 1½" wider. (10.2) Place one of the narrow edges of the silesia so it covers the zip on the waistband, and turn back the other narrow edge so it slots neatly behind the front hook. (10.3) Turn back the bottom edge of the silesia and place it ⅛" from the edge of the extension. Fell around the edge anti-clockwise from the zip. Make extra stitches at the corners of the hook to add strength. (10.4) Turn under the top edge of the silesia and place it ⅛" from the top edge of the waistband extension. Make sure the silesia is not tight, any fullness will press away. Finish felling into place. •

11   BACK HOOK

Hand-sew down the back hook on top of the waistband extension lining, in line with the edge of the fly, in the middle of the waistband. •

13   BARS

(13.1) Lay the trousers the right way up on a flat surface. Fasten the zip and close the waistband, placing the left waistband extension over the right fly guard. With chalk, mark the placement of where the back hook sits on the right waistband. (13.2) On the marks, use an awl to poke small holes through the cloth and waistband canvas. Push through the round end of the bar. Connect hook and bar and lay the trousers flat to make sure they're positioned correctly with no twists or drags. Fell the round ends of the bar to the band canvas, on the wrong side of the waistband. (13.3) Repeat steps 1 and 2 for the front hook and bars. •

12   LEFT FLY FACING & WAISTBAND LINING

(12.1) Cut a piece of silesia 3" by 2½". Place one of the narrow, cut edges ½" past the fly facing. Turn a seam back on the other narrow cut edge and slot the folded edge neatly behind the back hook, covering the top of the zip tape. (12.2) Fold the bottom edge of the silesia in line with the edge of the extension band lining. Fell around the edge anti-clockwise. Make extra stitches at the corners of the hook, to add strength. (12.3) Ensure the pieces of band lining line up with each other. (12.4) Turn in the top edge of the silesia and place it ⅛" from the top edge of the waistband. Make sure the silesia is not tight, any fullness will press away. Finish felling into place. •

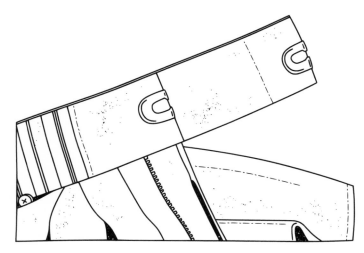

Fig. 12

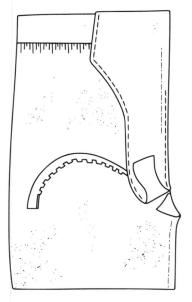

FIG. 14.1

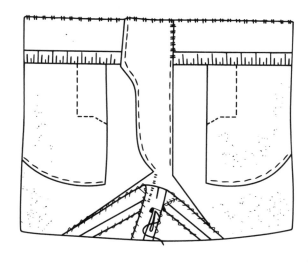

FIG. 14.4

14   RIGHT FLY GUARD LINING

(14.1) Trim the silesia back at the bottom of the fly guard so around 2½" is extended down past the left fly facing. Turn the edges back until the strip is ½" wide and baste into place at the crotch seam intersection. (14.2) Starting at the bottom, catching only the fly seam, prick stitch the silesia ⅜" back from the folded edge, along the fly seam and into the waistband. (14.3) Turn under the raw edge of the silesia across the top of the waistband ⅛" down from the edge and fell in place. Continue down the front edge of the fly guard, prick stitching through all layers, from top to bottom. (14.4) Prick stitch the other side of the strip made in step 1. •

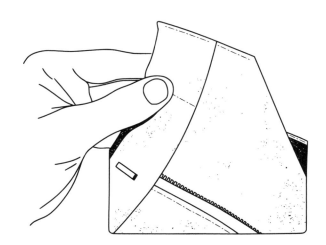

15   BEARER BUTTONHOLE

The bearer buttonhole is created by cutting a small 1" opening on the waistband seam of the right fly guard.

(15.1) On the right fly guard, ½" back from the front edge, sew a ¼" bar tack through the waistband seam (⅛" either side). Sew another bar tack in the same way, 1" back from the first. (15.2) Cut the machine stitches in between the bar tacks to create an opening. Then, along the opening, cut open the silesia, stopping at the bar tacks. A 1" hole should now be visible on the waistband seam. Turn back the cut edges of the silesia ⅛", either side of the waistband seam to neaten the hole. Fell the silesia in place. •

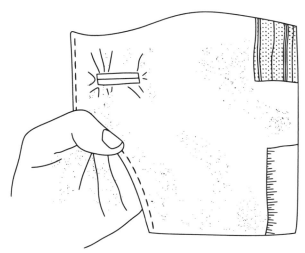

FIGS. 15.1 & 15.2

Fell the raw edges of the waistband inlay down to the waistband canvas, at the side and across the top. •

17 CURTAIN

The curtain serves as a way of hiding the seams and raw edges of the waistband.

(17.1) Cut a long strip of lining 6" wide and approximately 59" long (across the width of a piece of lining fabric). This will make up the curtain. Press the curtain lining in half horizontally, creating a long 3" strip. (17.2) Starting at the side seam, hide 1" of curtain underneath the pocket bag. Lay the raw edge of the curtain along the top edge of the waistband seam. Baste it in place along the seam. (17.3) At the dart, make a 1" pleat facing towards the side seam and at the centre back make a 1½" pleat facing the centre back. Baste these in place. (17.4) Continuing with the piece of lining, mirror steps 3 and then 2 on the other side. (17.5) Stitch the curtain in place along the waistband seam. At the pleats, tack the curtain to the inlay and darts with a few small stitches. •

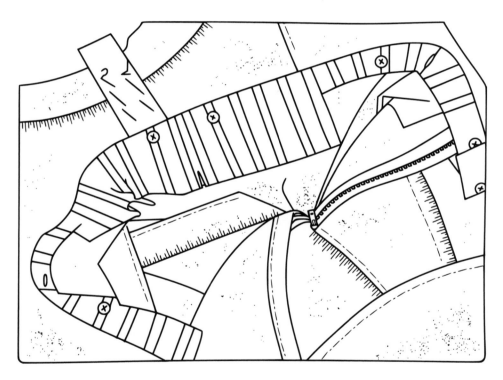

Fig. 17

18 POCKET BAGS

At the side seam, fell the folded edge of the pocket bag to the side seam inlay, making sure to cover the side seam stitch line. Only catch the inlay; do not sew through to the right side. •

The waistband lining attaches to the wrong side of the waistband, covering the seams and making the waistband look neat. Cut a strip of lining fabric 3" wide and approximately 8" longer than the finished waist measure. This will be more than enough, and the excess can be trimmed away during the sewing stage. (19.1) Start by placing the narrow end of the waistband lining 1" past the edge of the left fly facing. Lay the raw edge of the lining piece parallel with the edge of the curtain, with the wrong side facing up. (19.2) Using the waistband seam as a guide, back stitch along the length of the waistband from the left trouser front, towards the centre back. (19.3) Make a pleat the same depth as the inlay (for future letting out) at the centre back. Continue stitching back around to the right front. (19.4) Turn the lining up towards the waistband so the right side is now facing up and the seams and waistband canvas are covered. (19.5) Turn the raw edge of the lining inside and baste it in place ⅛" down from the top edge of the waistband. Turn back the sides of the lining in line with the edge of the left fly facing and the zip on the right fly guard. Baste in place. (19.6) Fell across the top and sides to fix it into place. •

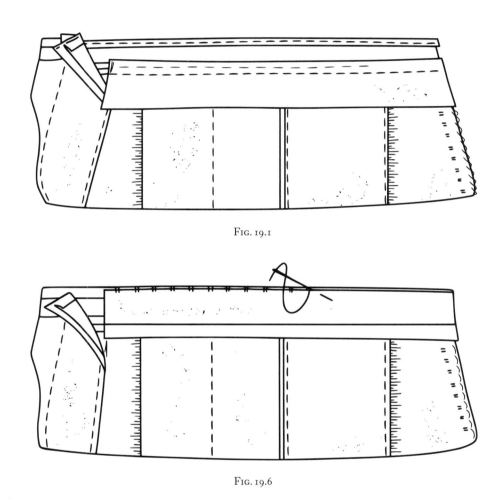

Fig. 19.1

Fig. 19.6

20   BUTTONS

(20.1) Fasten the trousers and lay them on a flat surface, with the backs facing up. From inside, mark the position of the bearer button by chalking through the buttonhole. Sew the bearer button in place using double thread. (20.2) Using chalk, mark the brace button position on the waistband lining. The front buttons should line up with the edge of the front pleat, in the middle of the waistband. The second button is positioned 3" back from that. At the centre back, the buttons sit 1½" back from the seat seam on either side, 3" apart. (20.3) Sew through all layers with a double thread. •

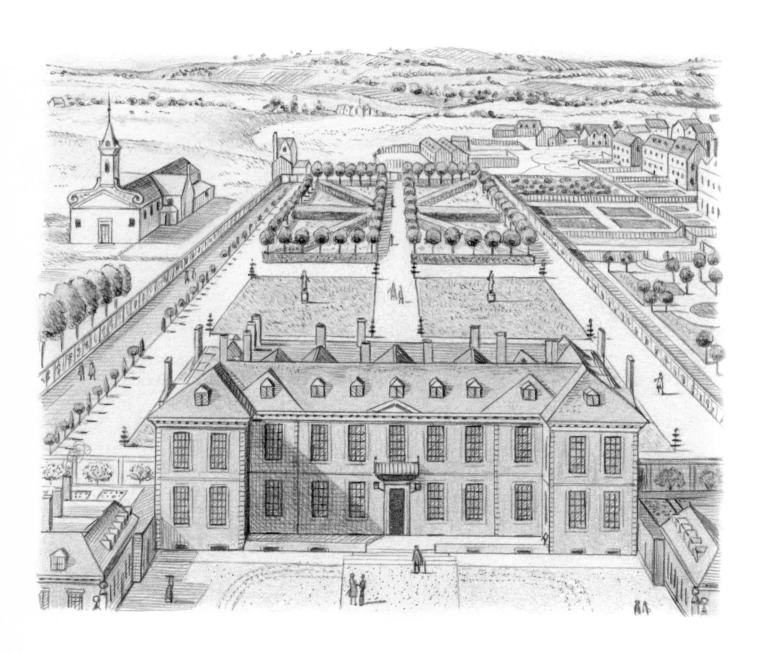

A HISTORY OF SAVILE ROW

Eight centuries of made-by-hand dressing for the power
brokers and cultural leaders of the ages

ABOVE The Earl of Burlington and his wife Dorothy Savile.
OPPOSITE Burlington House in the former gardens of which Savile Row was built.

THE ART of hand tailoring in London can be traced back more than 700 years to the 13th century, when a radically new style of creating garments was developed in Europe, taking its name from the French *tailler*, meaning 'to cut'.

Tailored garments were different from previous styles of clothing, as they were made from pieces of fabric that had been cut out, shaped, and assembled to create closer-fitting and more practical garments. The coat was an early tailoring innovation. With a front opening, button closure, and more anatomically accurate overall shape, it replaced the very basic over-the-head tunic constructed from flat rectangles of cloth.

The first organised company of tailors in England began as the Fraternity of St John the Baptist of Tailors and Linen-Armourers, which was formed to ensure high craft standards and fair pricing, and was formally recognised with a Royal Charter in 1327.

In 1600 the son of a Somerset cloth merchant named Robert Baker moved to London to set up shop with his wife, a flaxwoman, on the Strand. Baker became tailor to the nobility and gentry and developed a particular reputation as a maker of 'pickadils' or 'pickadillies' (from the Spanish *picado,* meaning 'pierced' or 'cut') – the large, elaborate cutwork ruffs and collars favoured by the fashionable elite. Baker's thriving enterprise employed 60 workers and his business received royal patronage, making the collars for the lavish wedding of Princess Elizabeth, daughter of King James I.

In the early 17th century, the City of London (now Britain's financial district) was a fetid place, a foul cocktail of open sewers, sooty air, plague, and various other forms of pestilence. Like many others, Robert Baker looked longingly to the green countryside, a few miles west of the City, an area that was home to the famous annual May Fair. He took the money he had earned from his now waning ruff business and invested in land. In 1623 the foundations were laid on a grand residence that, thanks to the source of his fortune, became known by the wits of the day as Pickadilly Hall. (It was rumoured that the Queen herself had coined the name.) It was from this hall that the nearby street, still one of London's most famous thoroughfares, took its name.

Some 20 years later in the City of London, a young man named Thomas Firmin became apprenticed to The Girdlers Company, makers of belts and girdles for fine dress and workwear. By 1655, in the short period during which Oliver Cromwell was Lord Protector of the Commonwealth of England, Firmin had completed his apprenticeship and set up in business under his own name. The business would go on to achieve unequalled success as a manufacturer of buttons and badges and thrives to this day, as Firmin House, having served through the reigns of some 16 British monarchs. Firmin's has held Royal Warrants for George II (who reigned from 1683–1760) and every successive monarch in an unbroken line. It is still the only choice for buttons for the bespoke uniforms and blazers tailored on Savile Row, and its buttons and badges adorn the clothes of senior officers of the armed forces (Admiral Lord Nelson wore Firmin buttons) and royal families of every country in the world. At 369 years (and counting) they are the oldest manufacturing business in the United Kingdom.

In 1663 work began on the neo-Palladian Burlington House, the grandest house built on the north side of Piccadilly, which until that time had been a country lane. In 1666 the Great Fire of London destroyed large sections of the City and this was the final straw for many

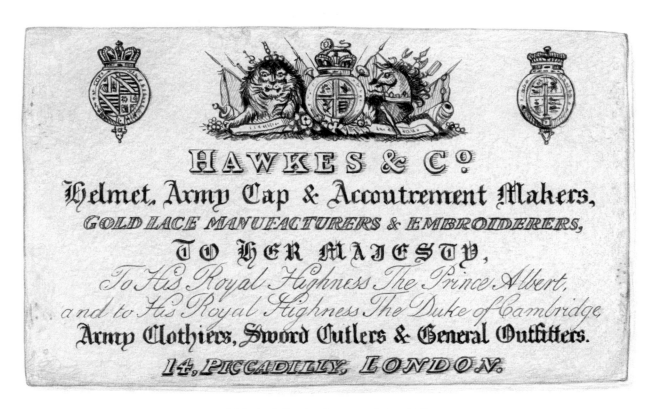

A Hawkes & Co advertisement card, circa 1845.

of its wealthiest residents. In 1667 Burlington House was acquired by Richard 'The Rich' Boyle, the wealthy Anglo-Irish first Earl of Burlington and Second Earl of Cork, courtier to King Charles II at the nearby court of St James. His great-grandson, the third Earl, Richard Boyle, had grand tastes, honed on his European Grand Tour, and would be nicknamed the 'Apollo of the Arts'. Unhappily for him, despite a sizeable inheritance and his marriage to the wealthy Dorothy Savile, his tastes exceeded his means. To raise money, he began developing the land behind Burlington House, naming the streets using family names – Burlington, Cork, Boyle, and Clifford. When his financial position worsened, he began a new development of houses on a new street he named Savile Row, after his wife. Originally just a single row of homes along the east side of the street, it became home first to military officers and then a fashionable location for many in the medical profession before their move to Harley Street. It was at one time home to William Pitt the Younger – the last Prime Minister of Great Britain and the first Prime Minister of the United Kingdom – and the politician and playwright Richard Sheridan. The third Earl's legacy is a self-contained corner of Mayfair that is architecturally refined and uniquely tranquil.

The blueprint for the modern suit was established by Charles II in the period immediately after the Great Fire of London. Designed to placate the Puritans, it was simple and modest and cut in black cloth, but the fashion did not take hold and more lavish styles quickly returned. However, in the second half of the 18th century, men's dress in London began to change. The simple practical clothes worn by the English nobility in the countryside, principally cut to be worn riding, began to appear in town. With the support of George III, who had acquired the nickname 'Farmer George' thanks to his love of agricultural pursuits, the more elaborate dress worn at court began to disappear. In France, meanwhile, the Revolution of 1789–99 meant that the lavish clothing of the aristocracy was now reviled and simpler styles began to dominate there, too.

However, it was a young man named George 'Beau' Brummell who would take this newly simplified mode of dress and elevate it to the very height of fashion. From upper-middle-class beginnings (his father rose to be Private Secretary to Prime Minister Frederick North), Brummell promoted himself through sheer force of personality and style to become something of an obsession amongst the fashionistas of Georgian London. Revered by the Prince of Wales, feted and lampooned in equal measure by the writers of the day, he rejected completely the ornate clothing of the previous period and embraced an outwardly austere mode of dress.

It was the simplicity of his clothes, and the perfection with which each outfit was assembled, that made him remarkable. He favoured dark-coloured coats – cut to perfection by the first generation of tailors who had followed the wealthy to the area around the Burlington Estate and Savile Row – accompanied always by dazzlingly white linens, a perfectly knotted cravat and trousers, when previously breeches had been the gentleman's choice.

> The blueprint for the modern suit was established by Charles II in the period immediately after the Great Fire of London: simple, modest and cut in black cloth.

Brummell's dressing routine was said to be a mesmerising performance lasting several hours, involving bathing in milk, scrubbing himself with pig bristle, and polishing his boots with champagne. He was a fanatic for understatement and despised showy or ornate clothes. He relied upon the excellent quality of his clothing, the perfection of his proportion, and his grace of manner to create an impression. Brummell is famous for saying that if anyone passing you in the street should have cause to give you a second glance then you are not well or correctly dressed.

Because of its simplicity it was a style surprisingly difficult to replicate, and it could not be achieved without the assistance of a first-rate tailor. Brummell employed the services of several, including the firms of Schweitzer and Davidson, both at 12 Cork Street, and Meyer at 36 Conduit Street. Jonathan Meyer, an Austrian, was also tailor to the Prince of Wales (later George IV) making for him personally; for his pet regiment, the 10th Royal Hussars; the Hussars' regimental band; as well as several friends and members of his household, including, it was noted in one bill, the royal cook. Meyer later joined forces with an Edinburgh-based sword manufacturer, and the firm became Meyer & Mortimer, which survives to this day at 40 Piccadilly.

By the late 18th century, several tailors and a variety of other purveyors of gentlemen's requisites had established workshops in the area around Savile Row on nearby Sackville, Maddox, Clifford, and New

The original east side of Savile Row today.

Burlington Streets. In 1760 Thomas Hawkes walked from Stourbridge to London to seek his fortune and was taken on as a journeyman at the shop of Mr Moy, a velvet cap maker. Moy, a heavy drinker, died in 1771 and Hawkes took the opportunity to set up under his own name, cultivating a clientele for his headwear that included George III.

In 1803 the tailoring firm of Davies & Son opened and one year later made a short move to Hanover Street, where it prospered, announcing not long afterwards that it dressed 'all the crowned heads of Europe'. A few years later in 1806, James Poole set up shop as a linen draper in nearby Bloomsbury. By 1822 the firm was making military tunics and doing well enough to enable a move to more fashionable premises on the newly created Regent Street, a stone's throw from Savile Row.

Reputedly the greatest of the early tailors was George Stultz, who had German military origins. When he set up shop on Clifford Street in 1809, he quickly became the most talked about tailor in town. At its peak the

firm employed more than 300 staff. The lead character in novelist William Thackeray's *Pendennis* was a Stultz customer, as was novelist Edward Bulwer-Lytton's young dandy in *Pelham*. Of Stultz, *The Town* magazine claimed in 1838, 'This establishment has no rival. It stands so far above all competition that comparison would be idle.' A distant second in its review of the tailoring houses of London was the firm of Burghart. Neither have any remaining connection. Meyer also received a mention in *The Town*'s top 10, as, further down the list, did the house of James Poole.

In 1811 Joseph Ede joined the firm of William Webb on the Strand. Established in 1689, William Webb was a robe maker and counted King George III among its clientele, producing several robes for his coronation. In 1834 Webb sold the firm to Ede's uncle, Thomas Adam, and it took the name Adam & Ede. In 1868 the firm moved to Chancery Lane and changed names once again to Ede & Son, before another Joseph – son of Joseph – married Rosanna Ravenscroft, uniting her family wig-making business with that of the Edes to create the firm of Ede, Son & Ravenscroft. The firm, today known simply as Ede & Ravenscroft, is now found on Burlington Gardens, facing down Savile Row to the west. It has made robes for the Church; state; legal and academic professionals; and every monarch from William III and Mary II to the present day and can lay a claim to be the oldest tailoring business in London.

A flourishing community of makers of high-quality clothing and accessories traded with great success in the streets built on the former Burlington estate. This community included boot makers, shirt makers, hatters, cap makers, cutlers, and purveyors of the many other essentials that fashionable London men required in their wardrobes. Tailors comprised about one-fifth of all the residents of the area, but few of note were on Savile Row itself. Today, there are nine fully bespoke houses on the Row, featured below, and it was a man named Henry Poole who put the quiet Mayfair side street on the world's sartorial map.

HENRY POOLE & CO

In 1828 James Poole made the short move from Regent Street to number 4 Old Burlington Street, a property that backs onto Savile Row. Poole had made his name and his fortune tailoring uniforms for the British officers fighting Napoleon during the Hundred Days war of 1815. The firm was hugely prosperous and James's son, Henry, was well established in London society. When his father died in 1848, Henry rang the changes at the family firm, including removing the main entrance to his emporium on Old Burlington Street and creating a grand Italianate façade to what had been the rear of the building at numbers 36–39 Savile Row.

Poole made military and sporting clothes and specialised in livery (uniforms for officials and servants). The firm courted clients from all walks of life and, through Baron Mayer de Rothschild – one of its first notable clients – secured the patronage of Emperor Napoleon III.

Unlike many of its august neighbours, Poole is fortunate to have an archive of ledgers (many other firms lost theirs through negligence or during the Blitz), and these treasured records are held in pristine condition by the firm. They read like a Who's Who of English and European society. In Poole's golden age, between 1860 and 1876, it was making more than 12,000 bespoke orders every year and built a list of clients that no other house is ever likely to come close to matching. In total it has dressed 6 British prime ministers, 15 emperors, and 20 kings.

One early client was Edward VII, Prince of Wales, a sartorial leader in his day, who commissioned the creation of a short smoking jacket, cut in midnight-blue cloth, to wear at informal dinner parties at Sandringham. A Sandringham houseguest, Mr James Potter, took a fancy to the prince's jacket and ordered a facsimile from Henry Poole & Co, which he subsequently wore to the Tuxedo Park Club in upstate New York, and the tuxedo was born.

Emperor Napoleon III in Henry Poole.

In 1876 Henry Poole died, and *Vanity Fair* magazine recorded his passing with a simple eulogy: 'So Old Pooley is dead.' Poole himself left a note behind that read, 'There will be nothing much to leave behind me', for despite his 16 Royal Warrants, the tailoring tradition of extending unlimited credit to its customers left the firm in great financial difficulty. Following Henry's death, his cousin Samuel Cundey stepped in to save the firm and the Cundeys remain in charge to this day.

Poole later opened branches in Paris, Vienna, and Berlin, and by the early 1900s, Henry Poole was the largest tailoring establishment of its type in the world, employing 300 tailors and 14 cutters. In 1961 a redevelopment of the west side of Savile Row led to the demolition of Henry Poole's shop and forced a move to nearby Cork Street. Poole remained there until 1982 when it was able to return to the Row, occupying the beautiful Victorian building at number 15, where they remain a custodian of the great traditions of bespoke.

Today the Poole cut is noted for its chest drape, a distinctly nipped waist, and a flair to the hips. And its separate livery department retains a unique tailoring expertise, its clothes gracing many state occasions including the Coronation of King Charles III.

HRH Prince William being inspected by his grandmother HM The Queen.

GIEVES & HAWKES

In 1771, upon the death of his master Mr Moy, Thomas Hawkes established a hat-making business under his own name on Brewer Street in what is now Soho. What set Hawkes apart from his rivals was his development of a superior method for the making of a leather shako, the tall military hat adopted by the British Army from the late 18th century. Toughened through a unique curing process, the Hawkes shako was more resistant to sabre cuts. He also perfected and patented a variation of the sola topee, or pith helmet, made of durable cork, which replaced the brass helmet. Mandated by the British Raj, and adopted by British colonial forces globally shortly thereafter, it made Hawkes's firm indispensable. His clientele came principally from the British Army but also from royal ranks, and in 1803 the firm received the ultimate seal of approval: the Royal Warrant to King George III.

Following the death of Hawkes in 1809, the firm passed into the control of his wife's nephew Richard Mosely, becoming Hawkes, Mosely & Co. It diversified into tailored clothing, predominantly military, at a time when, it was said, 'the sun never sets on the British Empire'. This was a profitable moment to be in the business of making military uniforms. From Brewer Street the firm moved closer to the moneyed customers of Piccadilly and remained there at several addresses for just over a century. In December 1912 however, Hawkes made the ultimate move, acquiring the building at number 1 Savile Row.

While Hawkes was busying himself in London with the Army, down the road in Portsmouth a man called James Gieve was making his way with another branch of the military, in a tailoring firm founded by Melchizedek Meredith. Meredith was the pre-eminent Portsmouth tailor and held the illustrious appointment to the Royal Navy. It reputedly made the uniform Lord Nelson was wearing when he was killed at the Battle of Trafalgar (although conclusive proof remains elusive), and it was also tailor to Nelson's famous Flag Captain, Thomas Hardy. Meredith made for the Navy during the peak of Britain's sea power, and much like Hawkes with the Army, being tailor to the Navy at this time was something of a goldmine.

After Meredith's death in 1830 his firm was acquired by Joseph Galt, for whom Gieve made his debut on the tailoring scene. Rising rapidly up the ranks, he became partners with Galt in 1852 and shortly before his death in 1888 assumed sole ownership of the firm. He was succeeded by his sons, James and John.

James Gieve the younger followed a policy of targeting naval cadets, his motto being 'get 'em young'. The Gieve patented sea-chest would accompany every cadet to sea, and he later boasted that more than 90 percent of all naval officers were outfitted by the firm. Firmly ensconced with the Navy's top brass, the firm innovated its supply of equipment across all aspects of naval life. In the 20th century it introduced an early model of the life jacket, as well as the 'Secret Service button', containing suicide pills, razor wire, a compass, and maps.

Gieves opened a London branch at the close of the 19th century and made its home on New Bond Street in 1916. Bombed in the Blitz of 1940 it temporarily relocated to Piccadilly, but returned to Bond Street at the end of World War Two.

While the war years were a boom period for London's military tailors, the post-war years were a bust. With many former clients killed, and lucrative military contracts slashed, this was a period of great upheaval among London's tailors, and many either closed or merged. Gieves Ltd and Hawkes & Co were no exception, and in 1974 the former acquired the latter. Initially undecided as to whether to base themselves at Gieves's Bond Street shop or Hawkes's premises on Savile Row, the decision was made for them in 1975 when the IRA blew up Gieves's, mercifully whilst unoccupied, their military connections having made them a target.

Today the firm continues to make both bespoke and made-to-measure uniforms for the Navy and RAF (Royal Air Force), including uniforms for William, Prince of Wales. It also makes for the Honourable Corps of Gentlemen at Arms, the Monarch's ceremonial bodyguard.

NORTON & SONS

Norton & Sons was established in 1821 on the Strand by Walter Grant Norton, as a tailor of bespoke clothing for the gentlemen of the City of London. The firm prospered, and in 1859 Walter's son, James, was granted the Freedom of the City of London in recognition of his services to tailoring. In the mid-1860s, along with many others, the firm made the move to London's newly prosperous West End, occupying two grand buildings at 18 and 19 Conduit Street, in the heart of the old Burlington estate.

In 1862 Emperor Wilhelm I of Prussia conferred his Royal Warrant on the house, having been introduced when visiting London as a guest at the wedding of Queen Victoria's daughter, Princess Alice, to Louis IV, Grand Duke of Hesse.

As a business built on civilian rather than military origins, Norton & Sons fared better than many in the difficult post-war years. While other houses shrank, Norton's thrived, and in the sixties and seventies it acquired the celebrated military and sporting houses of Hammond & Co; Todhouse Reynard & Co; and Hoare & Tautz, formed earlier by the merger of E Tautz & Sons and J Hoare & Co.

Hammond & Co was founded by Robert Hammond in 1776. It was noted for its sporting tailoring, particularly equine sports, but also other gentlemanly sports including cycling and golf. Hammond laid claim to having been the inventor of knickerbocker breeches, and in early advertisements advised potential customers to beware of imitations. Its York golfing coat was advertised as offering 'perfect freedom of arms and shoulders'. With grand emporiums on London's Oxford Street and branches in the most prestigious addresses in Paris, Brussels, and Vienna, it was internationally revered. Hammond held Royal Warrants not only to Britain's Queen Victoria, King Edward VII, and King George V, but also to the King of Belgium, the Emperor of Austria, the King of Spain, and the King of Portugal. In a letter from Buckingham Palace dated 1928, it is stated that Hammond 'are the only breeches makers to satisfy the King'. It made clothes for America's great military leader, General John J Pershing, commander of the American Expeditionary Forces on the Western Front during World War I. Other celebrated customers include the famed Paris couturiers

Norton & Sons was established in 1821 on the Strand by Walter Grant Norton, as a tailor of bespoke clothing for the gentlemen of the City of London.

Anthony J Drexel Biddle Jr, America's best dressed man.

45

Charles Frederick Worth and Paul Poiret – the start of a tradition of making for the fashion world that continues at Norton & Sons to this day.

Hammond & Co's pre-eminence in the world of sporting tailoring was challenged, however, when on 14 May 1867 Edward Tautz, its foreman, placed a notice in *The Times* to 'inform the nobility and gentry that he has commenced business for himself'. Tautz made a confident debut, opening right up the street from his alma mater at 285 Oxford Street. Building upon his Hammond experience, the original House of Tautz specialised in 'the hunting field and military men' and was particularly celebrated for its breeches. Edward Tautz fought to protect what he saw was his invention of the original style of knickerbocker breeches and in 1886 successfully proved it in court.

Tautz was a fashionable name in both London and Paris, where it had a shop on the Rue du Faubourg Saint-Honoré. An article in *The Times* wrote, 'The Tautz's make is as easily recognised by a connoisseur as the best brand of claret or the choicest Havana.' A young Winston Churchill wrote to his parents from Harrow School demanding they send him Tautz breeches, and Tautz went on to make a young Churchill everything from cashmere racing breeches to jockey silks.

Tautz also had a great name in the United States. It dressed Anthony J Drexel Biddle Jr, an American diplomat proclaimed in a long article in *Esquire* magazine to be 'America's best dressed man'. There was also a Hollywood connection. Cary Grant was a customer, and Norton claims to have made the famous grey suit in the crop-duster scene in *North by Northwest*. (Kilgour French & Stanbury also claim this.) When Seth Rogen recreated the scene for the March 2008 *Vanity Fair Hollywood* issue it was Norton that tailored the suit.

John Granger became Head Cutter at Norton & Sons in the mid-sixties and bought the firm from the last of the Norton family in 1970. It was Granger who oversaw the acquisition of Hammond, Tautz and others as he expanded the firm, continuing the tradition of making for sportsmen and adventurers.

Granger, like Edward Tautz before him, was something of an innovator. He developed a unique measuring harness that customers were strapped into. A Heath Robinson-esque precursor to modern body-scanning technology, it comprised around a dozen measuring tapes, mounted on a brass frame and equipped with a series of spirit levels for checking balance. Granger believed the system allowed for accurate creation of bespoke garments without the need for fittings. At the time, he regularly took the Norton trunk show to 28 cities in the United States and would send his measurements back to his tailoring team in London, where they finished the garments and dispatched them directly to customers. Another Granger innovation was his work with famed British couturier Sir Hardy Amies, cutting and making the Hardy Amies ready-to-wear menswear collections. He also cut Amies' own clothes, and the Norton ledgers record huge quantities of clothing tailored for the former royal couturier.

Norton remained on Conduit Street until 1980, when it took the opportunity to move onto the Row itself, taking a lease on the elegant white stucco townhouse at number 16 Savile Row, one of just two remaining original buildings built by the Earl of Burlington back in 1735.

Success with a sporting clientele continued under John Granger's two sons, who took over the business from their father in 1990, when Norton was making sporting clothes for, amongst others, King Juan Carlos I of Spain and Presidents George and George W Bush. Norton customers have always included adventurers, such as World War I flying ace Baron Manfred von Richthofen, 'the Red Baron', and Lord Carnarvon, the Egyptologist who discovered Tutankhamun's tomb. This tradition continued in the late 20th century with Brigadier General Charles ('Chuck') Yeager, the first man to break the speed of sound, and the great British explorer Colonel John Blashford-Snell CBE, who led expeditions of the Blue Nile and Congo.

The house also retains connections with Hollywood, and in recent years made for both Robert Pattinson and John Turturro in *The Batman;* recreated that aforementioned Cary Grant suit for Seth Rogen; dressed Edward Norton for a *Vanity Fair Hollywood* issue; made clothes for Bill Nighy and Andrew Lincoln; and Tautz clothes have been worn by Javier Bardem, Dev Patel, Clive Owen and Dominic West, amongst many others of note.

Norton's connection with the world of fashion has continued over the last decade, during which time the house has worked with celebrated designers including Christian Louboutin, Alexander McQueen, Kim Jones, Erdem, Christopher Kane, and many others, as well as working in close association with many of the world's finest luxury brands including Cartier, Tricker's, John Lobb, and Rolls-Royce, for whom they make the famous lab coats worn by customers visiting the firm's factory at Goodwood.

H HUNTSMAN & SONS

Established in 1849, Henry Huntsman remains a Savile Row heavyweight. At one time the largest – and today amongst the most expensive – houses on the street, its original expertise lay in the cutting of gaiters and riding breeches. Originally trading from premises on Dover

Street, Huntsman moved to Albemarle Street in 1898, before making the short move to number 11 Savile Row, its home to this day.

Amongst the firm's early patrons were Queen Victoria's son, Prince Alfred, who became a customer in 1876 and was later joined by the Queen herself. In 1886 the company earned its first Royal Warrant from HRH the Prince of Wales (later Edward VII), who was followed by his grandson, David Windsor (later King Edward VIII), who introduced many of his high-rolling friends to Huntsman.

Prince Alfred, patron of H Huntsman.

In the inter-war period, ownership of Huntsman passed to Robert Packer, who navigated the firm to prosperity when many other firms suffered. Packer possessed a combination of great personal style, affability, and warmth, but he also had an eye for quality and efficiency. It was Packer who revolutionised Huntsman through the introduction of the 'sectional' system. Until this point, most Savile Row houses ran a system by which one tailor would make one complete garment. Each tailor had a different hand, different tension, and often a slightly different method, the result being a different feel to each finished garment. The cutter would always give a customer's order to a particular coat maker or trouser maker to ensure that they would always feel the same

when worn. But Packer introduced a system by which his tailors would undertake just one part of the construction process: one would baste canvases; one would apply collars; and another would set-in sleeves. The result was not just efficiency, but also consistency, so a customer's job could go down any one of several production lines and emerge roughly the same. It was a system that Huntsman continued to use until the 1980s.

If Packer introduced efficiency, it was Head Cutter Colin Hammick who brought flair. Hammick joined Huntsman as a 15-year-old apprentice in 1942 and rose quickly to the ranks of Head Cutter by the 1950s. Hammick's refined aesthetic ensured that Huntsman's tailoring became highly sought after by Hollywood royalty. The firm's books from the era record orders from stars such as Clark Gable; Rex Harrison; Laurence Olivier; Paul Newman; Dirk Bogarde; Katharine Hepburn; and Gregory Peck. Under Hammick's guidance, the firm grew to a staff of more than 130 tailors and cutters in its workrooms. The modern Huntsman cut, with its high armhole, pronounced waist and skirt, and one-button fastening, traces its lineage directly to the cutting prowess of Colin Hammick.

ANDERSON & SHEPPARD

Anderson & Sheppard was founded on Savile Row in 1906 through the alliance of coat cutter Per Anderson and trouser cutter Sydney Sheppard. Anderson, a Swede, had worked at 7 Savile Row for the great Dutch tailor Frederick Scholte, who initiated the softening of tailoring at the turn of the century, and Anderson's style can trace its lineage directly to the heavy use of drape that was favoured by his master.

It was this ease that became the house's stock-in-trade and set it apart from the rest of the street, who tailored in the traditional English fashion with a cut and construction following a more structured military and sporting tradition. Legendary Director, Colin Harvey, said of Anderson & Sheppard's style, 'We drape bodies, we don't build them.' Recent Head Cutter John Hitchcock said Anderson's coats are cut to be as comfortable as a cardigan. It is not a look for all, but it is distinctive. The Anderson coat is roomy, the shoulder is soft, often extending beyond the natural shoulder, with little or no pad, and it has a very full sleeve.

Originally established at number 13 Savile Row, the growing business decided to move across the road to larger premises at number 30. In 2005, only one year short of a century on Savile Row and with its building due for redevelopment by the landlord, Anderson & Sheppard

A ledger at Anderson & Sheppard signed
by actor Gary Cooper.

relocated to its current premises at 32 Old Burlington Street and in 2012 opened a second store at nearby 17 Clifford Street selling ready-to-wear clothing.

By the 1930s the business was hugely successful in America, where they liked a roomy coat, and the popularity of the Anderson style had much to do with its close alignment to the hugely successful American outfitter Brooks Brothers. It was a look the wealthy American was familiar and comfortable with.

When Fred Astaire was given his marching orders by Teddy Watson at the old Hawes & Curtis for daring to suggest they make him a copy of the Prince of Wales' shirt and waistcoat, he turned instead to Anderson & Sheppard, which was more than happy to oblige. Astaire became a long-term customer, one of many of the early greats of Hollywood to be clothed by the house. Other customers of the era included Rudolph Valentino and Noël Coward, all drawn to the soft-shouldered comfort of the Anderson cut. Douglas Fairbanks was another star from the early years of Hollywood to patronise Anderson, and his influence brought a long list of leading actors and actresses of the 1920s and 1930s, including Marlene Dietrich, to their door. It was not just actors who put their faith in the house, however. Victor Fleming – director of *Gone with the Wind* and *The Wizard of Oz* – was a customer, as was Sam Spiegel – producer of *Lawrence of Arabia,* and studio heads including Joe Schenck, one of the founders of 20th Century-Fox. The irony was that Scholte, Anderson's master, had publicly shunned the flashiness of Hollywood types.

Despite its relatively late start, Anderson's is the largest of the bespoke tailors on Savile Row, a position it has enjoyed since the 1980s at least, when its books revealed a turnover of more than £1.5 million (about £7.5 million in today's money). Its trade then, as today,

was dominated by America. Anderson & Sheppard workshops turn out twice as many garments as the second-largest firm, and its output accounts for close to one-third of all Savile Row bespoke suits.

DEGE & SKINNER

The story of Dege & Skinner (the 'Dege' rhymes with prestige), is a family affair. It began in 1865 when German tailor Jacob Dege opened his first shop at number 13 Conduit Street. Jacob had a big family and his two eldest sons joined him in the business, so in 1900 his youngest son, Arthur, set up on his own, with his school friend William 'Bill' Skinner, whose family were tailors in Jermyn Street. Together they formed the rival firm of Arthur Dege & Skinner, trading from nearby Grafton Street until Bill died in a riding accident, aged just 42, leaving behind a widow and two young sons. In 1914 Arthur Dege & Skinner closed and Arthur joined his father in J Dege & Sons, while Jacob Dege paid for the schooling of William 'Tim' Skinner, Bill's son, and in 1916 took him on as an apprentice. Tim went on to serve the company faithfully until his retirement 54 years later.

Winston Churchill at the coronation
of Queen Elizabeth II in 1953.

In 1939, J Dege & Sons Ltd bought Wilkinson & Son, robe makers by appointment to HM King George VI, and two years later opened outposts in the military garrison towns of Aldershot and Catterick. Military uniforms have been a vital part of the firm's success, especially since 1967, when Dege bought Rogers & Co and John Jones, both tailors to the Household Division and the Cavalry, making the firm a pre-eminent force in Army tailoring.

Tim Skinner bought the firm in 1947, 31 years after first joining, and in 1953 his son Michael entered the business. That year saw Dege & Sons dress several peers of the realm for the Coronation of HM Queen Elizabeth, including Sir Winston Churchill, upon whom Her Majesty had conferred the honour of Knight of the Garter.

Dege & Skinner have held Royal Warrants to HM Queen Elizabeth II, the Sultan of Oman, and the King of Bahrain. For Oman and Bahrain, Dege made everything from personal uniforms to the uniforms worn by the Royal Camels and Royal Pipe Bands. Most recently they made the Blues & Royals uniform worn by Prince Harry at his wedding.

Today the firm is run by another William Skinner, the third William and the fifth generation of his family to take the helm.

RICHARD ANDERSON

The youngest of the genuine bespoke tailoring houses, Richard Anderson opened for business in 2001. It used to be commonplace for head cutters, or foremen, to leave one house and set up under their own name, but when Richard Anderson – former head cutter at Huntsman – and Brian Lishak, Huntsman's former managing director – moved a few doors down to establish their own house, it had been 50 years since anyone else had done so.

Richard started in the business at 17, serving his apprenticeship under the great Colin Hammick, the man who cemented Huntsman's place in Savile Row lore. Richard's cutting ability was clear, and he quickly rose to become the youngest head cutter in Huntsman's long history.

Brian began his career in 1956 in the era of Robert Packer, the other great Huntsman tailor. As a fresh-faced, 16-year-old junior sales assistant, he was the youngest employee at Huntsman. In his 45 years at the house, his considerable charm ensured that Hollywood royalty – including Katharine Hepburn, Paul Newman, and Gregory Peck – were loyal customers. He once had the unwelcome job of turning away Steve McQueen (his

Fred Astaire, Rudolph Valentino and Noël Coward were all drawn to the soft-shouldered comfort of the Anderson & Sheppard cut.

Richard Anderson at the board.

demands for the speed of delivery could not be met), and was lucky enough to watch from the roof of number 11 Savile Row as The Beatles played their famous gig on the roof of number 3 in 1969. Brian has been plying his trade on the Row for more than 60 years and is universally admired and respected by the Savile Row community.

Richard has built a fantastic reputation for the excellence of his cutting and his management of the tailoring team, and Brian has a customer list and charm that has been a perfect combination. Richard's style is synonymous with Huntsman, but his overheads have been significantly lower, so his prices are keener. It has been no surprise that between them they have built a strong client book and a fine reputation.

DAVIES & SON

Davies & Son has the longest history of any independent tailor on Savile Row. The firm was founded in 1803 and taken over by Thomas Davies from his brother the following year. Through his work for Army agents Greenwood, Cox & Co, Davies had established exceptional connections within military circles. Moving to grand quarters at number 19 Hanover Square, it counted Admiral Lord Nelson as an early customer and not long after claimed to dress all the crowned heads of Europe.

The Duke of Windsor.

In the 1820s it made for Sir Robert Peel, twice British Prime Minister and founder of the UK's first police force. When a scandal concerning outbreaks of fever in sweatshops operated by Davies hit the papers in 1892, it named the sons of Edward VII among its loyal patrons. The scandal engulfed other firms too, including Henry Poole and Meyer & Mortimer, and new provisions setting out minimum labour standards were established.

Davies dressed King George V from 1910 for the remainder of his reign and also tailored garments for his sons, the future Kings Edward VIII and George VI.

The last of the Davies family left the firm in 1935, and the Hanover Street shop was vacated in 1979, after several years and addresses, finally making its way to number 38 Savile Row in 1997, under the stewardship of Master Cutter Alan Bennett.

Bennett had worked at several of the great houses on the Row, including Kilgour, Huntsman, and Dege & Skinner, and it was Bennett who had had the foresight to purchase many of the grand old names of Savile Row and incorporate them into the business. These included Johns & Pegg; Fallan & Harvey; James and James; Wells of Mayfair; and Watson, Fagerstrom & Hughes, each one adding to the unique history of a house that, in more than two centuries of bespoke tailoring, has made for four kings, seven crown princes, and two presidents of the United States.

CHITTLEBOROUGH & MORGAN

Roy Chittleborough and Joseph Morgan, along with the late Edward Sexton, were the tailoring talents who gave life to the glorious creativity of the much-celebrated sixties designer and stylist, Tommy Nutter, who turned Savile Row on its head.

Nutter arrived on Savile Row at a time when it looked like it might be on its last legs. He brought sex appeal, star power, and much-needed buzz to the tired old street. During an eight-year run, he made for all of London's celebrity elite. Three of The Beatles were wearing Nutter suits when they crossed Abbey Road for their famous album cover (George Harrison chose to wear denim); John Lennon and Yoko Ono were both customers, as were Mick and Bianca Jagger, for whom he designed her celebrated white wedding suit; Elton John wore Nutter, as did Diana Ross; and from the fashion world Nutter dressed Bill Gibb and Twiggy.

Nutter was not a tailor, however. To turn his designs into wearable reality he called upon the sartorial know-how of Chittleborough, Morgan, and Sexton.

The Beatles crossing Abbey Road for their famous album cover; John, Paul and Ringo are wearing Tommy Nutter.

Chittleborough and Sexton had learned their trade at Kilgour, French & Stanbury in the fifties under the great Louis Stanbury, while Morgan trained at Meyer & Mortimer before moving to Dennis Wilkinson and then Jarvis & Hamilton on Conduit Street. Nutter lived nearby and would wave to Morgan as he passed the workshop window, so when Tommy started his own business in 1969, Morgan joined him.

Nutter's star burned bright but fast and by 1976 it was all over and Sexton bought out the business, establishing his own firm. In 1981 Chittleborough and Morgan established their own bespoke tailoring firm on Savile Row, and their style retains something of the character of their Nutter's heritage, with all its finery. Today, it is one of the smallest and most discreet houses on the street and continues to produce bespoke clothes only. •

Required trimmings: *0.35 m × 0.10 m 265 g 100% cotton canvas, cut on the bias; 0.35 m × 0.10 m 265 g 100% cotton canvas, cut on the straight; 0.20 m × 0.10 m 185 g 100% cotton canvas, cut on the straight; 0.50 m lightweight 1¼" fusible cotton-canvas tape; sewing thread, polyester, 120s; button-hole thread, polyester 80s; 1 × 16 line 4-hole button for collar; 7 × 16 line 4-hole button for fronts and cuffs plus spare if required.*

MAKING A SHIRT

A step–by–step guide to making a shirt by hand,
following the method of Lizzie Willett

W HAT SAVILE Row is to tailoring, Jermyn Street is to shirt making. This short street, a stone's throw from Savile Row, one block to the south of Piccadilly, is home to many of the most celebrated and finest shirt makers on earth.

Just as with Savile Row bespoke tailoring, so shirt making is taught through a lengthy apprenticeship, building through the simpler stages and culminating with learning to make collars and cuffs. The collar was once so important that up to the late 1950s many men wore shirts with separate collars. They were laundered and starched separately from the shirt and replaced more frequently to ensure they were always crisp and beautifully white.

Shirt making requires less handwork than tailoring, and a shirt-making apprenticeship typically lasts no more than a year, but it requires great skill; perfect hand-eye coordination; unparalleled control over the sewing machine; and exceptional manual dexterity to handle what in many cases are extremely lightweight and often delicate fabrics – much lighter than anything used by the tailors of Savile Row.

To make a shirt you will need a sewing machine with variable stitch length and a metal sewing plate to which a magnetic guide can be attached. You will also need a rotary cutter, shears, small scissors, snips, a magnetic sewing guide, and an iron.

The great majority of English handmade shirts are cut and sewn from high-quality two-fold cotton or linen shirt fabric, typically in qualities from 'two-fold 80S' to 'two-fold 140S', most often poplin or Oxford weaves. White remains by far the most popular choice, as are pale and deeper shades of blue. Finer fabrics including Sea Island cottons are also used, and linen is rising in popularity because of its great comfort in the heat, its durability and its incredibly low environmental footprint. Also popular are brushed flannel-finish cottons, chambrays, and lightweight denims. Most good shirt cotton today is made either in Italy or Turkey, where a lot of cotton is grown. The best-quality linen is grown in Belgium, the Netherlands, and northern France.

The list of required trimmings is short – just the floating canvases used in the collar and cuffs, and the fusible canvas that stiffens the front hem. Two weights of canvas are used – a heavier one for the top collar and collar band, and a lighter one for the cuffs. This canvas is bought on a roll: the top collar is cut on the bias and everything else on the straight. A fusible canvas, which is bought cut-to-width on a roll, is used in the front hem.

Just as with bespoke trousers, there is a cutting-out stage to prepare and cut your chosen fabric. Following a lay play, a card pattern is laid on to ensure no fabric is wasted, and pieces are typically cut directly without marking using a rotary cutter, as well as shears for some steps. As with bespoke tailored clothes, considerable attention is paid to matching the stripes and checks often found in men's shirts.

Making a shirt is typically divided into seven distinct stages: yoke to back; sleeves; fronts; side seam; collar and cuff; collar and cuff attach; button and buttonhole; ending; and press.

The combination of machine sewing during the setting stage and hand sewing during the finishing stage results in a functional and immaculately crafted garment that showcases the artistry, attention to detail, and exceptional quality that defines this age-old tradition. •

CUTTING OUT THE JOB

CUTTING THE FABRIC

*Use a good-quality cotton or linen shirt fabric; a two-fold cotton is best,
with typically fine shirts being made in qualities from two-fold 80S to two-fold
140S and Sea Island. Linen fabrics also make an excellent shirt.*

(1.1) The fabric should be laid out folded in half, carefully lining up selvedge to selvedge. With the fold to the back, iron out any wrinkles. If it is a plain fabric you can press the fold. (1.2) Lay out the pattern pieces according to the lay plan. (1.3) Flip the yoke piece to cut bias yoke, flip the top collar piece to cut collar stay pocket piece. (1.4) If using card patterns there is no need to mark around the pattern pieces; simply use weights and cut around using a handheld rotary cutter. If you prefer, you can mark around the pieces, either with a heat-removable pen, or some shirt cutters use a pencil. (1.5) **Fronts**. Cut 2 fronts with different widths. Cut a pair. Leave a piece for overfront (buttonhole side) at full width, (front hem piece 3¼" from the centre front line). Reduce the width of underfront (button side), narrower, reducing the width of the centre hem piece to 2½" wide measured from the centre front line; mark at 2½" at the top and bottom. Lay a metal ruler between the lines and cut with the rotary cutter. Mark notches at the hip point. (1.6) **Collars**. Cut a pair of collars and a pair of collar bands. Fold both in half and cut a small notch to mark where the collar stay fold is, bare ⅛" to mark the centre. If using collar stays, cut an additional pair of collar ends, cutting only around about 4" from the end of the pattern. (1.7) **Sleeves**. Cut a pair of sleeves. Checking the centre of the sleeve is running down the grainline, mark the end of the gauntlet slit, draw a straight line 6¼" long, parallel to the centre line, then cut with scissors and iron off pen. (1.8) **Back**. Cut back on the fold. Turn the fabric round and bring the folded edge to the front of the board for ease. Cut out and mark hip and back pleat notches. (1.9) **Gauntlet Pieces and Gusset**. Cut pairs of small and large gauntlet pieces and gusset. The gusset piece is easiest cut held in the hand using scissors. (1.10) **Yoke Pieces**. When using cotton fabric cut one pair with the long edge on the straight and one pair on the bias. For linen or silk fabric cut both on the straight. The bias yoke is largely aesthetic, with checks and stripes running on the diagonal on the outer yoke. (1.11) **Cuffs**. Cut 2 pairs from the same pattern piece by folding the fabric over again to create a layer of four and cutting once around pattern. •

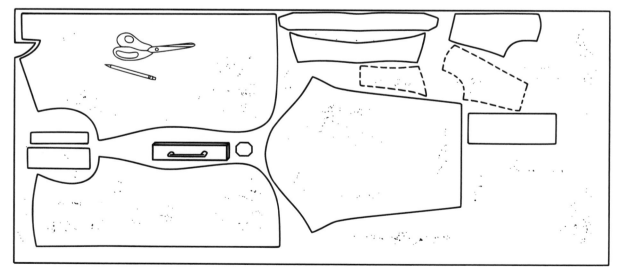

Fig. 1.2

*Two weights of floating canvas are used in the production of the
bespoke shirt: a lightweight and a heavier weight.
Collars and cuffs are cut from large rolls of canvas. Front canvas comes
on a pre-cut narrow strip so does not need to be pre-cut.*

(2.1) **Collar.** For the top collar, cut from the heavier canvas weight, on the bias, cutting around the full pattern piece using a rotary cutter. Check the symmetry by folding in half. If not symmetrical trim the larger side. (2.2) For the collar band cut from the heavier canvas weight, on the straight, but reduce the depth of the pattern piece by ½". Lay the collar band pattern piece on canvas, cut around the bottom edge using a rotary cutter, then move the pattern piece down by ½" (to the notch if the piece has one marked) and cut around the top edge. Check symmetry and correct as per top collar. (2.3) **Cuffs.** Cut one pair taking ½" off the long edge of the pattern piece. Fold the canvas in half, lay the pattern piece on, cut along the bottom edge, move the piece down by ½" then cut round the three remaining sides. Check symmetry and correct as per collar. •

3 CUTTING STRIPES & CHECKS

*Both stripes and checks need to be pattern
matched when cutting out.*

(3.1) Centre fronts must align. Put the centre front on the centre of the most obvious stripe. For check place the bottom edge on the edge of a horizontal line. (3.2) The centre back must align across all pieces. When cutting a stripe or check do not press fold into the cloth until you are ready to cut out the back. When ready to cut, press a finger crease into the centre of the most prominent stripe. Then press with the iron. Make sure the checks have not swerved off. Match the bottom of the armhole to the same point on back and front armholes. (3.3) Match points of both collar bands and the collar points. Align the bottom of the collar band to the same stripe. Align collar points on same stripe/check. Align the centre of the collar and band to the prominent stripe. (3.4) The sleeve centre line must run down the centre of the prominent stripe. On a check, align armhole points with the horizontal stripe. Cut the gauntlet slit straight down the stripe. Align the centre of the top of the sleeve with the edge of the yoke. (3.5) The large gauntlet piece must be matched to the gauntlet slit. The pattern piece has a notch at ½". Line this up along the same stripe as the slit and line up with horizontal lines on a check. (3.6) On a check, line up the centre back of the yoke (the line of the seam allowance on the patterns) with the prominent stripe. On a bias piece, align the point with the centre back stripe. •

SETTING THE SHIRT

1   SEWING

(1.1) The cut pieces are now ready for sewing. Keep the pieces flat. (1.2) Select the correct thread colour and thread the machine. Typically a 120S thread is used. (1.3) Bespoke shirt making requires minimal pinning. At the original Turnbull & Asser factory, staff were only allowed 3 pins, and all of these had to be accounted for (in case they were left in a shirt). The only processes in which pins are used are the setting of the pleats where the sleeve is inserted into the cuff, and attaching any pockets. (1.4) The sewing of a shirt is divided into sections which in some workshops are undertaken by a number of different team members, as is the case at Emma Willis workshop. In most workshops it would be normal for the collars and cuffs to be made by a specialist collar hand. Whilst most shirtmakers have the capability to do so, it is rare, for reasons of efficiency, that a full garment will be made all the way through by one maker. •

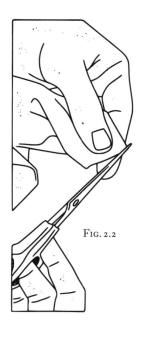

Fig. 2.2

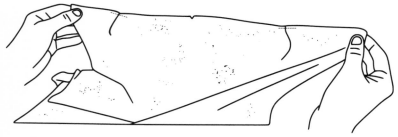

Fig. 2.3

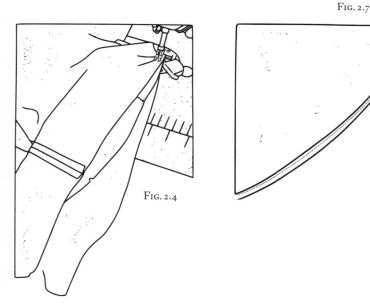

Fig. 2.4

Fig. 2.7

YOKE TO BACK   2

(2.1) **Yoke**. Attach a magnetic sewing guide at ⅜". Join the yoke pieces, back tacking both ends. Finger press the seam open. The outer yoke is sewn using bias pieces, inner yoke using those cut on the straight. (2.2) **Back**. Cut a bare ⅛" nick at the centre back by folding in half and cutting a small corner off the folded edge. (2.3) Fold pleats towards the centre back, finger press then tack in place about ⅛" from the top edge, tacking about 1" across. (2.4) Lay the bias yoke on the board seam allowance down, then lay the back on top with the pleats facing inwards on top. Next, lay the straight yoke on top, seam up, sandwiching the back between the two yoke pieces, ensuring the nick on the centre back is lined up to the centre seams on the yokes. (2.5) Attach the magnetic guide to ⅜" and sew across the top, no need to back tack. (2.6) Fold up the bias yoke. Ensuring all seam allowances are pointing up, edge stitch along the edge of the seam, catching in the seam allowance, no need to back tack. (2.7) **Hem**. First, working from inside, at first nick fold ¼" to the inside and edge stitch all the way to the other nick, letting the machine take the fabric – don't pull or force it. Fold ¼" again and oversew on top of the original sewing line, at the start and end running into a point at the nick. •

(3.1) **Gauntlets.** Starting with the right sleeve, place the sleeve wrong-side up under the machine and put the needle down at the top of the narrow side of the gauntlet slit. Finger press the small gauntlet piece in half lengthways. Lay the folded small gauntlet piece against the slit on the narrow side, with all three raw edges aligned, and sew down at a foot's width, tapering at the bottom of the slit. (3.2) Place the unfolded large gauntlet piece onto the larger side of the gauntlet slit, raw edges aligned, and sew down at a foot's width, tapering at the bottom of the slit. (3.3) Repeat for the left sleeve, but reverse the order, sewing the large gauntlet piece first. (3.4) Make sure you have a mirrored pair. (3.5) Starting now with the left sleeve, fold the small gauntlet piece through the slit to the right side of the sleeve. Edge stitch down the folded side curving slightly towards the slit at the bottom. Trim off ½" from the bottom point of the gauntlet slit. (3.6) Fold the large gauntlet piece through the slit to the right side. Finger press the bottom of the right hand edge about ¼" following down the seam previously sewn (A). Fold and finger press the free edge ¼" towards the sewn edge (B). Fold in half placing the pressed edge on top of the sewn seam (C) and edge stitch the folded edge, stopping 2" from the point of the gauntlet slit. ☞

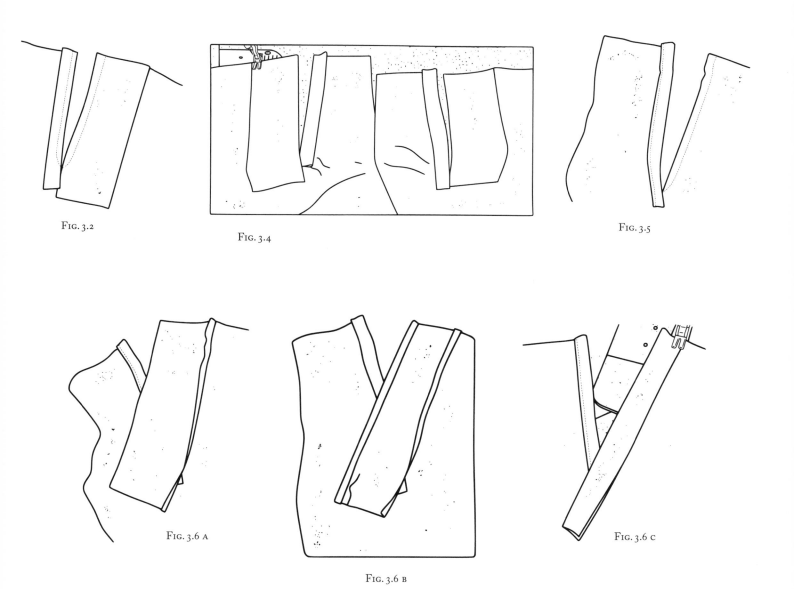

Fig. 3.2

Fig. 3.4

Fig. 3.5

Fig. 3.6 A

Fig. 3.6 B

Fig. 3.6 C

(3.7) Now create the mitred end of the gauntlet. Fold the free end diagonally, twice to create a mitred point (A). Hold down the point, then continue sewing around the point following the angle's edges. At 1¾" from the point, turn 90 degrees and sew across to the stitch line on the other side and back tack creating a box at the bottom of the gauntlet (B). A rectangular guide 1¾" long is handy. (3.8) Moving to the head of the sleeve, fold the top ¼" and edge stitch all the way around the head of the sleeve. (3.9) Repeat all steps on the right sleeve. •

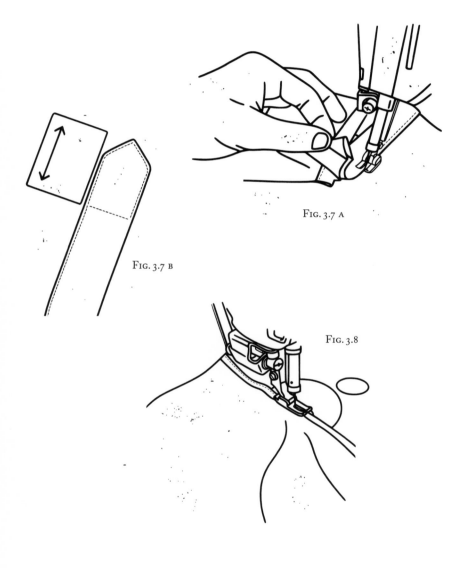

FIG. 3.7 A

FIG. 3.7 B

FIG. 3.8

(4.1) Starting with the underfront, lay your front piece on the pressing board with the top of the shirt to the right and the wrong side facing up. (4.2) Fold the top edge down at a point ⅝" from the centre front line, and press an even crease down the front moving from right to left, from the top to the bottom of the underfront. (4.3) Open up and now fold the top edge down so the distance from the pressed crease to folded edge is 1" (A). Now evenly press all the way down from right to left. Fold down again, from the original crease, folding the raw edge inside, to give a 1" front hem (B), turned to the inside of the underfront. (4.4) Move on to the overfront. Working with the right side up, lay the bottom edge of fusible canvas strip (1¼" wide) ⅝" from the centre front (A). Iron the fusible canvas in place, keeping an even distance from the top edge, stopping about 1" from the bottom. Cut the fusible canvas and iron down the end (B). (4.5) Now begin sewing. Starting with the underfront, on the wrong-side edge stitch all the way down the inner edge of the fold, starting at the neck hole edge – no need to back tack. (4.6) Replace a standard foot with a ⅜" foot ('front foot'). Take the overfront and fold the edge over the lining piece. Trim off any excess which overhangs the lining all the way up the front. ☞

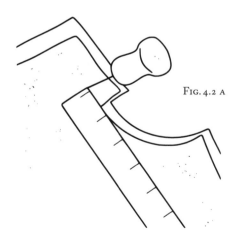

FIG. 4.2 A

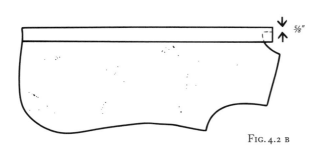

Fig. 4.2 b

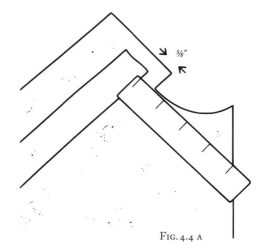

Fig. 4.4 a

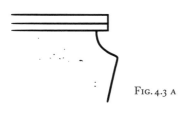

Fig. 4.3 a

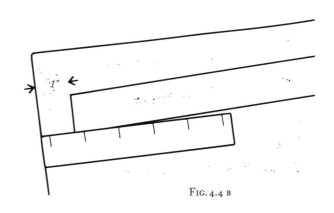

Fig. 4.4 b

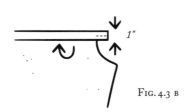

Fig. 4.3 b

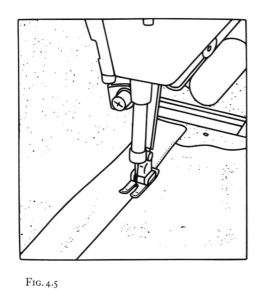

Fig. 4.5

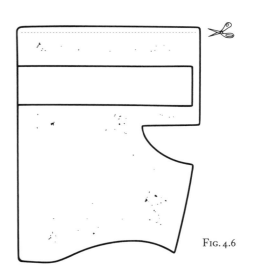

Fig. 4.6

(4.7) Fold the front edge tight to the lining, then fold over again, tight to the lining such that the lining is fully enclosed. Sew ⅜" from the edge, starting at the bottom (a), making sure that the fabric is tightly wrapped around the lining as you sew. Sew to the top, then turn the shirt and sew down from the top of the outer edge of the front hem. (4.8) Trim off excess hem at the neck hole. Match the front at the top and trim off any excess at the bottom. (4.9) Change back to the regular foot to begin hemming. Hem the underfront, starting from the nick, fold ¼" to inside and edge stitch all the way round to the front, and back tack at both ends. Fold again and then stitch again following on top of the original sewing line. Hem the overfront starting from the raised front hem and sewing back to the nick. Back tack at both ends.

(4.10) **Shoulder Join**. Attach ⅜" guide. Take the back piece and place on the board inner-side up, keeping the outside yoke down (a). Take the underfront and lay it right-side up so that the wrong sides are together. Sew along the shoulder seam (b). (4.11) Repeat with the overfront on the other side of the yoke. (4.12) Remove the guide. Turn the work over and, starting with the left side, turn the outer yoke up. Fold and finger press the edge of the yoke ⅜" inside. Lay the folded edge of the yoke on top of the shoulder seam sewing line, ensuring the seam allowance is folded inside the yoke. Edge stitch along. (4.13) Repeat on the other side. (4.14) Tack closed the open edges of the yoke with a running stitch, at the side and neck hole about ⅛" from the edge. (4.15) **Set Sleeves**. Place the guide on the machine at ⅜". ☞

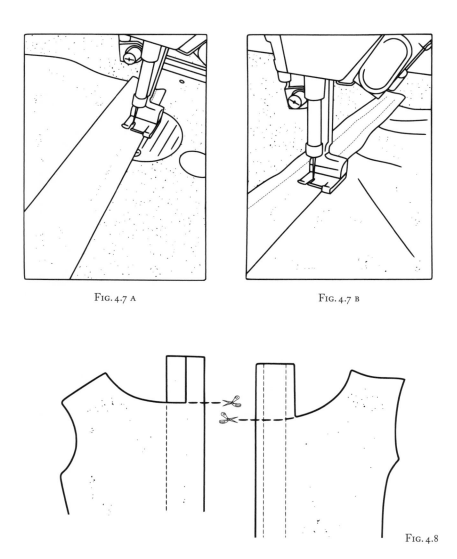

FIG. 4.7 A   FIG. 4.7 B

FIG. 4.8

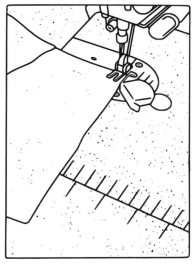

FIG. 4.10 A   FIG. 4.10 B

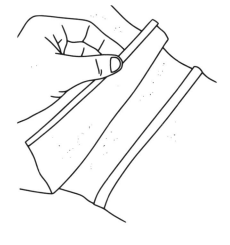

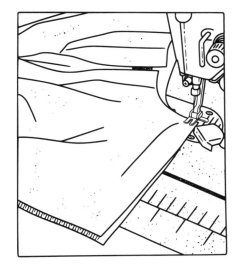

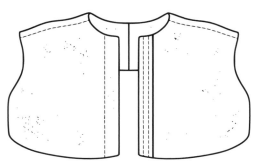

FIGS. 4.11

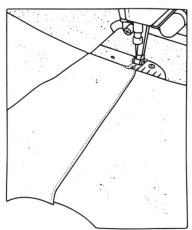

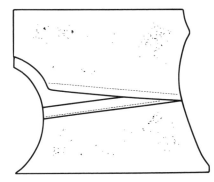

FIGS. 4.12

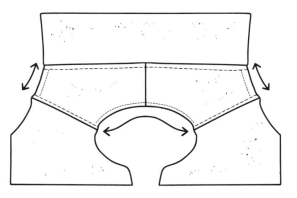

FIG. 4.14

(4.16) Starting with the right sleeve, lay the sleeve on the machine bed gauntlet (right-side up), laying the folded edge at the sleeve head against the guide. Lay the back on top, on the underfront side, right-side down so the right sides are together, with the top edge of the body just overlapping the raw edge of the folded top of the sleeve head, leaving ¼" space to the edge. (4.17) Sew all the way around the sleeve head towards the front, using the folded edge of the sleeve head to guide your sewing. (4.18) Repeat for the other sleeve. Place the left sleeve on the machine bed gauntlet (right-side up), laying the folded edge at the sleeve head against the guide. Lay the overfront right-side down, and starting at the side seam, sew all the way round to the back of the armhole. (4.19) Open out the shirt. Remove the guide. Starting at the underarm fold the sleeve seam onto the body, covering all of the raw edges, and sew on top of the original sewing line to the head of the sleeve. (4.20) Repeat on the other sleeve. •

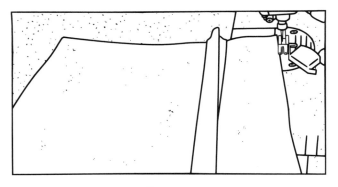

FIG. 5.1 A

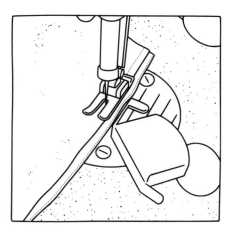

FIG. 4.16

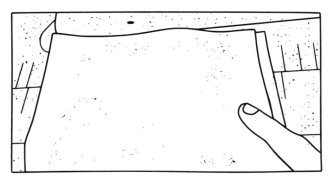

FIG. 5.1 B

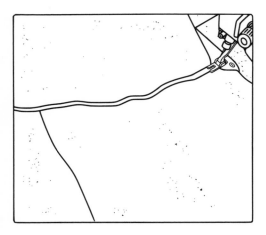

FIG. 4.19

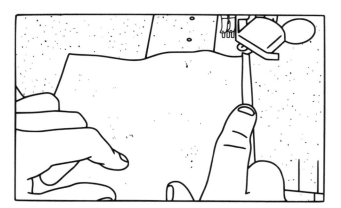

FIG. 5.1 C

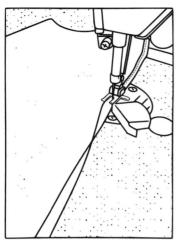

FIG. 5.2

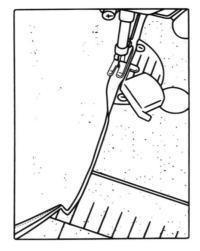

FIG. 5.3

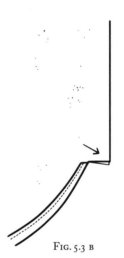

FIG. 5.3 B

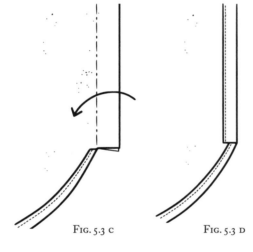

FIG. 5.3 C

FIG. 5.3 D

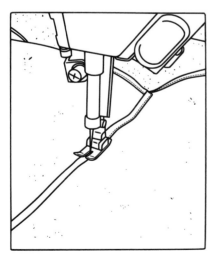

FIG. 5.5 A

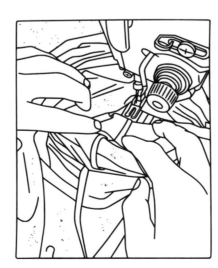

FIG. 5.6 B

(5.1) Place the guide against the foot of your machine. Lay the right sleeve gauntlet-side up (A). Fold the sleeve in half lengthways, left-side over, with the upper edge ¼" inside the lower edge (B). Fold the edge of the lower-side edge over enclosing the raw edge (C). (5.2) Place the folded edge against the guide and sew; the stitch line should be along the raw edge. (5.3) Continue to fold and sew all the way along the seam, ensuring matching at the bottom of the seams where the sleeve has been set, and at the nicks. Pause about 1½" from the bottom and move the upper piece across so that the two raw edges are aligned (B). Fold both raw edges over together (C) and sew straight down, still with the folded edge against the guide. Back tack at the bottom (D). (5.4) Repeat on the other side, this time starting at the back, ensuring the nicks are matched and raw edges lined up. This time sew up, back tacking at the start, to about 1½" up, then separate by ¼" and fold over. Next, sew all the way to the top and down the sleeve – no need to back tack at the bottom where the cuff will be attached. (5.5) Turn over and start with the underfront side. Starting at the bottom (no need to back tack), fold the seam to the front, and edge stitch all the way up the side seam (A). Continue down the sleeve, taking care not to catch the fabric, as you will be working inside the sleeve. Gather material carefully in your hand as you sew and ensure all seam material is pushed to the back and the seam is kept flat. No need to back tack at the end. (5.6) Repeat for the left sleeve. This time starting at the sleeve end, gather the sleeve in the hand and with the body of the shirt to your left side push the seam to the right (B) and edge stitch all the way up the sleeve and down the side seam. No need to back tack at the end. ☞

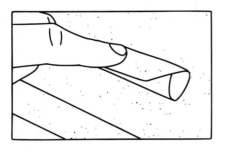

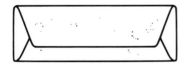

FIGS. 5.7

(5.7) **Gussets.** Take your hexagonal gusset piece and fold it into thirds. Fold the bottom edge up, then fold the top edge down over the top, creating an envelope shape, but make sure the raw edge does not overhang. (5.8) Fold in half, folded pieces inside, and place the middle under the centre of your sewing foot. (5.9) Lay the bottom of the side seam over your folded gusset piece and sew a V shape, about 1 cm long each side, with the open part of the V facing the gusset, inside the existing stitch lines. (5.10) Turn over (b), and starting at the left end of the gusset piece, fold the corners in to create a mitred point (c), folded sides down, and stitch down the two sides of the point, starting at the bottom (1 & 2). Leaving the needle down, fold the corners of the right side of the gusset piece to create a matching mitre, then continue sewing round, leaving the one side of the hexagon facing you open, back tacking at the bottom (3–7). (5.11) Repeat on the other side. •

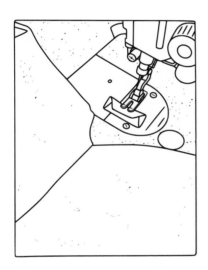

FIG. 5.8

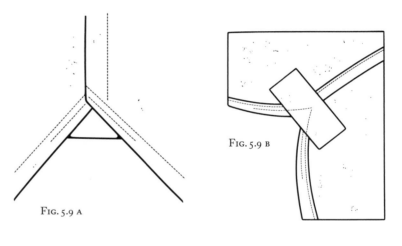

FIG. 5.9 A

FIG. 5.9 B

FIG. 5.9 C

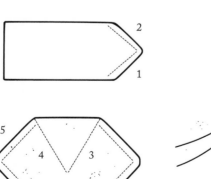

FIGS. 5.10

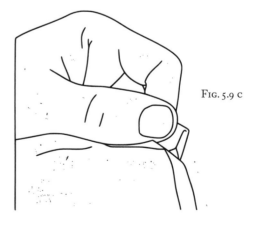

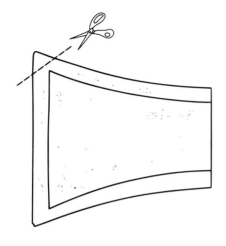

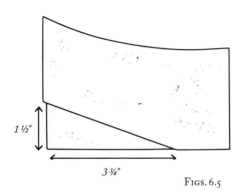

1 ½"

3 ¾"

Figs. 6.5

(6.1) The collar is formed of two parts: the top collar and the collar band. The top collar has a topside and an underside. The collar band has an inner and outer side. A pocket to contain collar stays is often included on the under top collar. The collar is sewn with a small stitch at between 18 and 20 stitches to the inch, and a longer running stitch about 10–12 stitches to the inch. (6.2) Fold the collar pieces in half and check symmetry. Trim if required. Also check for flaws in the fabric. (6.3) Snip the corner off the collar lining at the point, about ⅜" from the point to reduce bulk at the collar point. Do the same with the collar stay pocket pieces. (6.4) Fold the band lining in half, check symmetry and cut a bare ⅛" nick at the centre back. (6.5) **Top Collar.** Start by making the pocket for the collar stays. Take the underside of the top collar, lay down with the point towards you. Fold down the corner furthest from you 3 ¾" from the right edge and 1 ½" from the top and place on top of the pocket piece. (6.6) Following the stitch lines shown in Fig. 6.6, beginning just beyond one end of the fold in the collar piece, sew down the edge, then turn through 45 degrees and sew in a straight line to a point ¼" to the side of the collar point. Now starting at the other edge of the fold in the collar piece sew up the folded edge then turn through 135 degrees and sew towards a point ¼" to the side of the collar point, forming a sewn channel just wide enough for your collar stay. (6.7) Repeat on the other side. (6.8) Lay under top collar piece with the point towards you right-side up. Lay the top collar topside piece on top, right-side down, so the right sides are together. Lay the lining piece on top and the cut point towards you. Set the machine to a running stitch. Starting on the right side, at the inner edge of the collar, stitch ¼" all the way round three sides of the collar. You can sew this with a ¼" guide, but it is preferable not to so that the fabric is always able to lie naturally. ☞

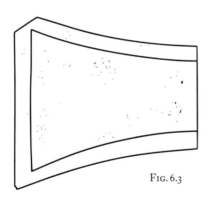

Fig. 6.3

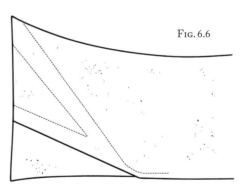

Fig. 6.6

Fig. 6.8

(6.9) Trim back the lining away from the points, and remove a small piece at the inside corner where the collar will be sewn to the neck band to reduce bulk in the seam. Snip three small-angled nicks into the curved edge of the top collar. Snip the corner of the collar point on the fabric. (6.10) Repeat at the other side. (6.11) Turn out the collar, using a bradawl, knitting needle or similar to push out the points. Use a needle mounted in a cork to poke out the collar points perfectly. (6.12) Take the collar and roll the edges between the fingers until the seam is perfectly in the centre between the top and under collar. Attach the guide at ¼". Change back to small stitch. Starting at the right side of

the collar, do a small back tack and then sew ¼" top stitch all the way around, using your hands to encourage the fabric away from the seams as you sew to get a nice flat seam. Leave your needle down at the collar points as you turn the collar. Do a small back tack at the end. (6.13) Using a running stitch, close the open end ⅛" from the edge and make sure all pieces are well aligned. Trim the raw edge a bare nothing just to tidy stray threads. Fold in half, lining up the points and trimming any excess. Cut a ⅛" nick at the centre back. (6.14) **Collar Band.** Lay the outer collar band fabric on top of the lining fabric, aligning at the curved edge. Fold the overlapping fabric under the straight edge of the

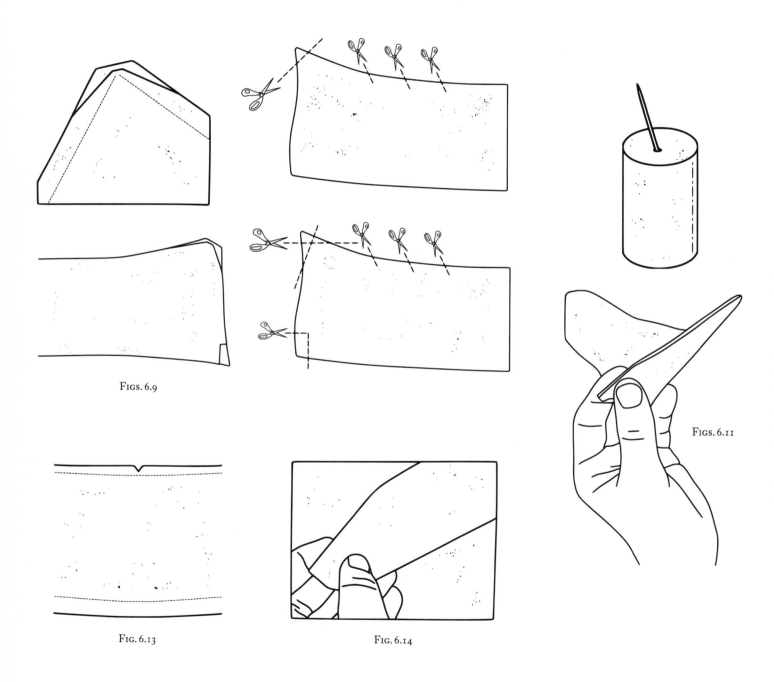

FIGS. 6.9

FIGS. 6.11

FIG. 6.13

FIG. 6.14

band lining. (6.15) Drop the needle to hold in place. Place the sewing guide at ¼" and set to small stitch. Sew all the way down, ¼" from the edge, wrapping the edge of the canvas as you sew. Use thumbs to ensure a tight wrap. No need to back tack at either end. (6.16) Take the top collar and lay it top-side up. Lay the collar band on top, fabric-side down (canvas showing), aligning the notches at the centre back. (6.17) Starting at the centre back notch, sew a running stitch at ¼" from the edge, from the centre to the edge, attaching the unwrapped side of the collar band to the top collar. Turn the collar round. Sew from the centre to the other edge. (6.18) Fold the collar in half and check symmetry.

If not symmetrical, unpick and re-sew; the band can be eased or the top collar stretched to make it symmetrical. (6.19) Take the inner collar band piece and lay with the curved side closest to you, then lay the assembled collar and band on top with the band uppermost, so the top collar is sandwiched. (6.20) Starting at the end of the band, back tack and sew using a small stitch ¼" from the edge, making sure to enclose the holding stitch. You can use a guide for this. Make sure to line up the edges and match the notches. Do not force the fabric – allow the machine to take it. Back tack at the end. Trim back canvas around the curve of the collar band. ☞

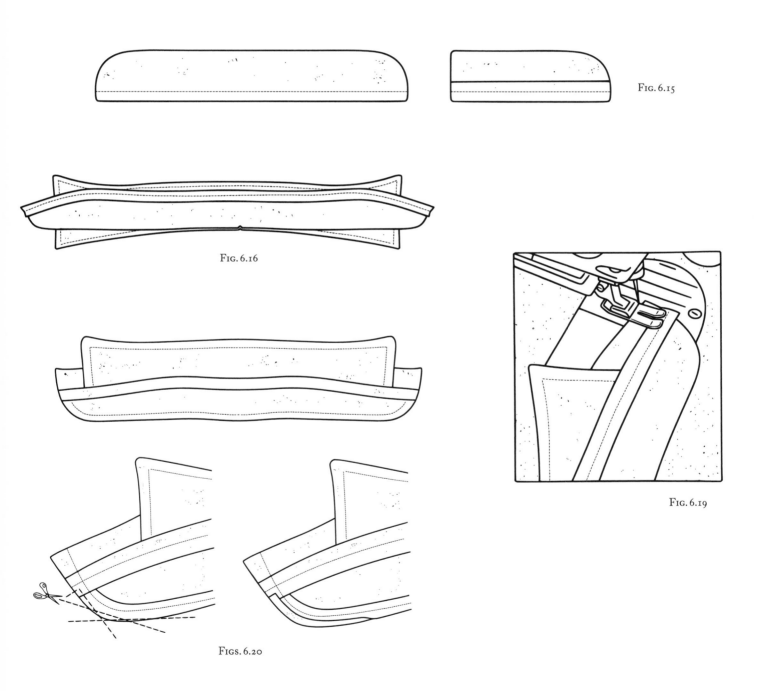

Fig. 6.15

Fig. 6.16

Fig. 6.19

Figs. 6.20

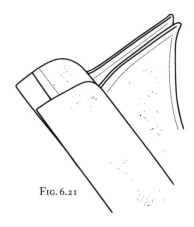

Fig. 6.21

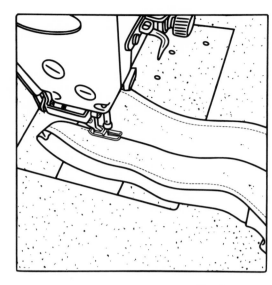

Fig. 6.22

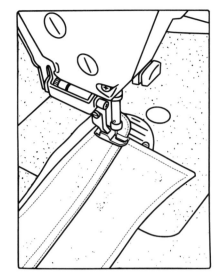

Fig. 6.23

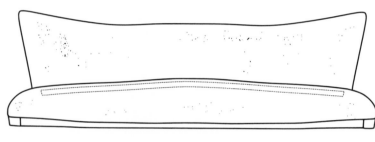

Figs. 6.24

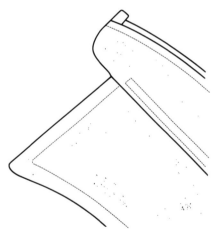

MAKING THE COLLAR AND CUFF (CONT.)

(6.21) Turn the collar band out and use fingers to roll the edges until the seam is perfectly in the centre between the inner and outer collar band. Use your thumbnail to crease the band where it meets the topside of the top collar. Fold in half and check that the point and bands match. (6.22) You will now top stitch the band to the collar. Lay the collar with the topside of the top collar up and the top collar to the right. Place the foot on the edge of the collar band, where the band meets the top collar, and lower the needle in line with the top stitch on the top collar. With a small stitch, sew on the edge of the band, making sure that the band is pulled to the left. (6.23) Sew down making the last stitch at the point where it lines up with the top stitch at the other side of the top collar. Turn the machine 90 degrees and sew 3 stitches. (6.24) Turn 90 degrees again. With the edge of the foot on the edge of the band, sew all the way down, stopping in line with the starting point. Again turn right 90 degrees and sew 3 stitches, turn 90 degrees again then back tack over your starting stitches. You will have sewn a long narrow rectangle of stitching. (6.25) Trim off excess from the outer collar band, leaving ¼" below the inner band. (6.26) Quarter the collar; first fold in half, cut a small nick at the centre of the outer band fabric. Fold the ends of the collar bands into the centre, finger crease lightly, open out and make a small mark at the quarter creases with a heat-removable pen. (6.27) **Cuff**. Fold the cuff lining in half and check the symmetry. Trim if required. (6.28) Lay the top cuff fabric over the lining, with the top overlapping ⅜" to ½". (6.29) Wrap the fabric round the edge of the lining; with the guide at ¼" and using a small stitch, sew from top to bottom, ensuring the fabric wraps the lining tightly. Repeat for the other cuff. (6.30) Take the back cuff fabric and lay the lining and top cuff fabric on top, lining uppermost, with the right side of the fabric together. (6.31) Starting on the corner of the back cuff fabric, back tack then sew with a running stitch ¼" down the side (you can use a guide if you need). At the corner, turn through 90 degrees, sew along the bottom, turn 90 again and sew up the other side back tacking at the end. Snip the corners off the lining at both outer corners. Same for round, square or mitred cuffs. ☞

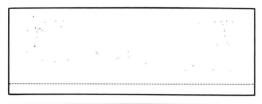
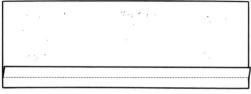

FIGS. 6.29

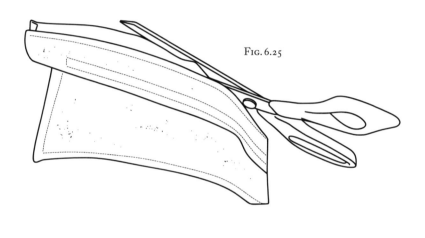

FIG. 6.25

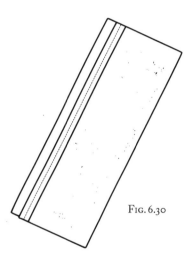

FIG. 6.30

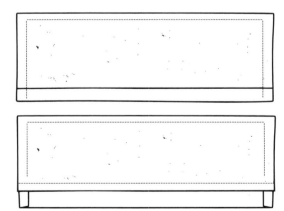

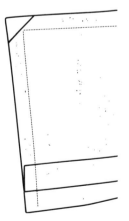

FIGS. 6.31

(6.32) Turn the cuff out using a bradawl, knitting needle or similar to push out the points. Use a needle mounted in a cork to poke out the cuff points perfectly; roll edges between fingers until the seam is perfectly in the centre between the top and back cuff, and use the edge of the sewing table to lightly crease the edge. (6.33) Put the guide at ¼" and starting ¾" from the inner edge of the cuff back tack and top stitch three sides, ensuring that the seams are sitting flat, finishing ¾" from the inner edge of the cuff with a back tack. (6.34) Collar and cuffs are now ready to be attached. •

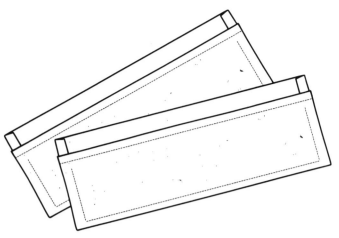

FIGS. 6.34

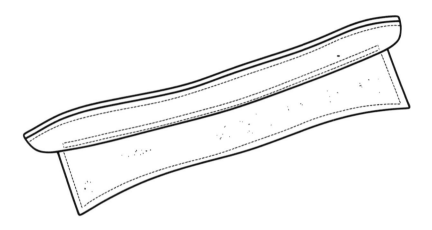

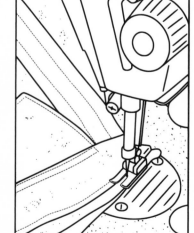
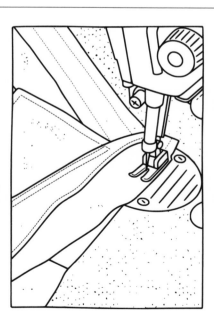

FIGS. 7.2

(7.1) **Attach Collar**. Double check the front line up. Lay down the overfront with the neck opening to the right, right-side up and place the collar, inner-band up, on top with the raw edges lined up. (7.2) Sew the single layer of the outer collar to the shirt body. When about 1" along, once you are able, move the band lining to the left, away from the foot. (7.3) Make sure the middle nick of the collar matches with the middle nick of the yoke, then make sure that the two quarter marks are attached at the same point on the shirt body. Sew a foot's width all the way along, making sure that the edges line up. About 1" from the end put the band lining back down and sew to the end being careful not to sew over the band lining. (7.4) Turn the collar up. (7.5) Line up the quarter marks. Starting on the quarter mark on the underfront, sew out towards the front edge. Edge stitch along the collar band, ensuring that the stitch sits on top of the sewing line

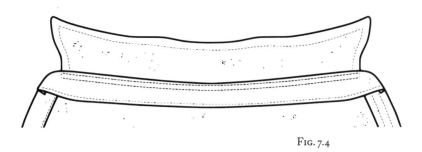

FIG. 7.4

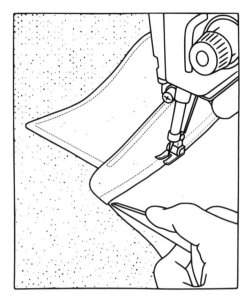

FIG. 7.5

below. Use the point of scissors or similar to ensure all seam allowances are tucked inside at the end of the collar band. (7.6) Sew to the end of the band then turn 90 degrees and sew along the upper edge following the curve of the collar band, overstitch 1" past the start of the box stitch. (7.7) On the other side sew in the reverse direction, starting 1" inside the box, sewing round to the quarter mark, and then carry on all the way along, overstitching the starting point by 1". (7.8) **Attach Cuff**. Check that the gauntlet and the edge of the sleeve line up. Trim if needed. (7.9) Make two small pleats on the end of the sleeve, about 1" from the large gauntlet facing towards the gauntlet, and pin in place. (7.10) Lay the cuff onto the sleeve, and adjust the size of the pleats if needed so that the cuff and sleeve end are matched. ✑

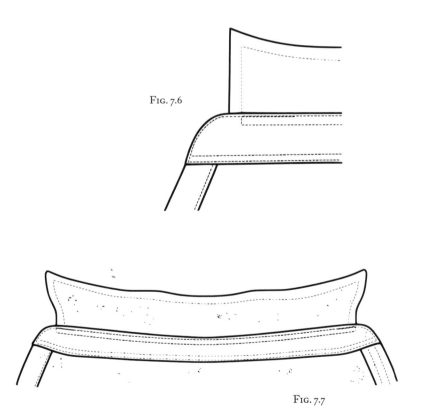

FIG. 7.6

FIG. 7.7

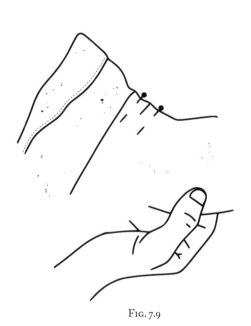

FIG. 7.9

(7.11) On the inside of the sleeve, line up the cuff, with the outside of the cuff facing up, ¾" from the edge of the sleeve. (7.12) Sew the cuff to the sleeve, making sure not to catch the lining. Go all the way along, no need to back tack. (7.13) Turn over and push all of the raw edges of material inside the cuff. (7.14) Starting 1" from the end of the cuff topstitching, sew down to the edge of the cuff to the point where it joins the sleeve, turn through 90 degrees, back tack to the edge, then sew along the edge with the stitches sitting above the sewing line below. (7.15) At the other end of the sleeve seam, back tack at the edge, about 3 stitches, turn 90 degrees, and sew up, over the existing stitches by 1". (7.16) Repeat on the other cuff. •

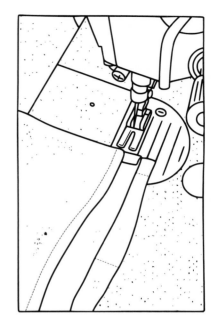

FIG. 7.11

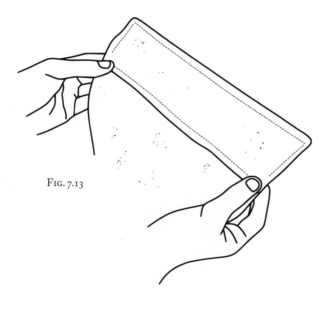

FIG. 7.13

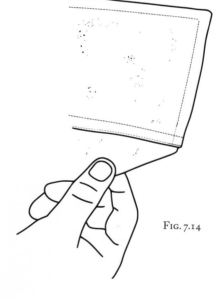

FIG. 7.14

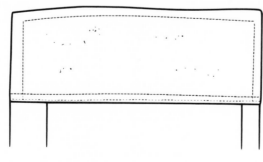

FIG. 7.15

FINISHING THE SHIRT

1   BUTTON AND BUTTONHOLE

(1.1) Iron both front hems. (1.2) Mark the position of your holes starting with the fronts. Mark the edge of the buttonhole on the collar band ½" from the front edge, centred in the band. Mirror the position at the other end of the band. Measure dot-to-dot to check the final collar measurement. Turn the shirt 90 degrees and mark the next buttonhole 3" down from the bottom of the collar band on the overfront. Then mark the position of each additional button in turn 3½" down. On a typical man's shirt there will be 6 buttons in total. (1.3) Mark the cuffs. For a single button cut a mark in the centre, for a two-button divide in half and centre each button in a half, ⅛" away from the stitch line on the cuff. Use a needle to make a small hole to mark the position of the hole or holes. (1.4) Thread the machine with correct thread, typically a slightly coarser thread than the standard sewing thread. Select the correct buttonhole programme, and always do a test on a scrap, even with a professional buttonhole machine, ideally something like a scrap cuff with the same weight of cloth and canvas. Check the front and back of the test. (1.5) If OK, move on to buttonholing. (1.6) Start by buttoning the front of the shirt. Line up the back edge of the hole with the red dot on your collar band and press to sew; the buttonhole should be running along the band, perpendicular to the front edge of the shirt. Moving onto the holes on the front hem, line up the centre of the buttonhole with the red dot and press to sew; buttonholes on the front hem should run up and down the hem. Making marks on your machine to show the centre point and back of your most commonly used hole sizes helps ensure accuracy. Repeat for all holes. (1.7) Moving to cuffs, line the edge of the hole up with the dot and sew with the buttonhole running around the cuff. (1.8) Next mark the button positions. Fold the shirt in half, inside out, lining up the fronts. Fold the back half of the overfront hem and, using magic pen, mark the position of the centre of the buttonhole. (1.9) Traditionally a 16-line natural mother of pearl button is used for the button on the collar band, and an 18-line for the front hem and the cuffs. (1.10) Place the button in the buttonhole machine, align the holes on the button as per machine instructions, align the marked button position under the machine head and sew the button, using a cross stitch. •

2   ENDING

Check the shirt for sewing errors, and trim all stray ends. •

3   PRESS

(3.1) Start with the back yoke, lay it flat on the nose of the pressing board. Press both the left and right yoke. Button the cuff and lay the sleeve gauntlet-side up on the pressing board. Press the sleeve, from the sleeve head, using the point of the iron to press either side of the gauntlet. Repeat for the other sleeve. (3.2) Press the overfront, then the back, then the underfront, pressing the full shirt, pressing between the buttons using the point of the iron. (3.3) Do not press the collar. Insert the collar stays and button the shirt. •

THE ART AND CRAFT
OF BESPOKE

The unequalled excellence of made-to-measure clothing

ABOVE Cloths and linings on the roll.
OPPOSITE Gieves & Hawkes, No. 1 Savile Row.

THE WORDS 'bespoken' and 'bespeak' were first recorded in the late 16th century, coming from the Old Saxon *bisprecan,* meaning 'to speak out'. Originally, to bespeak of something had two meanings: to speak up against or oppose something; or to request, reserve or order goods. In the realm of the tailor a customer would *bespeak* a length of cloth. By the middle of the 18th century the verb had become an adjective, one describing an item that had been made to order, particularly tailored clothing.

King Charles II is credited with the invention of the suit in 1666: mindful of public opinion after a Civil War, the Plague and the Great Fire, he decreed that his courtiers should no longer wear French fashion with big wigs, high heels, and ruffled accessories, but instead a 'Persian vest' – a long waistcoat to be made of English wool – with knee-length breeches and a long coat. Its form was refined and popularised by Beau Brummell in the early 1800s. In Brummell's day, only the wealthy

75

Bespoke patterns on the rail at Norton & Sons.

could afford new clothes, and the only choice was bespoke. Less affluent men wore second-, third-, or even fourth-hand suits, repaired and cleaned by an army of 'clobberers'. Bespoke remained the only choice until the second half of the 19th century, when the invention and subsequent improvement of the sewing machine – a device Karl Marx described in Volume 1 of *Das Kapital* as a 'decisively revolutionary machine' – along with the invention of the factory system transformed the manufacture of clothing. 'Ready-tailored' clothing was originally developed for the supply of low-cost uniforms for the military. Pre-made in factories in standard sizes, its low prices undercut the bespoke tailors and made new clothing affordable to the middle class for the first time, making it an immediate success.

By 1860, 80 percent of the UK population bought their clothes ready-made, and by the start of the 20th century there were 54 factories making ready-to-wear suits in Leeds alone. Tailoring shops continued to thrive up and down the country, however, and in London's West End, on Savile Row and the small coterie of streets that surrounded it, around 200 of the finest and best-known bespoke tailors served a wealthy, often aristocratic clientele. British and European royalty, prime ministers, presidents, military officers, industrialists and bankers wore fine clothes made by the world-famous tailoring houses of Savile Row.

By the start of the 21st century, however, all that changed and only a dozen or so of the very best and most adaptable bespoke houses remained, collectively making just 10,000 bespoke suits each year. Two world wars had killed a generation of customers, and peace in Europe had vastly reduced military spending, putting an end to lucrative uniform contracts. In addition, in the second half of the 20th century a wave of branded luxury goods found favour with the nouveau riche, who wished to signpost their wealth in a way that Savile Row's clientele would never have dreamt of doing. Two decades later, a global pandemic and working from home accelerated the casualisation of the working wardrobe that had been gathering momentum since the rise of the T-shirt and hoodie 'tech bro' look of the 1990s.

> **While Savile Row shops today are largely informal and offer a warm welcome to all, the bespoke process still retains an appropriate air of mystique.**

Many commentators predicted the demise of the bespoke tailors of Savile Row but, for the time being, they appear to be in rude health. The grey or navy work suit that once dominated the rails in most bespoke workshops has been replaced by bespoke jackets and casual suits tailored in a vastly more varied, interesting, and sometimes exuberant selection of cloths. Dressing in such clothes requires vastly more skill than donning a charcoal two-piece, so the knowledge and advice of the Savile Row tailor has never been more valuable. With mass manufacturing causing huge environmental damage, a system of clothes production in which only what is needed is made – and made in a way that treads very lightly on the planet – represents the most sustainable way to dress oneself. Connoisseurs still wish to enjoy experiencing the odd hour in quiet contemplation of cloth in the elegant salons of Savile Row, and enjoy discussing and debating clothing and style with experts whose opinions they respect and value.

Savile Row remains a special place, both staunchly traditional and yet well suited to the modern world. While the shops today are largely informal and offer a warm welcome to all, the bespoke process still retains an appropriate air of mystique. The roles of the men and women who are engaged in the production of bespoke, and its arcane language, are unique to this small community.

Broadly, those involved in making bespoke are divided between cutters and tailors – two very different and highly specialised roles. Cutters measure customers, cut patterns, fit garments and supervise production; tailors sew and alter garments. In some cases, typically in smaller houses, cutters may also sell, but sales are usually made by a dedicated salesperson with an encyclopaedic knowledge of many thousands of cloths, the styles and details of men's formal dress, and its suitability for the client and the occasion for which they wish to wear it. In some cases, the salesperson is trained to measure, but they never do fittings.

As with most crafts, bespoke tailoring is not learned from a manual; it is taught, master to apprentice, over many years of patient and often repetitive practice. An apprenticeship takes two to five years depending on the demands of the role and the aptitude of the apprentice. Once an apprenticeship is complete, it is commonly accepted that to be a master tailor or cutter requires 20 years of continuous practice. Cutters and tailors with many years of experience still consult the wisdom of the grand masters of the Row – a small handful of people, repositories of vast stores of knowledge – on aspects of the craft that might be infrequently practised, such as rarely cut garments or the method for dressing unusual figures. Master tailors and cutters advise their former apprentices throughout the entirety of their careers.

Not everyone has what it takes to be a bespoke tailor or cutter. To be a tailor requires manual dexterity, finesse, a great eye for shape and form, patience, and a dedication to quality. To be a cutter requires a different and quite unusual mixture of skills: the ability to see flat shapes transform themselves when joined to become something three dimensional; an ability to see perfection in proportion; a competence with fractions; and the diplomacy to sensitively manage very wealthy and successful men – to listen to and understand their wants and communicate with clarity the possibilities and limitations of the craft. Tailoring is not magic: a customer's appearance

A Norton & Sons buggy label.

can be greatly improved, but not wholly transformed. Communicating this with politeness but also firmness is requisite, as are the skills to manage a team of tailors with a wide variety of talents and egos.

For almost seven centuries, the tailors of London practised their craft in whatever way they chose, with no set rules about how things should be done, and no formal cooperation between the houses. Yet despite the absence of any formal ties between them, Savile Row has always been a tight-knit, deeply friendly and connected community with a great deal of personal amity between the staff of different houses. The sewing tailors, most of whom work freelance under the wonderfully arcane 'log system', work for at least two houses. Meanwhile, cutters have historically moved between houses as they rise up the ranks, taking relationships and tailors with them. Tailors and cutters eat lunch in one another's workrooms, sandwiches eaten beside hastily cleared sewing machines, and apprentices from all houses drink together after work and swap stories and gossip. Beyond the tailoring staff, cloth merchants visit almost every workshop nearly every day, delivering gossip with their bundles of fine worsted. The workshops of Savile Row are omniscient.

While the informal bonds between houses were legion, there was never any formal cooperation between them until 2004, when the forward-looking heads of five venerable bespoke houses decided to unite the hand-tailoring community, and the broader ecosystem of cloth and trimmings suppliers, through the creation of a formal association to preserve and advance this centuries-old craft as practised in this quiet corner of Mayfair. The Savile Row Bespoke Association (SRBA) was founded, dedicated to protecting and promoting the practices and traditions that have made Savile Row the home of the world's finest tailoring for more than two centuries.

Today, bespoke on Savile Row means something specific, a meaning enshrined within the articles of the Association, which is the arbiter of what can and what cannot be called bespoke. The rules are important, because the methods handed down over 700 years by the master tailors and cutters of this ancient and venerated community have been retained for very good reason: there may be cheaper or quicker ways to produce tailored clothes, but there is no better way. The precise method varies slightly from tailor to tailor, depending upon the lineage of their learning, but the principles of its construction do not vary. Only if the standards are adhered to is the garment allowed to bear the Association's marque – the cross shears – a visible brand of quality, sewn discreetly beside the 'buggy label' of the house that made it, its presence informing the customer that their garment is the genuine article.

The life of every bespoke garment must begin with a pattern – a stiff paper representation of the customer in two dimensions, made by the cutter by hand from a fresh blank sheet of pattern paper, using the customer's measurements and the cutter's interpretation of the intricacies of the customer's figure. Two people with identical measurements might be dramatically different in shape, so this figuration is a vital part of ensuring a good fit. The language used to record the vagaries of body shape is obscure and unique to bespoke tailoring: 'sway', 'drop', 'forward', 'erect', 'prom'. Each customer has their own set of patterns for the different garments that are made by their tailor: SB1 (one button, single-breasted); SB2 (two buttons, single-breasted); DB (double-breasted); SB overcoat; DB overcoat; dinner suit; morning coat; shooting coat; breeches. Prolific customers might have a dozen or more sets of patterns. Most cutters will attach a small square of every fabric used for a particular pattern so the pattern forms a wonderful visual record of a customer's wardrobe. They will also add to the pattern as a customer becomes larger or smaller, taping extra paper to the original pattern (or removing it) for a visual record of evolving physique as well as taste.

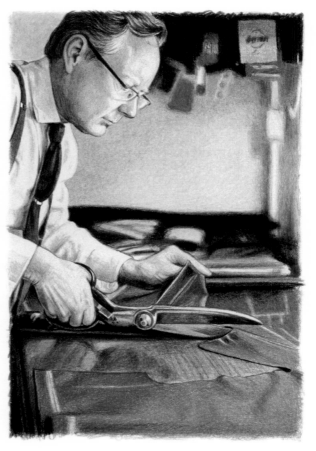

Norton & Sons Head Cutter Martin Nicholls at the board.

Next the garment is 'struck', or cut out. The customer's cloth, their 'bolt', is supplied by the cloth merchant at precisely the required length. Typically a coat will require about two metres of cloth, trousers about one and a half metres, and a waistcoat 80 centimetres, but the length ordered is not an estimate. When some cloth costs as much as £2,500 per metre, the cutter or undercutter must calculate the required length with care. A little more material might be required if it has a large check pattern, sometimes as much as one and a half metres more if the customer's circumference nears the 60-inch width of a standard bolt of fabric. (Alfred Hitchcock's did.)

The striking process begins with the cloth being laid out, smoothed flat and folded in two. The pattern is then laid on the cloth, aligned to the grain, and tessellated for economy, its shapes marked by hand using chalk, and the individual pieces cut by hand with large cloth shears by the cutter or their undercutter.

The cut pieces are then 'trimmed': their various canvases, interlinings, and other accoutrements are added to the bundle by the workshop junior or a specialist trimmer, before being passed to a maker for sewing. Today, rents in Mayfair have increased significantly and much of the original workspace on Savile Row has been let to wealthier tenants, so it is now often the case that tailors' sewing workshops are off Savile Row. In such cases the cut work is walked round to them by a 'trotter'. At this point, tailoring begins.

We do not sew jackets on Savile Row, we tailor coats or overcoats, and the people who tailor them are coat makers, coat finishers, coat alteration tailors, and pressers. A coat maker on Savile Row serves an apprenticeship of three (although this is rare) to five years, during which time they are taught to tailor, every day, five days a week, by a master coat maker. Every apprentice is employed by a bespoke house, and a master is engaged in a contract for their training.

The training begins with the simplest skills, such as holding a needle, for if it cannot be held correctly the bespoke method can never be mastered. It progresses through all aspects of the making process. A trainee may spend up to six months learning just one aspect of bespoke coat making, such as making and affixing collars, inserting sleeves, or padding and shaping foreparts. During their apprenticeship they will work for their master on customers' garments, making collars, padding foreparts, and sewing pockets – but only once they have passed out of their apprenticeship do they make a complete garment. In a quirk particular to Savile Row, once the house they work for considers them ready to graduate from their apprenticeship, their work is examined by master tailors from two other member houses of the

A basted fitting at Norton & Sons.

The training begins with the simplest skills, such as holding a needle, for if it cannot be held correctly the bespoke method can never be mastered.

SRBA – a practice that ensures every graduating tailor meets a standard of which all houses approve.

Not everyone can make it as a Savile Row tailor, and among those that do there is a natural variation: all Savile Row tailors are excellent, some are more excellent than others, some are modest, others less so. The names of the greats endure.

A tailor assembles, cuts, and shapes each piece of the coat. They stitch; shape; mould; draw in the cloth and canvases using heat, steam, and patience to sculpt; and use the feel of the thread in their hand to put precisely the correct tension in every stitch to draw together the cloth and canvases. A Savile Row coat emerges from

Basting a collar onto a fitting.

pocket, and it usually will, this should have a hand-stitched border. Front pockets must be top-stitched by hand. Buttonholes must be hand-sewn, and behind the left lapel buttonhole there should be a hand-sewn flower loop. Cuffs must feature an opening slit. Buttons should be attached by hand using a cross stitch. Finally, every Savile Row Bespoke garment must be sewn with inlays, additional cloth left in the seams, to allow adjustment to those seams (taking in, but mostly letting out) during the many long years of the garment's life. The process of cutting, sewing and fitting a bespoke coat can take upwards of 25 hours, with as many as seven highly skilled individuals (cutter, undercutter, trimmer, coat maker, alterations tailor, finisher and presser) having a hand in its creation.

On Savile Row, trousers are sewn by trouser makers, trouser finishers, trouser alteration tailors, and trouser pressers. A trouser maker serves an apprenticeship of two to three years. Just like the coat makers, they are trained under a master trouser maker and on completing their training they are examined by master tailors from other member houses of the Association.

Bespoke trousers must, like the bespoke coat, be hand-made. Pockets, band linings, and 'back curtains' must be sewn in by hand and seat seams hand-stitched. As with the coat, the finishing should also be made entirely by hand. The fly should be prick-stitched by hand, hems hand-sewn, buttonholes hand-sewn, and buttons sewn on by hand. As with the coat, bespoke trousers are not simply sewn, they are sculpted: calves stretched, back knees shrunk in. A bespoke pair of trousers should be adjustable over time, so waistbands and side seams must have significant inlays, typically enough for a combined adjustment (letting out) of up to three or four inches. The entire process of making a pair of bespoke trousers may take upwards of 10 hours and involves as many as seven skilled artisans, with the cutter, undercutter, and trimmer being the same people who work on the coat.

the workshop with human form, a three-dimensional sculpture in cloth.

At the end of the making and fitting process, if the coat requires additional alteration, this is carried out by a specialist tailor skilled in altering coats. They only alter – they do not make – and only once all final adjustments are complete will the coat be passed to a finishing tailor for hand finishing. From there the coat is passed to a presser, who applies its final finishing press. Some coat makers sew on buttons themselves, others leave it to another member of the team, often a junior, to complete. And that is the coat, complete and ready for collection.

To bear the mark of the SRBA a bespoke coat must be made entirely by hand. Sewing machines are used for the sewing of seams, but all other sewing must be completed by hand. Jacket foreparts and collars must be fully hand-canvased and these canvases must be hand-cut and hand-formed. The top collar should be hand-drawn and stitched onto the facing. Sleeves must be set in by hand and armholes should have a lining that is dropped in. The coat must also be hand-finished. It must have its linings felled by hand, its vents (typically two, sometimes one, occasionally none) and its front edges must be prick-stitched by hand throughout. If it has a breast

The excellence in making is just one part of the bespoke tailor's commitments to their customer. Beyond the process of making, the art of bespoke is also characterised by an unequalled level of service. Your bespoke tailor is an expert advisor on any and all aspects of formal men's dress. Need to attend the Lord Mayor's Banquet? A day at Royal Ascot? The Oscars, the BAFTAs, the Grammys? Your tailor makes sure that the dress code, and tone, are correct. They ensure that you do not stand out from the crowd for being either over- or underdressed; that you are not photographed wearing your medals on the wrong side of your chest, as one famous footballer did at a royal wedding. Your tailor helps you build a beautiful wardrobe of clothes and helps you keep that wardrobe in beautiful condition. They advise on dry cleaning, shoe polishing, and clothes hanging. Tailors also service your clothes for as long as you, or whoever you pass them on to, continue to wear them. As most of us have been in business for a century or two, there's a very fair chance we'll be there to honour all of those commitments.

Your Savile Row bespoke tailor and his or her trusted cloth merchant keep a record of every cloth you have ever made anything from – not just the design but the individual piece, so that should a customer require a repair, or wish to add a second or third pair of trousers to accompany a coat, a precise match for the original cloth can be sourced. The cloth merchants who supply the tailors of Savile Row keep a small length of every piece of cloth sold (for a certain time period at least).

A bespoke tailor also offers an alteration and repair service for the clothes they have made. They let out and occasionally take in. They re-line and send moth holes for repair by the very best invisible menders. If a coat is passed on, they can do a full re-cut. During my time in the Norton & Sons workrooms, we frequently saw clothing made 50 or more years ago come back for alterations and occasionally repairs – the oldest a riding coat dating from 1908.

A suit from Savile Row, in the right cloth, can last several lifetimes. It will be the best-made suit you ever wear, the best fitting, the most flattering, and it will certainly last longer than any other suit you own. Bespoke, as practised by the tailors of Savile Row, sets and upholds a standard that is unmatched by any other clothing maker anywhere in the world. •

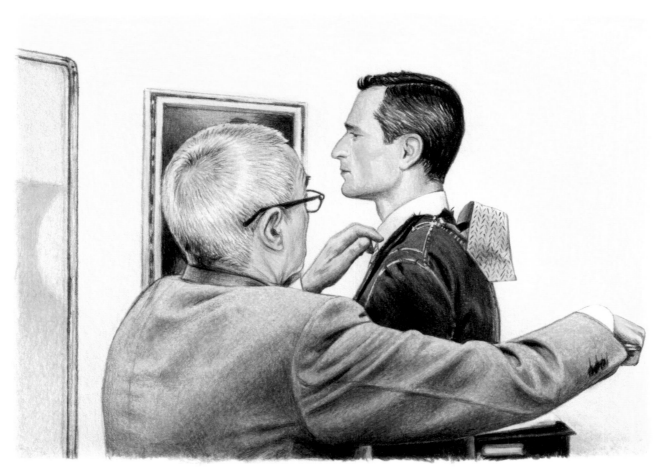

A cutter removes a collar during a fitting.

MAKING A WAISTCOAT

A step-by-step guide to making a waistcoat by hand,
following the method of Felicity Hamacher

I T IS QUITE unusual for a piece of clothing to have its origin precisely pinpointed in the annals of history. Remarkably, such is the case with the waistcoat. Quintessentially British, it was during the Restoration of the Monarchy in the late-17th century that King Charles II ushered in the waistcoat as an essential item of clothing. This royal decree first made reference to the waistcoat as a *vest,* but the later adoption of the term *waistcoat* served better to emphasise its defining feature – a coat cut off at the waist.

An interesting tradition surrounding the waistcoat is that the bottom button *should not be fastened.* Various explanations have been presented to shed light on the origin of this custom. The most common theory suggests that it was King Edward VII, when he was the Prince of Wales, who introduced the practice. Legend has it, with an ever-expanding waistline, the portly prince couldn't quite manage to fasten all the buttons on his waistcoat. As a mark of either admiration (he was a snappy dresser) or perhaps etiquette, his courtiers followed suit and the trend began. Another, more practical, theory is that the practice of undoing the lower button was to stop the waistcoat feeling restrictive and riding up while on horseback, or simply to make one more comfortable when sitting down to dinner.

A bespoke waistcoat is crafted to the customer's precise requirements, be it single- or double-breasted; with or without lapels; two or four pockets; back strap and side vents; or even with a pocket-watch hole for the real traditionalists. As a rule, the bottom button should conceal the waistband of the trousers, and just about an inch should show above the jacket's closure. The armhole is positioned an inch lower than that of the coat, keeping the waistcoat high and close-fitting, extending the proportions of the wearer. In its essence, the waistcoat maintains a formal allure, even when the coat comes off.

Traditionally, waistcoats are canvassed with a specific waistcoat canvas. This is similar to the linen holland used to stabilise pockets but is slightly more open and springy in its weave. More recently tailors have taken to using the wool/linen body canvas that is usually reserved for coats. This results in a softer construction and, more often than not, as a waistcoat comes as part of a three-piece suit, it makes sense to match the canvas throughout the garments. •

Required trimmings: *75 cm body canvas or waistcoat holland; 10" linen holland on the double; 50 cm silesia pocketing on the double; 20 cm fusible; waistcoat buckle; 10 m reel of buttonhole twist; silk thread for finishing.*

CUTTING OUT THE JOB

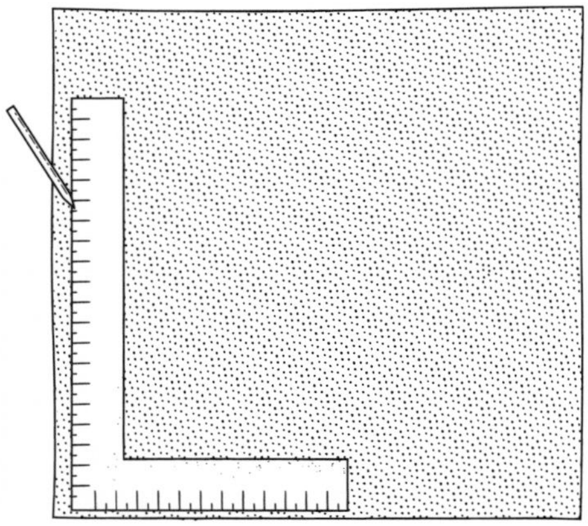

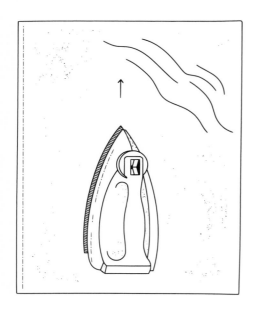

FIG. I.I

FIG. I.3

1   PREPARING THE CLOTH

(I.I) The cloth should be laid out folded in half, with the right sides together and the selvedge running parallel to the edge of the table. To ensure the cloth isn't twisted or warped, match the letters woven into the selvedge on either side. If the cloth has a check or stripe, ensure they match on both sides. (I.2) Concertina the cloth up and take it to the pressing board. Using only the weight of the iron, lightly steam the cloth on one side and then the other, making sure the selvedge (and check or stripe) is still aligned. The heat and steam will reset any twisted yarn, helping the cloth to settle back into its natural place. (I.3) This is a good time to look for damages or imperfections in the cloth. Many cloth suppliers will identify any damage before retailing the fabric. They are marked with a string tagged to the selvedge, directly in line with the damage. Extra cloth is given to allow for adjusting the lay and cutting around. If an unstrung damage is found, mark it clearly with chalk and avoid laying the pattern pieces over it when it is time to strike out (chalk around the pattern). (I.4) Lay the cloth back on the table as per step one and smooth it out ready to place the pattern pieces. •

2   THE WAISTCOAT LAY

The lay refers to the order in which the pattern pieces are arranged on the cloth. This is particularly important because it allows the maker to minimise the amount of cloth needed for each garment. The tighter the pieces slot together, the less cloth required, the more money saved.

(2.1) The first consideration should be whether the cloth has a nap or not. This will dictate whether the pieces are laid in one direction (one-way cloth) or opposite directions (two-way cloth). If the cloth does have a nap, the fibres are long and brushed in one direction (corduroy and velvet) and the waistcoat must be cut one-way. The colours can differ depending on what direction they are cut, given the way the light hits the nap. If the rough runs down the piece, the colour appears darker. If the smooth runs down the piece, the colour appears lighter. If the waistcoat pieces are cut in opposite directions, the shading created by the nap would make the waistcoat appear to be two different colours. Most cloths without a nap are fine to be cut two-way, but it is a good idea to check by looking down the piece of cloth from both directions and seeing if the colour changes. If there is a noticeable difference, it is best to presume the cloth is one-way. If there is no change, the cloth is two-way. (2.2) The second consideration should be the grainline. Always lay the pattern pieces with the grainline running parallel to the selvedge (warp). This is particularly important on stripes and checks, to ensure the waistcoat doesn't appear twisted on the wearer. (2.3) It is also important to consider the space around the pieces, and ensure that there is sufficient room for the inlays and fit-up, before striking out. Inlays are the extra cloth added to the seams (not seam allowance) for letting out in the future. **On the Forepart (Waistcoat Front)**: the inlays measure 0"/net across the shoulder; 1½" down the break line (this will be turned back to create the facing), stopping at the top button;

⅜" down the front edge; 0"/net around the armhole and side seam; 2" across the hem. **On the Back**: square up from the neck point 1"; 1" around the neck line; ⅜" down the centre back; 2" across the hem; 1½" down the side seam; ⅜" around the armhole; 0"/net across the shoulder. The fit-up is the cloth left over after the main pattern pieces have been cut out. This cloth is used for making the extra pieces within the waistcoat, for example the front facings, pocket welts and back straps. It is important to keep as large pieces of extra fabric as possible. •

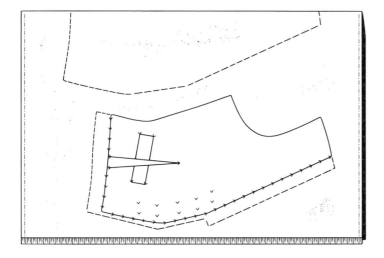
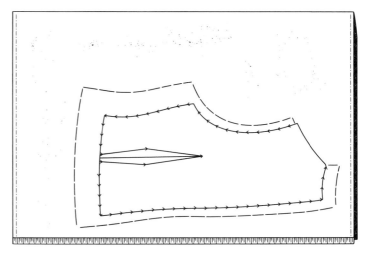

FIGS. 2

---

3 STRIKING OUT THE WAISTCOAT

Striking out is the act of chalking around the pattern pieces onto the fabric, and adding the inlays (extra allowance that is hidden inside the garment for future alterations).

(3.1) Ensuring the grainline of the pattern pieces run parallel to the selvedge, use weights to hold the pattern pieces in place. (3.2) Sharpen a piece of chalk using a chalk sharpener, or failing that, a sharp blade. Chalk around the pattern pieces firmly, but not enough to drag or pucker the fabric. Think of the chalk as a speedboat. Push with the back edge, lifting the front as it gathers speed. (3.3) Extend the chalk marks out beyond the pattern to ensure the finish points are clearly defined. Mark the darts and notches clearly. (3.4) Remove the paper patterns from the cloth and chalk in the inlays. •

4 CHOPPING OUT

Chopping out is the act of cutting the pieces out of the fabric. It is important here to be accurate, especially on the pieces that are cut net (without inlay).

(4.1) The bottom edge of most tailors' shears is flat on the blade and the bottom of the handle. As the cloth is cut, use the flat edge of the shears to keep contact with the board. This will help to maintain balance and control. (4.2) Let the cloth drape over each side of the blade and use the weight of the shears to guide the pressure. Use the entire length of the blade, making long, confident cuts. (4.3) Think of the shears like a race car. Go fast down the straights and slowly around the corners. At this stage, accuracy is much more important than speed.

(4.4) Start from the selvedge and cut out the forepart first. Then the back. Remember, lining is slippery and difficult to control, so pinning the pieces of lining fabric together might help. Cut neatly around the outer edge of the chalk lines and avoid cutting across any large pieces of the remaining fabric, as these odd bits of leftover fabric will become the fit-up. This will be needed later on in the making process. (4.5) Roll the waistcoat pieces, fit-up and trimmings into a bundle and tie them up with an off-cut of selvedge. •

SETTING THE WAISTCOAT

1   MARK STITCHING THE JOB

*Mark stitching (also referred to as 'thread marking'
or 'tailor tacks') is the process of hand-sewing threads through
two layers of fabric to transfer important pattern markings
and details to each layer.*

(1.1) Working with the right sides together, ensure both pieces align perfectly, matching any stripes or checks. With basting cotton, mark stitch down the break line (stopping at the first button) and along the hem. The inlay on the front edge is a ⅜" seam only, so this does not need to be mark stitched. Mark the button positions and the three points of the dart, the bottom and sides of the welt pocket, and any notches on balance marks. (1.2) Open up the layers of cloth and snip the mark stitches in between. Separate the forepart pieces. (1.3) Lay the back lining pieces on a flat surface with the right sides together. Smooth out the lining, making sure all edges and notches are aligned. From the centre back neck, baste down the centre back seam with a ⅜" running stitch, finishing at the bottom of the inlay at the hem. Take care with this initial step, as lining has a tendency to be slippery and difficult to control. Fixing it into place accurately now will not only help with the rest of the mark stitching, but the machine stitching too. (1.4) Mark stitch along the chalk lines across the hem, side seam, neck line and armhole. Mark stitch all points of the dart, as well as any notches and balance marks. Open up the layers of cloth and gently snip the mark stitches, transferring the lines to each side. •

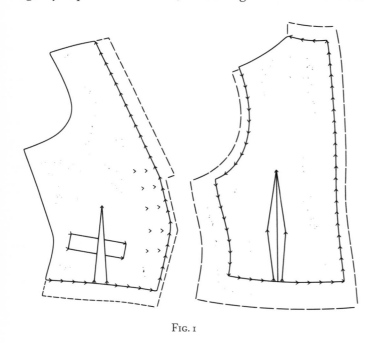

Fig. 1

2   CUTTING THE CANVAS

Lay the canvas on a flat surface and fold it in half horizontally. Place one of the forepart pieces onto the folded canvas, along the straight grain. Draw around the forepart with chalk, leaving a ¼" allowance around the whole piece. Cut the canvas out on the double (both pieces at the same time). If the waistcoat is too wide for the canvas to be cut on the double, open up the canvas and chalk them individually. •

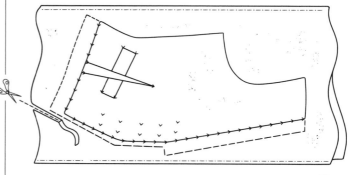

Fig. 2

3   SEWING THE DARTS

(3.1) Lay the forepart pieces with the right sides together, on top of the canvas pieces. Mark stitch through the points of the darts, through all layers, to transfer the dart position onto the canvas pieces. Open up the layers of canvas and snip the mark stitches in between. Separate canvas and cloth. On the wrong side of all pieces, mark in the darts with chalk. (3.2) Working on the wrong side of the cloth, on the forepart, cut through the middle of the dart, stopping ¾" from the top. Baste the dart together on the chalk lines and then machine stitch the dart closed on the edge of the bastes. Never back stitch on the dart, and always tie off both ends. (3.3) Slot the eye of the basting needle, with the thread attached, into the small pocket at the top of the dart. Even out the dart seam and press. Pull the needle out by the thread because it will be hot. Cut a 1" square of fusible interlining and press it to the top of the dart to hold it in place. (3.4) Repeat steps 2–3 on the other forepart and the canvas pieces. •

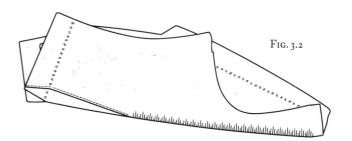

Fig. 3.2

(4.1) Lay the canvas with the open dart facing up. Place the forepart on top with the right side facing up, straight grains matching and the darts laying on top of one another. Move the dart seams about ⅛" from each other to avoid bulk. Smooth out the forepart piece until it's laying even. (4.2) Using a long, but not tight running stitch, baste the forepart onto the canvas catching all layers. With the non-sewing hand, gently ease the cloth with each stitch, creating a slight ripple effect in the canvas beneath. The most important thing to remember is to keep the canvas straight and not twisted during the basting. (4.3) **Line 1**: Start in the centre of the shoulder line, around 1" down. Follow the shape of the chest, basting towards the hem and right through the middle of the dart. Stop about ½" above the hem line. (4.4) **Line 2**: Start parallel to Line 1, about ½" in from the arm hole. Follow the shape of the arm hole and at the top of the side seam, begin to baste stitch in a curved line down towards the front edge. Finish when the stitches meet Line 1 at the waistline. (4.5) **Line 3**: Start parallel to Line 1, about ½" in from the break line. Follow the break line until the stitches hit the first button position, then stitch back towards the dart 1" and continue down the front edge. Finish ½" above the hem line. (4.6) Flip the canvassed forepart over, so the canvas side is facing up. Cut a 3" slash into the canvas from the centre of the shoulder line. This is to ease the tension across the shoulder for better freedom of movement.

(4.7) Cut a piece of ¾" linen tape for the bridle. The bridle is made up of a piece of linen tape cut on the straight grain, sewn along the break line. As the break line is cut on the bias, it has a tendency to stretch over the wearer's chest. Sewing the bridle along the break line stabilises the cloth so it cannot stretch. The bridle should start 1½" down from the shoulder line and finish 1½" above the first button position. Place the bridle on the outside edge of the break line, so the stitches are not visible when the inlay is turned back to create the facing. Starting from the top, cross stitch down the bridle, drawing it in over the chest about ¼". (Drawing in is the act of pulling the stitches slightly tighter to create shape in the fabric.) (4.8) Cut another piece of ¾" linen tape for the hem, measuring from the front edge seam to the dart. Place the linen on the outside edge of the hem line, so the stitches don't show on the right side of the waistcoat when the hem is turned back. Cross stitch the tape, drawing it in around the belly about ¼". This is to create a more three-dimensional shape around the wearer. (4.9) Trim back the canvas around the armhole ⅜". Turn back the seam and make little snips on the curve to relieve any tension. Baste the seam into place on the edge of the armhole and press. (4.10) At the side seam, 1¼" up from the hem line, snip into the forepart ⅜". Fold back the cloth below the snip and baste it down. This will become the side vent. (4.11) Repeat steps 1–9 for the other forepart. •

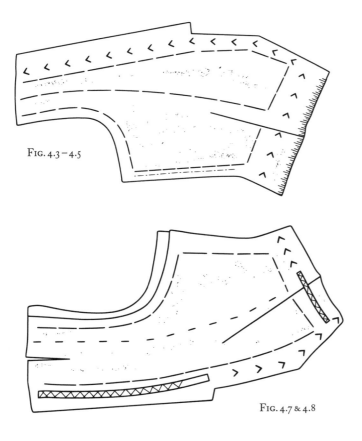

Fig. 4.3 – 4.5

Fig. 4.7 & 4.8

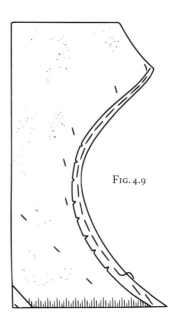

Fig. 4.9

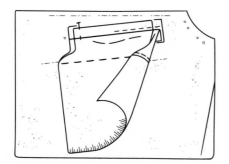

FIG. 5.3

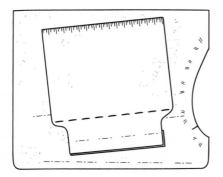

FIG. 5.11

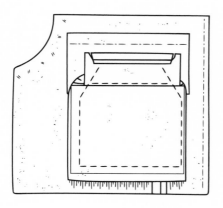

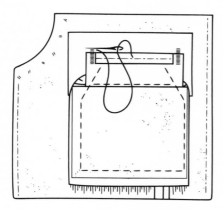

FIGS. 5.15

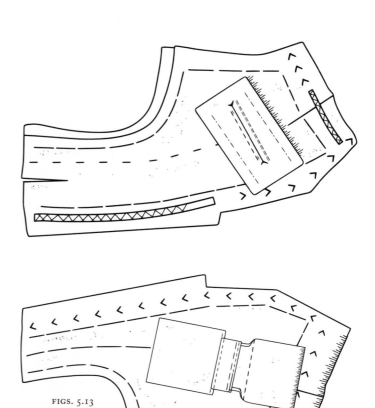

FIGS. 5.13

5   MAKING THE POCKETS

(5.1) Lay the forepart with the wrong side facing down. Press until smooth and flat. With chalk, mark the out-breast welt pocket position through the mark stitches. The pockets should start 3½" up from the hem edge and be a minimum of 5" long, usually 5½". (5.2) Cut 2 squares of linen roughly 3" deep and 6" wide. One piece will form the inside of the welt itself, giving it strength and body. The second piece will be placed behind the welt to give extra strength to the forepart fabric where the welt is sewn. Press one in half horizontally. (5.3) Lay the unpressed piece under the forepart, against the wrong side, making sure it overlaps all of the mark stitches at least ½" at the sides and bottom, with plenty of inlay at the top. (5.4) Using a piece of fabric from the fit-up (make sure it is at least 2" longer and wider than the welt size), mark the welt shape onto the right side of the fabric. Add ¾" inlay to the top and sides and a ⅜" seam across the bottom.

(5.5) Baste a running stitch across the top line of the welt chalk mark. This is so the pocket position is visible through to the other side. (5.6) Turn the fabric over to the wrong side and lay the creased edge of the second linen strip, along the baste line, and baste within the inlay. (5.7) From the right side, crease along the chalk marks at the ends. Trim away just the linen along the creases. (5.8) Turn in the edges of the welt and baste in place. Press flat against a straight edge (a wooden ruler is good). Fell down the turned-back inlay and cross stitch the raw edge. Remove all basting. (5.9) On the right side of the forepart, re-mark the welt shape: 1" wide at the front and 1⅛" wide at the back. The bottom line of the welt is the stitch line. (5.10) With the right sides of the welt and forepart fabric together, lay the welt upside down, matching the stitch lines. Baste through all 3 layers: welt, forepart and linen underneath. (5.11) Lay the facing piece right-side down, aligned with the bottom of the welt inlay. Machine stitch both seams, stopping the seam on the facing piece ¼" in at both ends. (5.12) Cut the pocket line in between the seams, stopping in line with the facing stitch line. Snip vertically up to – but not through – the end of the facing stitch, through all layers. Snip diagonally towards the end of the welt seam, through all layers except the welt seam. Press both seams open. (5.13) Cut a piece of silesia the same size as the facing piece. Turn back the edge of the silesia and hand-sew it onto the back of the welt, stopping ¼" in on both sides of the welt. Snip the silesia along the edge of your felling stitch and pull it through the pocket opening. (5.14) Mark the shape of the pocket bag on the silesia side. Machine stitch around the pocket bag and trim the excess fabric back to ½". (5.15) Repeat steps 1–14 for the other forepart. •

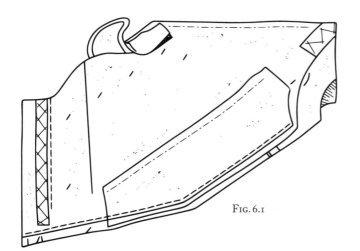

FIG. 6.1

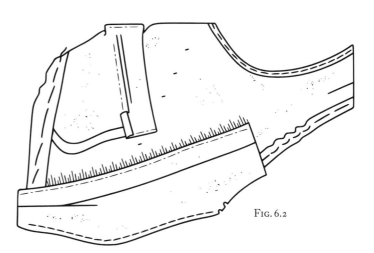

FIG. 6.2

6   ATTACHING THE FACING

(6.1) Cut a strip of linen the shape of the front edge, measuring from 1½" above the top button position to 1½" below the bottom button position and 3" wide. Baste it to the canvas side of the forepart, so it is aligned with the front edge. This will add strength for the buttons and buttonholes. (6.2) The fit-up used for the facing piece should mirror the shape of the front edge. It should measure at least 4" wide, and extend up past the top button position by 4" and down to the edge of the hem inlay. (6.3) Lay the forepart with the right side facing up. Place the facing piece, right sides together along the front edge. Baste the facing piece into position along the stitch line, ⅜" back from the edge, from the top button position, to 1" past the bottom point – into the hem inlay. Machine stitch along the basted line. (6.4) Trim the canvas back to ¼" on the seam to avoid bulkiness. Press the seam open. ☞

(6.5) Lay the forepart with the canvas side facing up. Turn back the hem inlay along the mark stitches, and baste it down about ¾" from the edge. Trim back the inlay to 1¼". Then, turn back the break line inlay along the mark stitches. Baste it down ¾" back from the edge, and trim the inlay back to 1¼". At this stage the facing should still be open, with only the break line and hem edge turned back and trimmed. (6.6) Turn back the facing, over the break line and hem inlay. Roll the seam back so the stitch line is hidden from the right side and sits on the inside of the waistcoat. Baste along the edge. (6.7) Trim back the bottom of the facing inlay at the point to avoid bulkiness. Baste it into place around ⅛" back from the hem edge, so it can't be seen from the front. (6.8) Trim the back edge of the facing piece. The finished measure should be approximately 3" wide along the front edge, curving around to 1½" wide as the waistcoat cuts away from the bottom button. Baste the facing piece down ¾" in from the raw, inside edge. (6.9) From the top button position, turn the raw, top edge of the facing piece back along the break line, angled upwards. Baste along the edge of the fold. (6.10) Repeat steps 1–9 on the other forepart. •

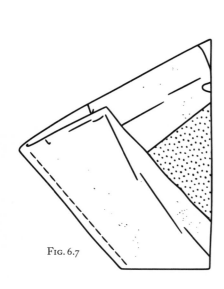

Fig. 6.7

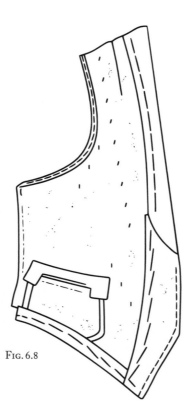

Fig. 6.8

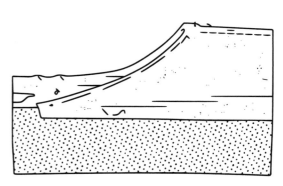

Fig. 6.9

7   SEWING DOWN THE INLAYS

(7.1) Catching only the canvas, cross stitch the edge of the hem inlay and the bottom back edge of the facing, where it meets the hem inlay. (7.2) Fell the vent allowance, around the armhole, down the break line inlay and back edge of the facing piece. (7.3) Fell the bottom of the facing to the hem inlay, and the top of the facing to the break line inlay. •

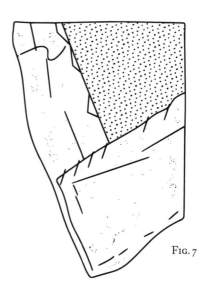

Fig. 7

8   MAKING
THE BACK STRAPS

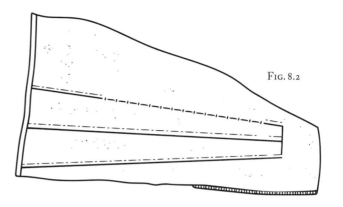

Fig. 8.2

(8.1) Measure the back lining piece across the half waist, including the inlay and seam allowance. Lay a piece of lining fit-up, a few inches longer than the half waist measure and at least 8" wide, onto a flat surface with the wrong side facing up. (8.2) With chalk, draw a horizontal line through the centre of the lining piece, the same length as the half waist measure, plus 1". At one end, square up 2½" and down 2½" (total 5"), and at the other end, square up 1" and down 1" (total 2"). Cut out the 5" by 2" strip. (8.3) Cut a piece of linen holland the same length as the lining strip and 2½" wide. (8.4) Fold the lining strip in half horizontally, with the right sides together. Machine stitch it through the middle of the linen strip, along the raw unfolded edge, with a ¼" seam. (8.5) At the narrow end of the lining, turn the folded edge in half again, back towards the raw edge, and top stitch it into place. The seam line should be in the middle. (8.6) Measure the finished size of the strap (it should be around 2¼" by ¾"). Trim the linen back equally on each side of the seam so it fits neatly inside. (8.7) Turn the strap the right way out so the linen is now on the inside and the right side of the lining is facing out. Make sure the points are sharp and press flat, with the seam running down the centre of the strap. (8.8) Repeat steps 1–7 for the other strap. (8.9) Affix a waistcoat buckle to the narrow end of one of the straps, with the seam facing down. Baste into place. •

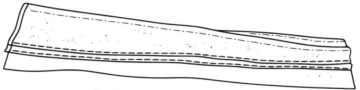

Fig. 8.4

9   CUTTING
THE LININGS

(9.1) Lay the forepart with the right side facing up, onto the wrong side of the lining. Cut around the forepart leaving a 1" allowance all the way around. (9.2) Lay the back lining piece onto the wrong side of the lining. Trace around it exactly, giving no extra inlays or allowances. Cut it out. •

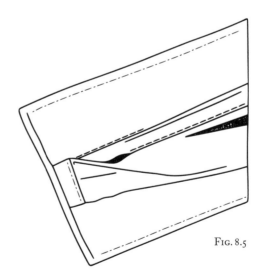

Fig. 8.5

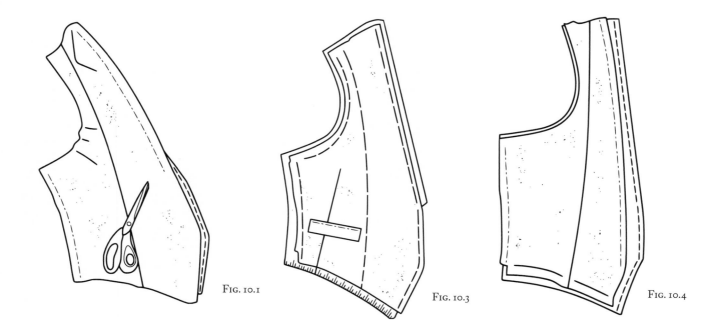

FIG. 10.1

FIG. 10.3

FIG. 10.4

SEWING THE FRONT LININGS 10

(10.1) With the right side of the lining facing up, press a ¼" pleat through the centre of the lining piece, from the middle of the shoulder line to the middle of the hem. Baste through the middle of the pleat to hold it in place. The pleat should be pressed towards the side seam on the right side. (10.2) Lay the forepart with the wrong side facing up. Place the lining piece on top of the forepart with the right side facing up (wrong sides together) and the

pleat running through the centre. Baste down the side of the pleat from the shoulder line, to the hem. (10.3) Flip the forepart so the right side is facing up. Trim away any excess lining around the forepart, leaving: ¼" down the break line and front edge; 1½" at the hem; 0"/net at the side seam and across the shoulder; and ¼" around the armhole. Flip the forepart over so the lining is now facing up, and trim the lining back ½" from the front edge.

(10.4) Turn back the lining and baste into place, catching only the turned back inlay: ½" from the edge on the break line; 1¾" from the front edge on the facing (for buttonholes); ½" at the hem; and ¼" around the armhole, making sure it covers all the snips. (10.5) Baste the lining down the side seam ½" in from the edge, catching all layers. Turn the lining in at the vent and baste ⅛" back from the edge. (10.6) Repeat steps 1–5 for the other forepart. •

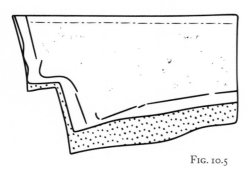

FIG. 10.5

11   SEWING THE BACK LININGS

(11.1) Lay the inner lining pieces on a flat surface with the right sides together. Smooth out the lining, making sure all edges and notches are aligned. From the centre back neck, baste down the centre back seam with small stitches around ⅜" long – finishing at the bottom of the inlay at the hem. (11.2) Using the outer lining pieces as a guide, mark the dart position on the inner lining in exactly the same place. (11.3) On both assembled lining pieces, machine stitch the centre back along the basting stitches and then machine out the darts. *Do not* cut the darts – press them flat to one side, in opposite directions. On the outer lining, press towards the side seam; on the inner lining, press towards centre front. (11.4) Lay both pieces with the right sides together and the inner lining on top. Align the centre seams and pin into place. Then align the darts, and pin them at the centre. (11.5) Machine stitch across the hem line, ⅜" below the mark stitches. Then, trim the hem inlay back to 1½". (11.6) Cut a strip of linen for the back neck, 1" wide on the bias and the same shape as the back neck curve. Baste around the neck on the mark stitches to create the neck line. (11.7) Open the assembled lining pieces and lay them flat. At the hem, press the inlay towards the inner lining, away from the mark stitches. Then close the pieces so the wrong sides are together. At the hem, press along the mark stitches so the inner lining finishes ⅜" above the outer lining and doesn't show on the right side. (11.8) Pin the wrong sides together (right sides out) through the centre back seam and place with the outer lining facing up. Trim away all the excess inner lining from around the edge so it aligns net with the outer lining. Remove the pins. (11.9) With the outer lining facing up, lay the back straps into position. The bottom of the back strap should sit about 2¾" up from the hem line. Baste on in the inlay and across each strap, through all layers, so they stay in place. The buckle side is always on the LEFT for menswear and on the RIGHT for womenswear. The centre of the buckle is in line with centre back seam, and the right strap should extend 2" past the centre back seam to allow it to turn back. •

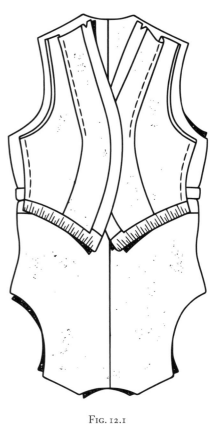

Fig. 12.1

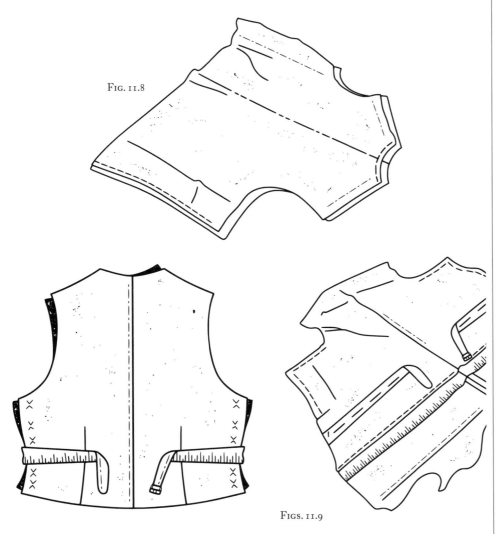

Fig. 11.8

Figs. 11.9

12   BAGGING OUT

(12.1) Lay the assembled back lining pieces open, with the right sides facing up. Place the foreparts, with the right side facing down on top, aligning the edge of the side seam to the edge of the mark stitches on the lining. For balance, match the notches at the waist. Leave one seam (⅜") at the top of the side seam. (12.2) Baste a seam ⅜" in from the edge, down the edge of the side seam. Machine stitch along the baste line and repeat with the other forepart. (12.3) Align the shoulders. As the back neck is curved, remember to match the break line to the neck line a seam down (⅜") – where it will be stitched, as the transition around the neck should be smooth. Baste across the shoulders with a ⅜" seam, adding in any fullness across the back shoulder if the pattern requires it. Machine stitch along the baste line and repeat on the other shoulder. ☞

(12.4) Turn up the inner lining so the wrong side is facing up and the foreparts are sandwiched in between the lining pieces. Baste along the side seams and shoulders, through all layers, to hold the inner lining into place. Then, about ½" back from the finished edge, baste around the armholes, catching only the lining. (12.5) Flip the assembled waistcoat over so the wrong side of the outer lining is facing up. With chalk, using the front armhole as a guide, mark the back armhole shape. Measure across from the centre back to the chalk mark, to make sure the distance is the same on each side. (12.6) Starting at the side seam hem, machine stitch up the side seam ⅜" in from the edge of the forepart. Make sure to sew right into the corner of the seam at the vent, and do not stitch further than the top of the side seam on the forepart. (12.7) Continue machining around the armhole, catching *only* the lining and not the forepart underneath. Sew right into the corner of the shoulder end. If the stitch does not meet the corner, the front and back pieces will not be aligned at the shoulder ends. (12.8) Finally, machine stitch across the shoulder, ⅜" in from the edge.

Stop and back tack at the neck point. Do not stitch around the neck. This remains open, in order to pull the waistcoat the right way out. (12.9) Repeat steps 6–8 on the other side. (12.10) Trim away the excess lining around the armholes to ½" and make small snips on the round to ease the curve. Trim away any other excess lining, leaving the inlay around the neck and 1½" at the side seams. (12.11) Reach into the neck hole and, grabbing the hem from the inside, pull the waistcoat the right way out. The waistcoat should now be fully assembled, with only the neck left to close. •

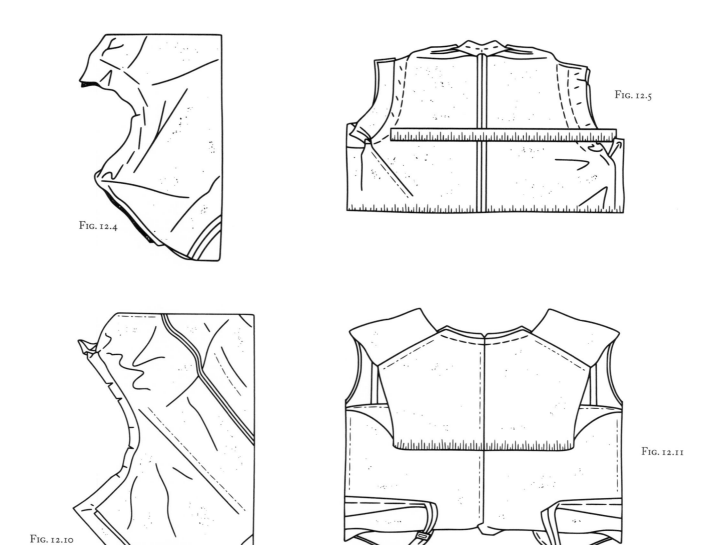

Fig. 12.4

Fig. 12.5

Fig. 12.10

Fig. 12.11

FINISHING THE WAISTCOAT

1   CLOSE THE BACK NECK

(1.1) Turn in the back neck inlay along the mark stitches at the neck line. Baste the two sides together about ⅜" from the folded edge. (1.2) Working on the outer lining side, prick stitch around the neck line ⅛" from the edge. •

2   FRONT LINING

Fell down the front lining, around the armhole, down the fronts and around the hem and vent. The stitches should be ⅛" apart and barely visible. •

3   EDGE STITCHING

(3.1) Starting from the neck point, prick stitch ⅛" in, around the edge of the forepart, finishing at the side seam. The stitches should be firm but not tight. (3.2) Prick stitch the side of the welt, ¼" in, trapping the raw seam inside. (3.3) Prick stitch across the top edge of the welt ⅛" in. •

4   BACK STRAPS

(4.1) Prick stitch through the back strap, in line with the back dart. (4.2) Fell the buckle into place. •

5   VENTS

(5.1) Working on the outer lining side, prick stitch the edge of the vent on the back lining. (5.2) Sew a bar tack at the top of the vent for strength. •

6   BUTTONHOLES

(6.1) Mark the buttonholes with chalk, on the right side of the cloth. (6.2) The buttonholes should still be indicated by the mark stitches sewn at the beginning of the job. Each hole should measure ⅝" long and start ¾" in from the front edge. They would ordinarily be spaced between 2" and 2½" apart. (6.3) Using the technique shown on p. 160, sew the buttonholes previously marked in step 2. •

7   PRESSING

(7.1) Remove all remaining basting and mark stitches from the waistcoat. (7.2) Place the waistcoat on a ham to retain its shape during the pressing. When pressing on the lining, avoid using steam, as any water leaks will stain and damage the lining. (7.3) Gently press the waistcoat around a ham. •

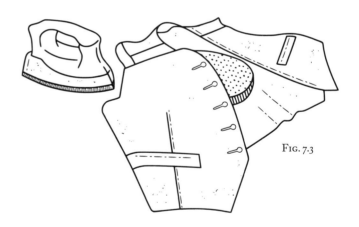

Fig. 7.3

8   SEW BUTTONS

(8.1) Turn the waistcoat inside out so the right sides are together. Lay it on a flat surface with the left side facing up. This will leave the back of the buttonholes exposed. (8.2) Align the front edges so the break line and cut-away run perfectly parallel. With chalk, mark through the back of the buttonhole, onto the right side of the cloth. Then sew the front buttons on the marks, through all layers, with double thread. Remember to leave at least a ⅛" shank on the button thread. •

AN APPRECIATION OF BRITISH CLOTH

Why bespoke suits demand cloths woven only in the British Isles

Above Cloth books at Johnstons of Elgin.
Opposite A tailor in front of shelves of cloth house bunches.

THE FINEST tailored clothes can only be made with the finest cloth – material made solely from pure cotton, linen and wool. So it is fortunate, and perhaps no surprise, that the home of the world's greatest bespoke tailors is also home to the world's very best woollen cloth manufacturers.

While Italian mills make beautiful fabrics, using some of the rarest and finest fibres known to man, the Italians tend to favour softness over structure. For my ready-to-wear clothing collections, I've used cloth from Italian mills as often as British and Irish, but for bespoke? At Norton & Sons we always used British.

British mills are terrible at self-promotion – a deep-seated modesty prevents them from blowing their own trumpet – but they are phenomenal at making cloth with the quality and structure required for the bespoke process of moulding and shaping by the tailor's hand.

A madras-style cloth on the loom.

Highly decorative clothing for men endured until King George III brought the simple clothes of the English countryside to London.

Softness is often mistaken for quality, but the reverse is true. On day one, your typical Italian cloth feels softer and has more drape than its British equivalent, which is a little flatter and firmer. But over time, while the Italian will more rapidly lose its form, the British cloth will improve: it will soften, develop a character and, most importantly, over decades of wear it will retain the form given to it by the skilled hand of its tailor.

In the British Isles we have a proud history of making the world's best cloth. In the Middle Ages, the wool trade was England's biggest employer and its most important industry. Worsted, named after the village in Norfolk that was the centre of its early development, became famous across Europe, its name synonymous with the finest quality British woollen cloth.

As early as 1130, the Worshipful Company of Weavers (the weavers' guild) was recorded in the Pipe Roll of King Henry I – the oldest series of English financial records. By 1155 the Weavers were granted a Royal Charter by Henry II, conferring the privilege and liberty to carry on their profession; they rank as the oldest livery company (trade association) in the City of London.

In the early 1300s, rival Freemen – the term for members of a livery company or guild – were authorised to set up their own weaving businesses in competition with the Company. By the 1330s, Edward III recognised the value of the flourishing cloth trade and allowed Flemish weavers to settle in England and establish another rival guild. In the late 17th century, as many as fifty thousand Huguenots escaped persecution in France and fled to England, bringing with them exceptional weaving skills. Throughout this period, Britain was successful in encouraging the most skilled artisans to establish businesses and provided them with protection that allowed their trade to flourish. The strength of the guilds and the intense competition between them ensured that British cloth was made to the highest standards.

'Sumptuary laws' – enacted in many countries across the centuries – restricted the wearing of sumptuous clothing to curb extravagance and ensure that distinctions between different levels of society were maintained. In England these lasted into the 17th century, dictating the colour and types of cloth worn by each social class. A duke, marquis or earl might wear crimson velvet; a wool merchant was allowed a little cat or fox fur, but a peasant was permitted just one tunic of the plainest wool. Until the late 18th century, wealthy men dressed with great flamboyance: they wore elaborate codpieces in the 15th and 16th centuries, ruffs, and sumptuous woven cloth. Highly decorative clothing for men endured as a style until King George III, or 'Farmer George' as he was known, brought the simple clothes of the English countryside to London.

George 'Beau' Brummell, close friend of the Prince Regent – the future George IV – was famed for his dress and took the simplification of men's clothing one stage further with his almost minimalist approach. Brummell made simplicity fashionable: decoration was frowned upon, excellence of cloth and cut was everything, and the cloth makers of Britain responded accordingly.

Another of George III's influences on the world of men's clothing was the introduction of merino wool. From 1780 he employed a small team to smuggle merino sheep into Britain from the dry mountain regions of Spain. After a decade or so, George had amassed a large enough flock to begin selling them. While the merino sheep did not like the cold, wet British climate, they did thrive in Australia, where British colonists established huge flocks and began exporting the fine fleece back to England.

Brummell's fashion revolution coincided with a revolution in Britain's manufacturing systems – especially in the methods of textile production. Huge advances in technology were made by the great British innovators of the period: in 1733 John Kay invented the flying shuttle; in 1764 James Hargreaves invented the spinning jenny and Sir Richard Arkwright developed the water frame in 1767 – the world's first powered textile machine; and in 1779 Samuel Crompton invented the spinning mule, rounding off a period of advancement that propelled British cloth making to its zenith. By the time

this first Industrial Revolution drew to a close in the mid-19th century, Britain was producing the best woollen and cotton cloth on the planet and had grown with incredible speed to dominate the global trade in textiles. At its peak, Britain's cotton textile manufacturers produced more than 70 percent of the global supply.

The 20th century was marked by two more great upheavals in the British textile industry. First, the invention of synthetic fibres was seen as the great panacea for the production of inexpensive clothing. Britain's largest industrial businesses, such as Imperial Chemical Industries Ltd. (a leader in the production of synthetic dyes) and Courtaulds (which recognised the future of man-made fibres as early as 1904, when it acquired the patents for viscose), battled to develop and expand production of fibres such as nylon, Terylene, Crimplene and rayon. Courtaulds became the largest manufacturer of synthetic textiles in the world and was the fifth-largest

Richard Roberts's self-acting spinning mule.

99

corporation in Britain, employing more than a hundred thousand people.

Additionally, the rise in offshoring was another significant change in Britain's textile-manufacturing industry. Prior to the First Industrial Revolution, cotton textiles had been manufactured extensively across Asia, with Indian textiles holding a position of pre-eminence thanks to their exceptional quality and the global power of British traders. Britain's technological advances allowed it to undercut the price of Asian-made textiles, but from the early 20th century, China, India, Japan and others had acquired British spinning and weaving technology and, combined with their lower labour rates, they began to replace British-made goods. When Gandhi was invited to visit the textile workers of Lancashire in 1931, following the Indian National Congress Party's boycott of British products, they appealed to him to help their plight. While he sympathised, he chose not to help them.

By the mid-1960s Britain's mass textile industry had begun an irreversible decline, with both ICI and Courtaulds slashing jobs and setting up operations in Asia, joining a global rush to relocate production close to the newly emerging clothing production centre of Hong Kong. Britain had grown rich on wool and pioneered the most rapid advance in technology in history, but by the 1990s, the movement offshore of UK textile manufacturing reduced the national textile workforce to less than a tenth of its size in the 1960s. Today, several specialist synthetic textile manufacturers continue to make advanced engineering textiles in the UK, but almost nothing remains of Britain's once dominant clothing textile industry, and our cotton textile industry, which once supplied more than 70 percent of the world's cotton textiles and employed nearly one million people. Today the industry employs just a few hundred.

The very best of Britain's woollen textile trade has survived, however, thanks largely to the difficulty in replicating the manufacturing techniques for the finest quality wool cloth – considerably more complex than manufacturing cotton – and to the fact that we have the perfect water for finishing woollen cloth.

A small number of exceptional specialist mills continue to thrive, producing the very finest wool cloth for the world's most discerning customers – firms such as William Halstead for mohair; Joshua Ellis for cashmere; Johnstons of Elgin for estate tweeds; Linton Tweeds for bouclé (extensively used by Chanel); Stephen Walters for cotton, wool and silk jacquards; Lochcarron of Scotland for tartans; and Hainsworth for wool melton. Several exceptional weavers of that iconic woollen cloth, worsted, also flourish, including Bower Roebuck – which I worked with every season for a decade on my E Tautz collections; Taylor & Lodge; and Pennine Weavers.

ABOVE Worsted wool.
TOP A fancy check Harris Tweed.

We also have the very best finisher of wool cloth anywhere on the planet in WT Johnson and Sons.

These specialists continued to supply not only the tailors of Savile Row and Britain's luxury brands, but the finest luxury houses in France, Italy, the USA and Japan. British cloth continues to have an extraordinary cachet around the world, and the mills I have worked with over the past two decades have counted amongst their customers Hermès, Louis Vuitton, Chanel, Prada, Tom Ford, Brioni, Dior and Yves Saint Laurent, among many others. The late Vivienne Westwood liked Harris Tweed so much that she appropriated its orb marque, in a dispute which runs to this day, while Ralph Lauren regularly uses Harris Tweed and Fox Brothers flannels.

The bespoke tailors of Savile Row do not buy cloth directly from the mills; instead a number of long-established London cloth merchants provide them with a selection of somewhere in the region of fifteen to twenty thousand different cloths, all of which can be delivered the next day in specific cut lengths. These cloth houses design and commission the weaving of cloth that they package into bunches – swatches of 100 or so fabrics bound in hard covers, typically in just a single weight and construction, such as a 9 or 10 oz plain weave or 7 oz twill. Occasionally, where fewer patterns exist, they are combined: a bunch of mid- and heavy-weight trouser fabrics say, including such rare and special items as cavalry twills and Bedford cords.

When I started out at Norton & Sons, there were a dozen British cloth houses whose bunches I stocked. I had a policy of using only local wool cloths because, in the opinion of my tailors, the UK still made the best in the world and experience taught us that they gave the best results with the Savile Row bespoke method. But I didn't carry every bunch in Norton's collection; I sifted and edited its collections to a more manageable number – around seven thousand or so – and I knew my way round these bunches like the back of my hand. I could take you instantly to the best winter jacketing, or the perfect summer trouser, or find a cloth in a specific shade or colour.

To those bunches I added a selection of cloth that I sourced myself from some of the small independent mills I had come to know: Luskentyre Harris Tweed; Garynahine Harris Tweed; Breanish Tweed; Lovat Mill; Islay Woollen Mill; and Ardalanish. I always enjoyed visiting their mills or small weaving sheds, and I became friends with the weavers and their families. At Ardalanish, I even met the sheep that provided the wool that went into their cloth. Each mill has beautiful, unique cloth and incredible stories to tell.

Cloth selection is vital not only to the look of the suit (colour, texture, pattern) but to how it feels when worn,

how it behaves and how it ages. Depending on how they are woven, two 7 oz Super 120 cloths can feel very different when worn. Whoever makes your bespoke clothes will devote much time to understanding where and how you intend to wear them. Are they for winter in northern Scotland, summer in the South of France, or spring in London? Will you stuff them in a suitcase and need to wear them on arrival, or will they travel in a large valise and be pressed by a valet? Do you feel the cold or do you sweat when the mercury hits 20°C?

In the weaving shed at William Halstead.

In the past few years, several of those great old English cloth houses have merged, but happily most have kept the original names – and famous bunches – alive. Huddersfield Fine Worsteds now incorporates J & J Minnis, famous for its flannels, and John G Hardy and Hunt & Winterbotham, both celebrated for their tweed bunches. Harrisons incorporates Lear Browne & Dunsford; H Lesser & Sons, famous for its Lumb's Golden Bale; Porter & Harding; the wonderful tweed merchant W Bill, and Harrisons of Edinburgh. And the great names of Holland & Sherry and Dugdale Bros & Co. continue to thrive.

The London cloth houses provide a service that is integral to the tailoring houses of Savile Row. The two exist in perfect symbiosis. •

Required trimmings: *1 m body canvas; 20" horsehair chest canvas; 5" collar canvas, bias cut, across the piece; 10" linen holland on the double; 20" domette on the double; 5" × 12" collar melton, bias cut, on the double ; 18" sleeve head roll; 2 × medium winged shoulder pads; 1 m silesia, on the double; 50 cm fusible; 10 m reel of buttonhole twist; silk thread for finishing.*

MAKING A COAT

A step-by-step guide to making a coat by hand,
following the method of Rachel Alice Smith

THE MOST frequent comment from first-time customers for a bespoke coat is about how it feels. They can't explain it necessarily, it just *feels different;* more comfortable, more connected to the body. It makes them feel more confident, and so it should. The time and attention taken by the cutter and tailor to make the piece are a labour of love. The coat is not simply assembled and thrown on, it is designed to mould and sculpt around the owner's body, creating shape, and redefining their proportions.

This starts with the *cutting*. For example, the armholes are closer, and cut higher into the armpit. This might sound counterintuitive, but the height of the armhole creates less resistance between the sleeve and the body of the coat at the chest, allowing for better rotation and freedom of movement. Furthermore, the longer seam under the arm elongates the body, making the coat feel lean and less boxy. Another concern is 'balance' – the difference in length between the front and back of the coat. The bottom of the coat should run parallel with the ground: if a person has a rounded back, the jacket will gape off the neck, and they require more back balance. If they have a more prominent chest or stomach, the coat will rise and cross over at the front, so they need more front balance. This is not just an aesthetic conundrum. Should a coat be short of back balance, for example, the owner will forever feel that it's falling off their neck – as if they're being pulled backwards – and will be obliged to constantly tug it back into position. A bespoke coat should hug the neck – this is the anchoring point from which the rest of the garment drapes.

Then comes the *tailoring*. When you hold a bespoke coat in your hands, besides the beautiful hand-finishing you will see one fundamental difference from anything off-the-peg: *shape*. The owner's shape is quite literally built into the coat through the canvas and interlinings. The tailor uses a series of 'pad' stitches, dart manipulation and iron work to create a three-dimensional canvas form, from which the rest of the coat is constructed. The canvas and interlinings are made of natural fibres – wool, linen, cotton – and, like an iron, the human body creates heat and moisture. So, over time, the more the coat is worn, the more it begins to cast itself around the body, becoming more comfortable, more shapely and unique.

A bespoke coat can be a welcome delight for someone who finds it difficult to wear off-the-peg clothes. The ready-to-wear system is flawed. How can the few billion people around the world who wear coats be pigeonholed into wearing ten common sizes? Bespoke offers a solution: a unique garment, designed by the owner, with form, function, and style all considered. Historically, this was *the only way* to buy clothes. That changed with the advances in technology and export, but now, with a consciousness for the environment and limiting waste, spending more on fewer pieces is very much in the fashion zeitgeist. A bespoke coat does just that. It's built to last. Inlays are hidden inside the garment, allowing it to be let-out up to four or five inches in its lifetime. The making process hasn't changed much in two hundred years, so, if you know how to put a coat together by hand, you can take it apart by hand, rebuild it and extend its life, perhaps even, as is common on Savile Row, beyond that of the original owner. •

CUTTING OUT THE JOB

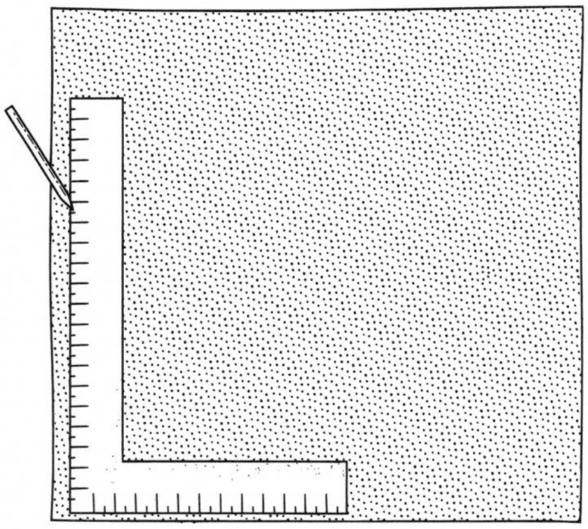

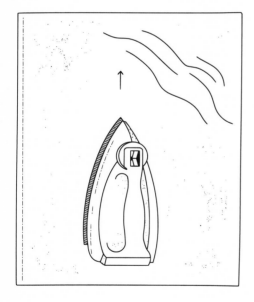

FIG. 1.1

FIG. 1.3

1   PREPARING THE CLOTH

(1.1) The cloth should be laid out folded in half, with the right sides together and the selvedge running parallel to the edge of the table. To ensure the cloth isn't twisted or warped, match the letters woven into the selvedge on either side. If the cloth has a check or stripe, ensure they match on both sides. (1.2) Concertina the cloth up and take it to the pressing board. Using only the weight of the iron, lightly steam the cloth on one side and then the other, making sure the selvedge (and check or stripe) is still aligned. The heat and steam will reset any twisted yarn, helping the cloth to settle back into its natural place. (1.3) This is a good time to look for damages or imperfections in the cloth. Many cloth suppliers will identify a damage before retailing the fabric. They are marked with a string tagged to the selvedge, directly in line with the damage. Extra cloth is given to allow for adjusting the lay and cutting around. If an unstrung damage is found, mark it clearly with chalk and avoid laying the pattern pieces over it when it is time to strike out (chalk around the pattern). (1.4) Lay the cloth back on the table as per step one and smooth it out ready to place the pattern pieces. •

3   STRIKING OUT THE JACKET

Striking out is the act of chalking around the pattern pieces onto the fabric, and adding the inlays (extra allowance that is hidden inside the garment for future alterations).

(3.1) Ensuring the grainline of the pattern pieces run parallel to the selvedge, use weights to hold the pattern pieces in place. (3.2) Sharpen a piece of chalk using a chalk sharpener, or failing that, a sharp blade. Chalk around the pattern pieces firmly, but not enough to drag or pucker the fabric. Think of the chalk as a speedboat. Push with the back edge, lifting the front as it gathers speed. (3.3) Extend the chalk marks out beyond the pattern to ensure the finish points are clearly defined. Mark the darts and notches clearly. (3.4) Remove the paper patterns from the cloth and chalk in the inlays. •

The lay refers to the order in which the pattern pieces are arranged on the cloth.
This is particularly important because it allows the maker to minimise the amount of cloth needed for
each garment. The tighter the pieces slot together, the less cloth required, the more money saved.

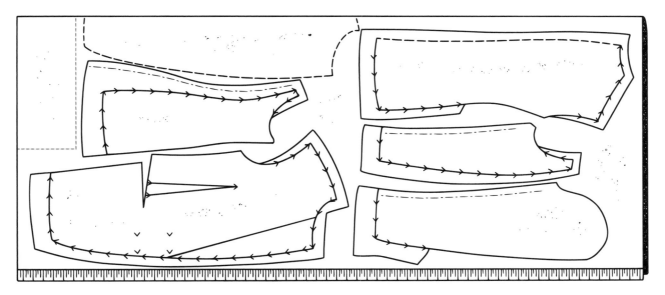

FIG. 2 & 3

(2.1) The initial factor to consider is whether the cloth has a nap or not. This will dictate whether the pieces are laid in one direction (one-way cloth) or opposite directions (two-way cloth). If the cloth does have a nap, the fibres are long and brushed in one direction (corduroy and velvet) and the coat must be cut one-way. The colours can differ depending on what direction they are cut, given the way the light hits them. If the rough runs down the piece, the colour appears darker. If the smooth runs down the piece, the colour appears lighter. If the coat pieces are cut in opposite directions, the shading created by the nap would make the coat appear to be two different colours. Most cloths without a nap are fine to be cut two-way, but it is a good idea to check by looking down the piece of cloth from both directions and seeing if the colour changes. If there is a noticeable difference, it is best to presume the cloth is one-way. If there is no change, the cloth is two-way. (2.2) The second consideration should be the grainline. Always lay the pattern pieces with the grainline running parallel to the selvedge (warp).

This is particularly important on stripes and checks, to ensure the coat doesn't appear twisted on the wearer. (2.3) It is also important to consider the space around the pieces, and ensure that there is sufficient room for the inlays and fit-up, before striking out. Inlays are the extra cloth added to the seams (not seam allowance) for letting out in the future. **On the Forepart**: inlays measure 1" across the shoulder; extend ½" past the shoulder end and down to 0"/net as the armhole starts to curve; 1" around the neck line and top of the lapel; 1" down the front edge of the lapel (stopping at the top button); ⅜" down the front edge (from top button to hem); 2" across the hem; 0"/net through the underarm seam and bottom of the armhole. **On the Side Body**: 1" across the top; extend 1" into the armhole and down to 0"/net as the armhole curves; 1½" down the side seam (stopping at the waist); kick out to 3" at the waist to 3½" at the hem (vent allowance); 2" across the hem; 0"/net through the underarm seam and bottom of the armhole. **On the Back**: square up from the neck point 1"; 1" around the neck

line; 1½" down the centre back; 2" at the hem; 1" up the side seam (stopping at the waist for vent allowance); 0"/net from the waist to the armhole cut; ⅜" from the armhole cut, kicking out to ½" at the shoulder end; 0"/net across the shoulder. **On the Top Sleeve**: 0"/net around the crown; 0"/net down the forearm seam; 3" across the cuff, kicking out 2" at the bottom of the hind arm; 2" up the hind arm (stopping 6" up for sleeve vent allowance); 0"/net up the hind arm from vent to crown. **On the Undersleeve**: 1" across the top; 1" down the underarm seam tapering to 0"/net as it begins to curve; 0"/net around the underarm; 0"/net down the forearm seam; 3" across the cuff, kicking out 2" at the bottom of the hind arm; 2" up the hind arm (stopping 6" up for button stand); 1" up the hind arm from button stand. (2.4) The fit-up is the cloth left over after the main pattern pieces have been cut out. This cloth is used for making the extra pieces within the coat, for example the front facings, jets, flaps and welt. It is important to keep as large pieces of extra fabric as possible. •

Chopping out is the act of cutting the pieces out of the fabric.
It is important here to be accurate, especially on the pieces that are cut net (without inlay).

(4.1) The bottom edge of most tailors' shears is flat on the blade and the bottom of the handle. As the cloth is cut, use the flat edge of the shears to keep contact with the board. This will help to maintain balance and control. (4.2) Let the cloth drape over each side of the blade and use the weight of the shears to guide the pressure. Use the entire length of the blade, making long confident cuts. (4.3) Think of the shears like a race car. Go fast down the straights and slowly around the corners. At this stage, accuracy is much more important than speed. (4.4) Start from the selvedge and cut out the forepart first. Then the sidebody, top sleeve, undersleeve and back. Cut neatly around the outer edge of the chalk lines and avoid cutting across any large pieces of the remaining fabric, as these odd bits of leftover fabric will become the fit-up. This will be needed later on in the making process. (4.5) Roll the coat pieces, fit-up and trimmings into a bundle and tie them up with an offcut of selvedge. •

(5.1) Lay the lining in half onto a flat surface, with the right sides together. Using a hot iron and trying to avoid steam, press the lining flat. The folded edge should be closest to the body and the selvedge edge further away. (5.2) Starting with the backpiece lay the raw edge of the inlay parallel with the folded edge, leaving a 2" gap at the top of the neck line. With chalk, mark around the backpiece: net at the bottom edge, net along the side vent inlay, 1" through the side seam, 2" through the shoulder, and 2" around the back neck. At the bottom of the centre back, draw a box in line with the inlay, 1¼" wide and ¼ of the back length long. Angle the top of the box upward, mirroring the shape of the side vent. This box will be sewn out later as part of the centre back pleat. (5.3) Lay the top sleeve next to the backpiece along the side seam edge, towards the selvedge. With chalk, mark net along the hind arm seam, net along the inseam, 1" past the finished cuff line, and 2½" across the top of the crown. (5.4) Lay the forepart on the straight grain, along the selvedge edge, with the lapel and front edge overhanging the edge of the selvedge. The lapel and front edge are not required to be cut in lining because they make up the facing, which will be cut later in fabric. Lay the side body next to the forepart with the underarm seams together, as if they have been sewn. With chalk, mark around the pieces: 2" through the shoulder, 1½" up the shoulder end, 2" across the top of the side body, 2" through the side of the side body, 1½" at the side vent, and ¾" past the inlay at the hem. (5.5) Lay the undersleeve along the folded edge, in the gap between the side body and bottom of the backpiece. With chalk, mark: net along the hind arm seam inlay, 2½" at the top of the sleeve around the armhole, net along the inseam, and 1" past the finish cuff line. Also mark the net edge of the hind on seam to show the position of the inlay. Turn over the top layer of lining and mark the same inlay line on the right side of the lining, as well as the cuff vent 6" up from the finish cuff line. (5.6) In the space along the selvedge edge, between the top sleeve and the forepart, mark a line 3" from the edge and the full length of the space. This will become the bridle. The spare lining in the other gaps will be used for pockets. •

SETTING THE COAT

1   MARK STITCHING THE JOB

Mark stitching (also referred to as 'thread marking' or 'tailor tacks') is the process of hand-sewing threads through two layers of fabric to transfer important pattern markings and details to each layer.

(1.1) Lay the back pieces on a flat surface with the right sides together. Smooth out the fabric making sure all edges and notches are aligned. For a check or a stripe take extra care in ensuring that the patterns match on each side. From the centre back neck, baste down the centre back seam finishing at the bottom of the inlay at the hem. Mark stitch across the hem, neck line, back armhole and top of the vent inlay. Stop at the top of the vent. From the top of the vent to the hem, chalk a new line ⅜" forward of the original chalk line. Mark stitch the new line. This is where the stitch line on the side seam meets the vent. Mark stitch all notches and balance marks. Open up the layers of cloth and gently snip the mark stitches, transferring the lines to each side. (1.2) Lay the side body pieces with the right sides together. Make sure all edges and notches are aligned. Mark stitch along the hem, along the back vent and side seam, and around the armhole. Mark stitch all notches and balance marks. Make sure to mark stitch the position of the top of the vent on either side of the side seam. Open up the layers of cloth and snip the mark stitches. (1.3) Lay the forepart pieces with the right sides together. Make sure all edges and notches are aligned. Mark stitch along the edge of the lapel, down the front edge, and along the hem; around the armhole, across the shoulder, around the front neck, and across the gorge line. Mark stitch the break line at the top and bottom only. This line will be drawn in with chalk later. Mark the top button position and the top and sides of the dart, the bottom and sides of the out-breast pocket, and any notches on balance marks. Open up the layers of cloth and snip the mark stitches in between. Separate the forepart pieces. Remove the mark stitches for the out-breast welt to the pocket on the right-hand side. The out-breast welt appears on the left forepart only. (1.4) Lay the top sleeve with the right sides together. Make sure all edges and notches are aligned. Mark stitch along the cuff finish line and along the cuff vent. Mark stitch the notch at the top of the hind arm. Open up the layers of cloth and snip the mark stitches in between. (1.5) Lay the undersleeve with the right sides together. Make sure all edges and notches are aligned. Mark stitch the cuff finish line, along with the hind arm, and around the armhole. Mark stitch the notch at the top of the hind arm. Open up the cloth and snip the mark stitches in between. •

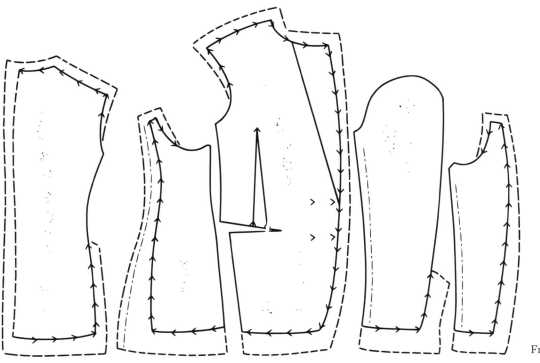

FIG. 1

(2.1) Fold the body canvas in half vertically and press it flat. Lay the right forepart, with the right side facing up, over the body canvas. Match the grainlines. (2.2) With chalk, on the body canvas, mark around the forepart net with the edge of the fabric: along the front edge, lapel, neck line, shoulder line and around the armhole. Mark the top button position and the top and the break line. Mark the dart at the top and two points at the middle (¾" wide) at the waistline suppression, making a triangle shape. (2.3) Curve a line from the bottom of the armhole, stopping at the waistline 1½" in from the side seam. Continue to chalk the line towards the hem, finishing around 1" forward of the side seam at the hem. (2.4) Cut out the body canvas shapes through both layers and mark the other piece to match. (2.5) The chest canvas should be cut with the long hairs running straight across the piece. The front runs parallel with the break line and net with the shoulder and armhole. At the bottom of the arm hole, it starts forward of the side seam ½" and curves into a horizontal bottom edge around 3" above the waistline. (2.6) The domette should be cut with the bias running along the shoulder line. This allows for freedom of movement. The domette follows the shape of the chest canvas, along the break line, through the shoulder and around the armhole. Under the armhole at the side seam and along the bottom edge, it comes ½" past the chest canvas. This layers the pieces so they are not too thick, and covers the sharp edges of the horsehair. (2.7) Repeat steps 2–6 for the other side. •

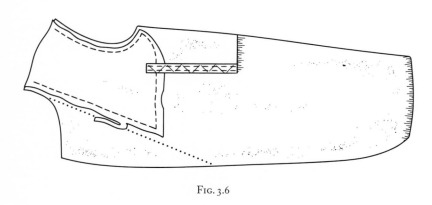

FIG. 3.6

FIG. 3.8

3   MAKING UP THE CANVAS

(3.1) If the body canvas is not pre-shrunk, spritz it with water and use the iron to dry. Press the body canvas until it is flat and crisp. (3.2) Re-mark any chalk marks from the previous steps so they are clear. (3.3) Lay the chest canvas in position on top of the body canvas, and the domette on top of the chest canvas, using the break line, shoulder and armhole as a position guide. (3.4) With the domette facing up, baste all layers together starting at the shoulder line, 1" back from the break line, basting down the chest and finishing 1" from the bottom of the domette, and a big stitch in towards the dart. From the shoulder end, starting on the shoulder line, baste down 1" in from the armhole and finish 1" up from the bottom of the domette, and a big stitch in towards the dart. (3.5) Cut along the waistline from the side seam, stopping at the front edge of the dart. Cut out the triangle shape that makes up the dart, through all layers. Take a scrap of silesia slightly wider and slightly longer than the dart. (3.6) Lay the body canvas with the domette facing up and place the silesia underneath the canvas, so the dart is visible to sew. Close the dart. Machine stitch up one side and down the other, and then up and down again. Then, from the bottom of the dart, zig-zag stitch all the way up the centre of the dart, ensuring it stays flat. Trim away the excess silesia from the edges of the stitching. (3.7) With the domette facing up, roll the canvas backwards in the hand from the top down, stopping around 1" above the line. (3.8) Pad stitch through all layers, in rows, back and forth across the domette, gently unrolling the canvas with each row. Start and end the rows at the basting stitches running through the chest 1" back from the break line and armhole. Stop padding at the shoulder line. (3.9) Pad all the way to the bottom edge of the domette, fixing the raw edge into place. (3.10) For a softer canvas, use fewer pad stitches sewn looser. For a firmer canvas, use lots of pad stitches sewn slightly tighter. (3.11) Repeat steps 1–10 to make up the other canvas. •

4   CUTTING OUT THE WEDGE & SEWING THE DARTS

(4.1) Lay one of the forepart pieces with the right side facing down. (4.2) Cut out the wedge marked below the waistline, ending the cut on the front dart line, closest to the front edge. (4.3) Cut up the middle of the dart, stopping ¾" from the top. (4.4) Working on the wrong side of the cloth, baste the dart together on the chalk lines, then machine stitch the dart closed on the edge of the bastes. Never back stitch on the dart as it causes bulk, and always tie off both ends. (4.5) Slot the back of the basting needle, with the thread attached, into the small pocket at the top of the dart to allow it to press out evenly. Pull the needle out by the thread because it will be hot. (4.6) Cut a 1" square of fusible interfacing and press it to the top of the dart to hold it in place. (4.7) Cut a strip of fusible interfacing 1" wide and slightly longer than the wedge cut. Close the wedge and fuse the raw edges together on the wrong side of the cloth. This will become the pocket line. •

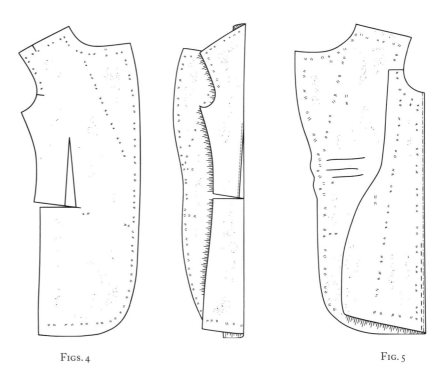

5   ATTACHING THE SIDE BODY

(5.1) Lay the forepart with the right side facing up. (5.2) Place the side body on top of the forepart with the right sides together. Aligning the underarm seams and matching the notches, baste along the seam ⅜" from the edge. With checks and stripes, match below the pocket and double baste, to secure when machining. (5.3) Machine stitch along the underarm seam just inside the baste stitches and press open the seam. (5.4) Repeat steps on the other forepart. •

6   MAKING & ATTACHING THE OUT-BREAST WELT

*Take care when constructing the out-breast welt pocket.
Remember, it appears on the LEFT chest of the coat only.*

(6.1) Lay the left forepart with the wrong side facing down. Press until smooth and flat. On the right side, with chalk, mark the out-breast welt pocket position through the mark stitches. (6.2) Cut 2 squares of linen roughly 3" deep and 6" wide. One piece will form the inside of the welt itself, giving it strength and body. The second piece will be placed behind the welt to give extra strength to the forepart fabric where the welt is sewn. Press one in half horizontally. (6.3) Lay the unpressed piece under the forepart, against the wrong side, making sure it overlaps all of the mark stitches at least ½" at the sides and bottom, with plenty of inlay at the top. (6.4) Using a piece of fabric from the fit-up (make sure it is at least 2" longer and wider than the welt size), mark the welt shape onto the right side of the fabric. Add ¾" inlay to the top and sides and a ⅜" seam across the bottom. ☞

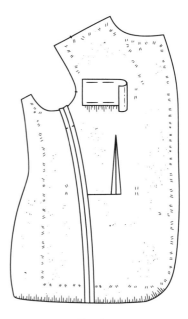

Fig. 6.3

(6.5) Baste a running stitch across the top line of the out-breast chalk mark. This is so the pocket position is visible through to the other side. (6.6) Turn the fabric over to the wrong side and lay the creased edge of the second linen strip along the baste line and baste within the inlay. (6.7) From the right side, crease along the chalk marks at the ends. Trim away just the linen along the creases. (6.8) Turn in the edges of the welt and baste in place. Press flat against a straight edge (a wooden ruler is good). Fell down the turned-back inlay and cross stitch the raw edge. Remove all basting. (6.9) On the right side of the forepart, re-mark your welt shape: 1" wide at the front and 1⅛" wide at the back. The bottom line of the welt is the stitch line. (6.10) With the right sides of the welt and forepart fabric together, lay the welt upside down, matching the seam lines. Baste though all 3 layers: welt, forepart and linen underneath. (6.11) Lay the facing piece right-side down, aligned with the bottom of the welt inlay. Machine stitch both seams, stopping the seam on the facing piece ¼" in at both ends. (6.12) Cut the pocket line in between the seams, stopping in line with the facing stitch line. Snip vertically up to, but not through, the end of the facing stitch, through all layers. Snip diagonally towards the end of the welt seam, through all layers except the welt seam. Press both seams open. (6.13) Cut a piece of silesia the same size as the facing piece. Turn back the edge of the silesia and hand-sew it onto the back of the welt, stopping ¼" in on both sides of the welt. Snip the silesia along the edge of the felling stitch and pull it through the pocket opening. (6.14) Mark the shape of the pocket bag on the silesia side. Machine stitch around the pocket bag and trim the excess fabric to ½". •

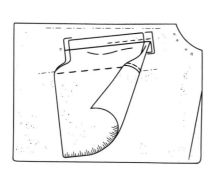

Fig. 6.6

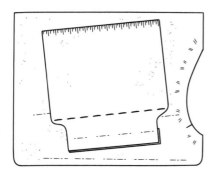

Fig. 6.10

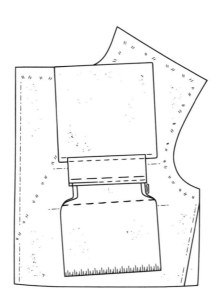

Figs. 6.12

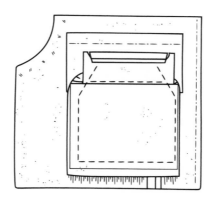

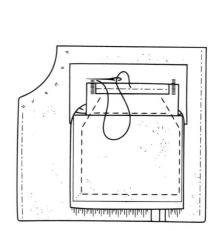

Figs. 6.14

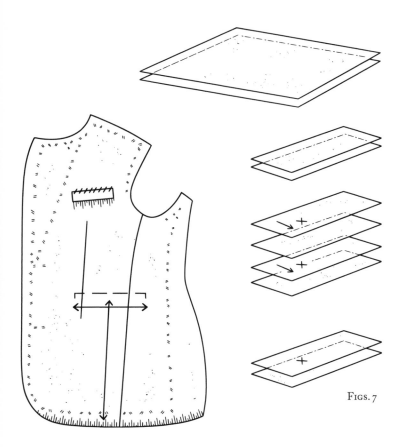

FIGS. 7

8   CUTTING THE POCKET FLAPS

(8.1) From the fit-up, place 2 small pieces of cloth together, wrong sides out, on a flat surface. (8.2) Use chalk to draw out the shape of the pocket flap along the straight grain, in the same direction as the forepart was cut. Below is a list of measurements for the flap. **Along the Top**: the width of the pocket opening (6"), 2¼" deep at the sides. **At the Bottom**: the width of the pocket opening, plus ¼" towards the back of the flap. (8.3) Draw a slanted line at the back of the flap. This should mirror the shape of the side seam. Draw a gentle curve around the front corner of the pocket flap. (8.4) Add a ¼" seam allowance to the sides and bottom of the flap and ½" seam allowance at the top. (8.5) Cut the flap out around the outside lines just made in step 4. (8.6) Place 2 pieces of lining fabric together, wrong sides out, on a flat surface. (8.7) Use the cloth flap pieces as a guide and use chalk to draw around the flap shape on the lining fabric. (8.8) Cut out the flap shapes from the lining fabric. Mark the wrong side of the lining fabric with an 'X'. This marking will help you distinguish the wrong side from the right side when assembling the pockets later. •

7   CUTTING OUT THE SIDE POCKET PIECES

(7.1) Place the foreparts on a flat surface with the right side facing up. Using chalk, mark the position of the pockets (pocket line) along the wedge cut. The pockets should come forward of the dart by approximately 1" and extend back past the side seam by around 1". Each pocket should measure around 6". (7.2) On one of the foreparts, measure the distance between the pocket line and the hemline. This measurement will be used later. (7.3) Cut out 2 rectangles from silesia. Each rectangle should have a height equal to twice the measurement taken in step 2, minus 2". The width of each rectangle should be 1" more than the length of the pocket line (for example, 7"). (7.4) Cut out 2 rectangles from linen. These pieces will be used to strengthen the pocket jets. Each piece should have the same width as the pocket bag (silesia fabric) and a depth of 3". (7.5) Use one of the linen pieces as a pattern, and cut 4 rectangles from the garment cloth. These pieces will become the jets above and below the pocket openings. Make sure to cut them on the warp (in the same direction as the selvedge) for strength. (7.6) Cut out 2 rectangles from the lining fabric. Each rectangle should have the same width as the pocket bag (silesia) and be 1" deeper. (7.7) Mark an 'X' on the wrong side of each lining and cloth piece. This marking will help you identify the wrong side of the fabric, ensuring that the pockets are assembled correctly later on. •

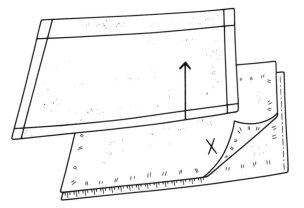

FIG. 8

(9.1) Place a cloth flap piece on top of a lining piece with the right sides together. Align the edges. (9.2) Baste the lining to the flap along the sides and bottom, keeping the stitches about ⅜" from the edges. (9.3) Machine stitch around the sides and bottom of the flap, using a ¼" seam allowance. Take care when stitching around the curve at the front corner. (9.4) Remove the basting stitches that were used to hold the pieces together initially. Trim the corners close to the machine stitching to reduce bulk and make it easier to turn the flap right-side out. (9.5) Turn the flap right-side out, making sure to pull the corners all the way out to achieve a neat finish. (9.6) Baste around the finished edges of the flap, rolling the lining back slightly so that it doesn't show on the right side of the flap. At the corners, make the basting stitches slightly smaller and tighter to ensure the flap will curve nicely over the hip when the coat is worn. (9.7) Baste the open edge at the top together, to fix both pieces securely. (9.8) Repeat the same process (steps 1–7) with the other flap piece and lining to create the second pocket flap. (9.10) Gently press the flaps. •

(10.1) Take one of the side pocket lining pieces cut earlier and place it wrong side up on a flat surface. (10.2) Fold back ⅜" on one of the long sides of the lining piece. This will be the edge that attaches to the pocket bag. Press it into place. (10.3) Place the lining piece wrong-side down at one end of the pocket bag piece. Align the raw edge of the lining piece with the edge of the pocket bag piece on the narrow end. (10.4) Baste along the raw edge of the lining, about ½" in from the edge of the pocket bag. Baste the folded edge of the lining to the pocket bag. (10.5) Machine stitch along the fold to secure the folded edge of the lining to the pocket bag. Remove the basting stitches and press the pocket to ensure a crisp and well-finished look. (10.6) Repeat these steps with the other lining piece and the second pocket bag. •

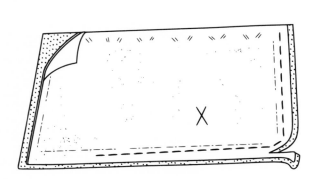

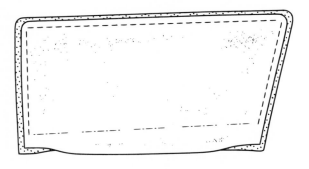

FIGS. 9

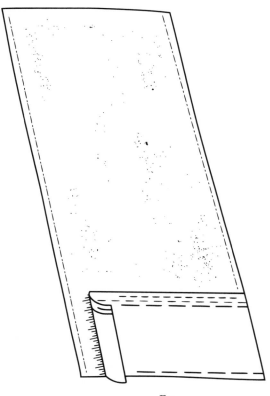

FIG. 10

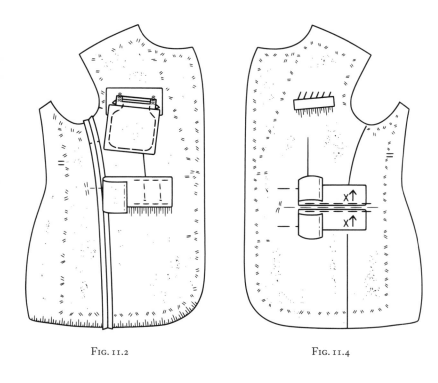

Fig. 11.2   Fig. 11.4

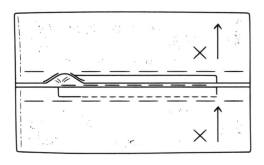

Fig. 11.6

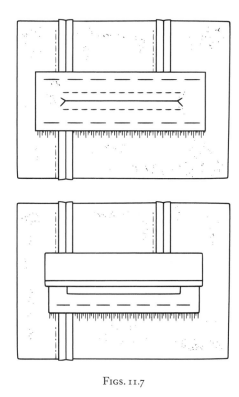

Figs. 11.7

11   MAKING THE SIDE POCKET JETS
& ATTACHING THE FLAP

(11.1) Take one of the jacket foreparts and place it wrong-side up. (11.2) Take one of the pieces of linen that was cut earlier. Place it over the basted line of the pocket mouth, with the pocket line in the centre of the linen piece. Baste the linen in place along the top and bottom edges. (11.3) Flip the forepart so the wrong side is now facing down. (11.4) Place two of the jet pieces (cut earlier) wrong-side up, one above and one below the basted pocket line. The long edges of the jet pieces should meet at the basted line and extend 1" beyond at the sides. Baste the jet pieces into place ⅜" back from the pocket line, on either side. (11.5) Lift the edges of the jet pieces at the sides to see where the pocket mouth starts and ends, and mark these onto the fabric. (11.6) On both jet pieces, machine stitch along the baste lines, with a ¼" seam, backtacking at each end. Turn the forepart so the wrong side is facing up. (11.7) Starting from the middle, cut along the pocket line, stopping ⅜" from the end of the machine stitching. Then, cut diagonally up to, but not into, the ends of the stitch lines. (11.8) Open the cut and pull the lower jet piece through to the wrong side. Press the seam open. Push the jet piece back through the cut to the right side of the forepart. Repeat the process with the upper jet piece. Flip the forepart so the wrong side is now facing down. ☞

(11.9) Push the bottom jet piece through the cut, folding it over the seam. This folded jet piece will become the pocket jet itself. If the jet does not sit properly, check the diagonal snips made in step 7 and ensure that the snip reaches all the way to the edge of the stitching. (11.10) Baste the jet into place through all layers using the seam as a guide. Make sure the jet is an even ¼" all the way across. (11.11) Fold the forepart up, right sides together, along the lower jet. Turn the lower jet piece away from the forepart so that the line of stitching on the linen is visible. Working on the wrong side of the forepart, machine stitch as close as possible to the line of stitching to fix the lower jet to the seam, ensuring it stays in place. (11.12) Lay the forepart with the wrong side facing down. (11.13) Turn the two small triangles that were created when the pocket line was cut, under the ends of the jets. This will make the jets neat and uniform. (11.14) Lay the forepart flat, with the right side facing up. Insert the top, raw edge of the flap under the top jet, into the pocket opening, so the seam line (½" from the top edge) is parallel to the bottom of the top jet. Baste along the top jet, through all layers, to hold the flap into place securely. (11.15) Fold the forepart in half horizontally along the seam of the top jet, with the right sides together and the wrong side facing up. Turn the top jet piece away from the forepart so that the seam line on the linen is visible. (11.16) Working on the wrong side, machine stitch as close as possible to the seam to fix the top jet and the pocket flap to the seam. Remove the basting stitches. Unfold the forepart and flip it around so the wrong side is again facing down. Press the jets and flap, ensuring that all layers are lying flat and aligned properly. •

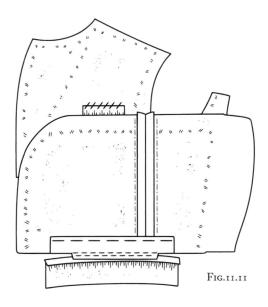

FIG. 11.11

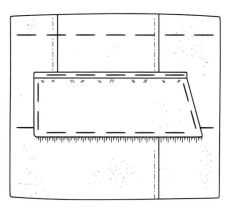

FIG. 11.14

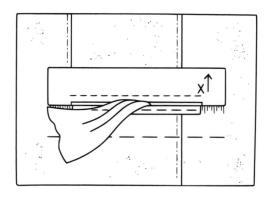

FIG. 11.9

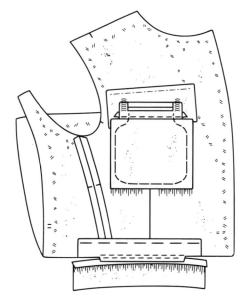

FIG. 11.16

(12.1) Lay the forepart with the wrong side facing up. (12.2) Place the pocket bag with the lined side down, aligning the unlined edge of the pocket bag with the bottom edge of the bottom jet. Baste the pocket bag to the jet piece, ⅜" from the edge. Be careful not to catch the linen or jacket cloth in the stitches. (12.3) Use chalk to draw a seam line ¼" from the edge of the pocket bag. Machine stitch the pocket bag to the jet piece along the same line. Again, be careful not to catch the linen or jacket fabric in the stitches. (12.4) Turn the pocket bag over, covering the seams, and press the seams towards the hem. (12.5) Fold the pocket bag upwards so that the lined, unattached edge is ½" above the seam line of the top jet. Baste the pocket bag to the flap seam allowance, making sure not to catch the linen or the jacket fabric as you stitch. (12.6) Fold the forepart in half, wrong sides out, along the seam of the top jet. Turn the top jet piece away from the forepart, so that the stitching on the linen is visible. Machine stitch the length of the seam as close to the seam line as possible. (12.7) Lay the jacket with the right side facing up, and fold back the forepart fabric and linen at the edge of the pocket opening on one side, revealing the pocket bag and jet pieces underneath. (12.8) Pull the small triangle away from the opening. Machine stitch back and forth over the triangle, catching all layers. Stitch as close to the pocket as possible. Repeat this step on the other end of the pocket opening. (12.9) Machine stitch around the sides and bottom of the pocket bag, starting 1" above the pocket opening and ½" inch out from the end. At the corners, curve the stitch line and finish back 1" above the pocket opening on the other side. (12.10) Smooth the forepart out and press the pocket nicely into place. (12.11) Repeat all of the steps, starting from MAKING THE SIDE POCKET JETS & ATTACHING THE FLAPS, to construct the other pocket. •

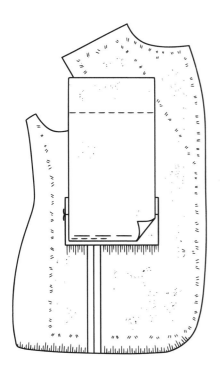

FIG. 12.2

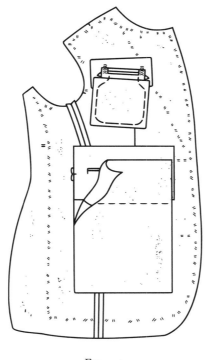

FIG. 12.5

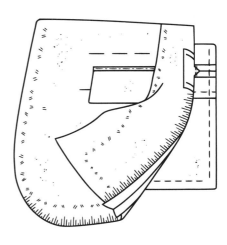

FIG. 12.9

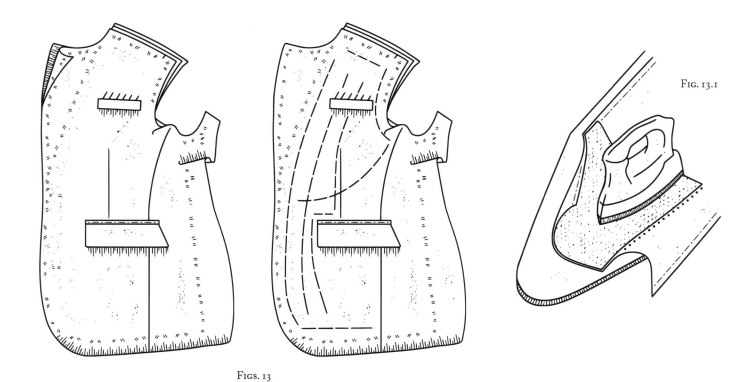

FIG. 13.1

Figs. 13

CANVASSING

(13.1) Lay the body canvas with the domette facing down, with the side body draped over a sleeve board or tailor's ham to create shape. Pull the shoulder taut and press along the dart and chest. Flip the canvas over and repeat on the domette side. (13.2) Lay the canvas with the domette facing down. Place the forepart on top with the straight grains matching and the darts laying on top of one another. Smooth out the forepart piece until it's lying happy and smooth. (13.3) Using a long, but not tight, running stitch, baste the forepart onto the canvas catching all layers. The most important thing to remember is to keep the canvas straight and not twisted during the basting. (13.4) **Line 1**: Start around 2½" down from the shoulder line, and 2" back from the neck line. Follow the shape of the chest, basting towards the hem around 2" in front of the dart with no ease. At the waist line, back stitch and continue to the hem adding slight ease with each stitch. (13.5) **Line 2**: Start parallel to Line 1, around 1" back towards the arm hole. Follow the shape of Line 1 and continue to baste through the out-breast welt and down the centre of the dart. At the top jet, come forward, following the line of the pocket and flap. At the bottom of the flap, stop and back stitch. (13.6) Flip the forepart over, so the canvas side is facing up. Just below the back stitch at the bottom of the flap, slice the body canvas horizontally towards the front edge, to just

beyond the pocket bag. Pull the pocket bag through the slice, so it now sits on top of the canvas. (13.7) Flip the forepart back over, with the fabric side facing up, and continue stitching Line 2 from the bottom of the flap to the hem. (13.8) **Line 3**: Start parallel to Line 1, but this time forward of it, around 1". Baste a good ¾" back from the break line and front edge. At the waist line, back stitch and continue to the hem adding slight ease with each stitch. Continue around the curve at the bottom and towards the side seam at the hem, sewing over the bottom of the first 2 lines. (13.9) **Line 4**: Start from just above the top of Line 3. Baste back towards the shoulder end, past Lines 1 and 2, and curve down around the armhole, around 1" from the edge. At the side seam start to curve in the opposite direction and stitch towards the front edge, through the dart and across the waist line, stopping just before Line 3. (13.10) With chalk, on the right side of the cloth, mark the front edge and the waist button. Make a new mark, parallel to the waist button, ¾" up from it. Mark the break line on the right side of the cloth. Place a ruler along the mark. Turn the cloth back and re-chalk the line between body and chest canvas. (13.11) Turn the forepart over so the canvas is facing up. Trim back the domette and chest canvas to ½" behind the chalk line. Then trim the chest canvas back a further small ¼". This is to layer the pieces and reduce bulk.

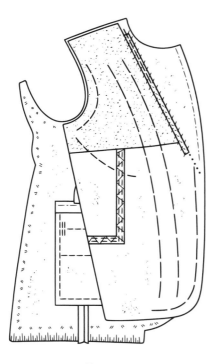

FIG. 13.12

(13.12) Take the bridle cut earlier from the lining piece. Place it over the edge of the domette, 1" down from the shoulder, with the selvedge edge overlapping the domette by ½". Baste in place along the selvedge edge, pulling taut with each stitch to create a slight curve in the chest. Trim away the excess lining ½" below the edge of the domette. Press out the fullness. (13.13) On the canvas side, chalk the break line through the bridle, and mark the rest of the shape of the lapel, but ¼" in from the original lines. This is the guide for pad stitching the lapel. (13.14) Place the forepart with the right side facing up. Holding the lapel with the less dominant hand, and rolling it slightly away from the break line, pad stitch the lapel. Make sure to stitch with a cotton matching the fabric colour. Starting from the break line, sew rows of pad stitches around ⅜" long up and down the lapel. Stay within the chalk marks made in step 13. To stop the stitches showing through on the fabric side, use the prick stitch technique, picking up minimal threads with each stitch. (13.15) Lay the forepart with the right side facing up. On the under-vent, chalk a horizontal line 1" above the top of the vent and 1" out into the inlay. From the side seam mark stitches at the hem, mark a diagonal line 3" wide and ½" up from the hem line. Connect the 2 lines with a curve. Draw another line parallel to the curved line, but ¾" back. Trim away any excess cloth outside of the ¾" line. Snip into the ¾" inlay, stopping at the 1" line above the top of the vent. Turn back the ¾" inlay along the first curved chalk line and baste into place. (13.16) Press the lapel and under-vent. (13.17) Repeat steps 1–16 on the other forepart. •

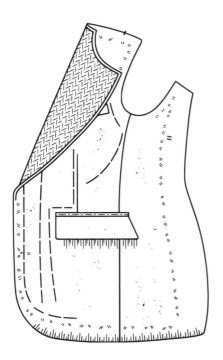

FIG. 13.14

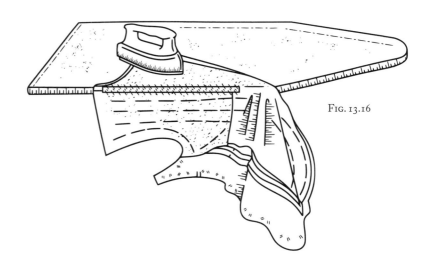

FIG. 13.16

(14.1) Lay the forepart with the canvas side facing up, smooth onto a flat surface. Press the lapel and front edge. (14.2) Trim back the inlay leaving a ⅜" seam along the mark stitches, starting from the notch on the gorge line, down the front edge, and finishing as the bottom curve starts to straighten off at the hem. (14.3) Lift the top of the lapel, locate the notch point on the right side, at the end of the gorge line, and mark onto the canvas side of the forepart. Do the same at the front edge and mark the button positions. (14.4) Trim back the body canvas along the hemline, front edge, lapel and gorge line, so the edge is aligned with the mark stitches on the jacket front. (14.5) Take a long piece of stay tape to tape the front edge. To start, place the end of the stay tape at the notch centred over the mark stitches and covering the edge of the canvas. Sewing through the canvas and forepart cloth, baste on the inner edge of the stay tape, along the gorge line, and down the lapel, stopping at the top button position. (14.6) Pull the tape taut in between the buttons and continue to baste down the front edge, stopping again 2½" from the curve. (14.7) As the front edge starts to curve, pull the tape taut and continue to baste, until the corner lifts into the shape of a hollow curve. Continue basting along the hem line, finishing at the back edge of the canvas. Trim away the excess tape. (14.8) Fell around the inside edge of the stay tape, catching only the canvas. (14.9) Flip the forepart around so the right side is facing up. From the notch, baste along the mark stitches with ⅜" long stitches, through all layers, down the lapel, front edge and hem, finishing at the front of the hem inlay. This will act as the sewing guide when the facings are machined on. (14.10) Repeat steps 1–9 on the other forepart. •

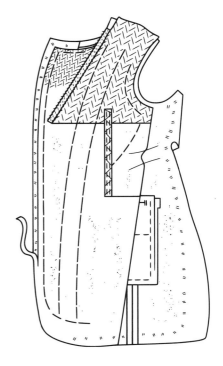

Fig. 14.2

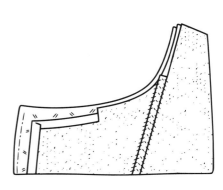

Fig. 14.5

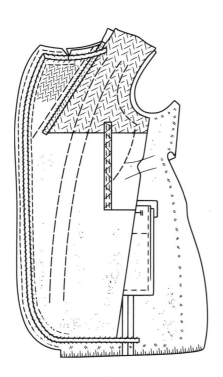

Fig. 14.8

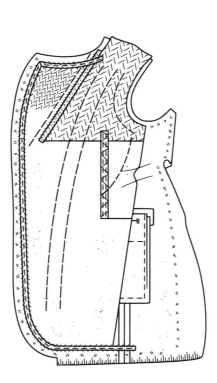

Fig. 14.9

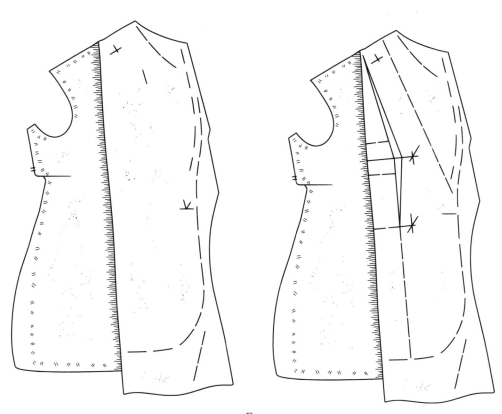

Figs. 15

15   CUTTING THE FACINGS

(15.1) Lay the forepart with the right side facing up.
(15.2) Place the facing fit-up piece, folded in half with the
wrong side facing up, over the front half of the forepart,
with the straight grain running parallel to the top edge
of the lapel. Make sure the cloth covers the shoulder
line at least 1½" back from the neck point and covers
the bottom curve around 4" back from the front edge.
(15.3) Using the forepart mark stitches as a guide, mark on
the facing piece with chalk: the neck point and the line
¾" above the top button made earlier. Draw in the break
line. Still following the mark stitches underneath, trace
around the edge of the lapel, the front edge of the forepart and around the curve into the hem. (15.4) Mark
the in-breast pocket line by placing a ruler (1¼" wide)
horizontally at the bottom of the armhole, angled down
¼" at the front and up ¼" at the back. Chalk the underside. The front of the pocket line should start 2" back
from the break line and measure 6" long. (15.5) From the
shoulder, starting 1¼" back from the neck point, chalk
a vertical line to a point 1" back from the front of the in-
breast pocket line. Continue the line down towards the
hem, finishing around 4" back from the bottom curve.
(15.6) Draw a parallel line 2" above the pocket line, and
another 2" below. Extend the lines 1½" past the back of
the pocket and square off. Curve the line made in step 5
as it meets the horizontal lines. (15.7) Cut out the new facing shape and re-mark the pocket lines on the right side
of the facing fabric. •

(16.1) Take one of the lining fabric pocket pieces cut earlier and place it wrong-side up on a flat surface. Fold back ⅜" on one of the longest sides of the lining piece. This will be the edge that attaches to the pocket bag. Press it into place. (16.2) Place the lining piece wrong-side down at one end of one of the silesia pocket bag pieces. Align the raw edge of the lining with the edge of the pocket bag on the narrow side. Baste along the raw edge of the lining, about ½" in from the edge of the pocket bag. Baste the folded edge of the lining to the pocket bag. (16.3) Machine stitch along the fold to secure the folded edge of the lining to the pocket bag. Remove the basting stitches and press. (16.4) Take one of the coat facing pieces and place it wrong-side up. Place a piece of linen, centred, over the pocket line. Baste the linen in place along the top and bottom edges. (16.5) Flip the coat facing so the wrong side is now facing down. Take another lining fabric piece, wrong-side up, and place it over the pocket line. Baste the piece into place, creating a ½" box inch around the pocket line with the basting stitches, ¼" on either side. (16.6) Machine stitch around the box, starting from the middle. Flip the coat facing so the wrong side is facing up. (16.7) Cut along the pocket line, stopping ⅜" from the end of the machine stitching. Then, cut diagonally up to, but not into, the corners of the box. (16.8) Open the cut and pull the lower jet piece through to the wrong side. Press the seam open. Push the jet piece back through the cut to the right side of the facing. Repeat the process with the upper jet piece. Flip the facing so the wrong side is now facing down. (16.9) Push the bottom jet piece through the cut, folding it over the seam. This folded jet piece will become the pocket jet itself. (16.10) Baste the jet into place through all layers using the seam as a guide. Make sure the jet is an even ¼" all the way across. (16.11) Fold the facing up along the lower jet. Turn the lower jet piece away from the facing so that the line of stitching on the linen is visible. Machine stitch as close as possible to the seam to fix the lower jet to the seam, ensuring it stays in place. (16.12) Lay the coat facing with the wrong side facing down. Turn the two small triangles that were created when the pocket line was cut, under the ends of the jets. This will make the jets neat and uniform. (16.13) Lay the facing wrong-side up. Place the pocket bag with the lined side down, aligning the unlined edge of the pocket bag with the bottom edge of the bottom jet. Baste the pocket bag to the jet piece, ⅜" from the edge. (16.14) Use chalk to draw a seam line ¼" from the edge of the pocket bag. Machine stitch the pocket bag to the jet piece along the same line. Turn the pocket bag over, covering the seams, and press the seams towards the hem. (16.15) Fold the pocket bag upwards so that the lined, unattached edge is ½" above the seam line of the top jet. Baste the pocket bag to the seam allowance. (16.16) Fold the coat facing in half, wrong sides out, along the seam of the top jet. Turn the top jet piece away from the forepart, so that the stitching on the linen is visible. Machine stitch the length of the seam as close to the seam line as possible. (16.17) Lay the coat facing with the right side facing up, and fold back the fabric and linen at the edge of the pocket opening on one side, revealing the pocket bag and jet pieces underneath. Pull the small triangle away from the opening. Machine stitch back and forth over the triangle. Do not catch the facing fabric. Stitch as close to the pocket as possible. Repeat this step on the other end of the pocket opening. (16.18) Machine stitch around the sides and bottom of the pocket bag, starting 1" above the pocket opening and ½" out from the end of the pocket mouth. At the corners, curve the stitch line and finish back 1" above the pocket opening on the other side. (16.19) Repeat steps 1–18 for the other in-breast pocket. •

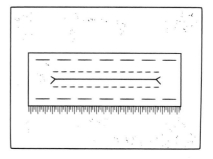

Fig. 16.7

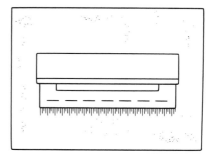

Fig. 16.8

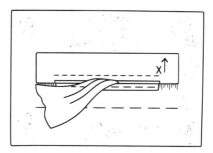

Fig. 16.9

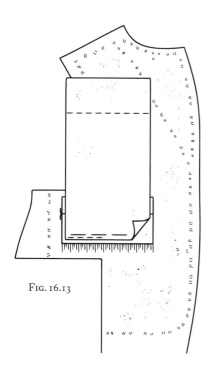

Fig. 16.13

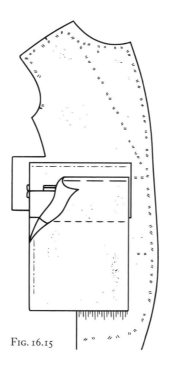

Fig. 16.15

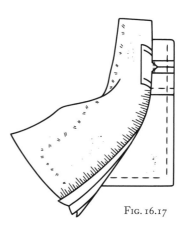

Fig. 16.17

17   ATTACHING THE FRONT LINING

(17.1) Place the front lining piece with the right side facing up. Fold a pleat horizontally across the piece, halfway between the armhole and shoulder, about 1" deep. Press it into place. (17.2) Press a ½" pleat down the piece where the side body meets the forepart, about ¾ of the length of the underarm seam. Leave a gap at the bottom. (17.3) Lay the front facing with the right side up, and place the front lining piece over it, right sides together. Baste the lining to the back edge of the facing. (17.4) Machine stitch along the baste stitches, leaving a 4" gap at the bottom (to allow the lining to be turned back). Stop 1" below the in-breast pocket jets, and start again 1" above, leaving a window to cut the lining and hand stitch around the in-breast pockets later. Take out the baste stitches and press the seams back towards the side seam. (17.5) Repeat steps 1–4 on the other facing piece. •

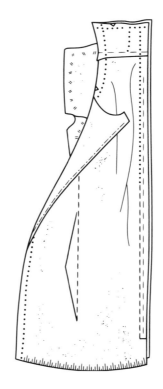

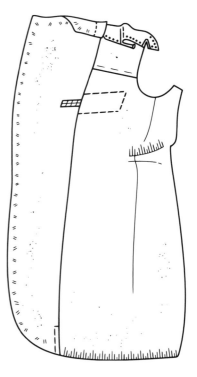

FIGS. 17

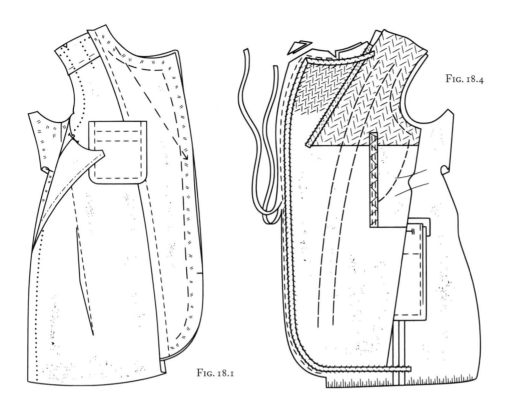

Fig. 18.4

Fig. 18.1

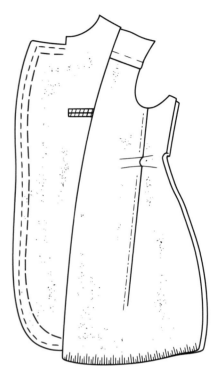

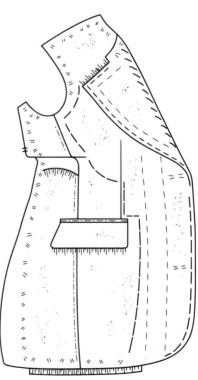

Figs. 18.7

18   ATTACHING THE FACINGS

(18.1) Lay the forepart right-side up. Place the facing over the forepart, right side-to-right side. Align the edges of the facing to the forepart and all of the chalk marks. From the top of the lapel to the bottom edge of the facing at the hem, baste along the front edge sew line, making sure the facing is happy and smooth, and not tight. Turn the back edge of the facing at the hem back ¼" so the cut edge does not show when the facing is turned out. (18.2) Starting a new baste 3" down from the top of the lapel and ½" back from the cut edge, sewing up the facing, baste around the corner of the lapel notch, easing a small pocket of fullness, so the point of the lapel is not tight when turned out to the right side. Continue to baste along the gorge line and stop at the break line. (18.3) Turn the forepart over so the canvassed side

is facing up. Machine along the basted seam line (⅜" back from the front edge). On the right forepart start from the bottom, and on the left forepart start from the gorge line, back tacking three stitches at the beginning and end. Walk the machine needle one stitch across the corner of the lapel, to remove the sharp angle of the point. (18.4) Trim back any excess fabric at the corner of the lapel. At the lapel notch (end of the gorge line), snip vertically into the seam, up to – but not into – the stitch line. (18.5) Using a sleeve board or a pressing point, press open the seam. Turn up the bottom edge along the mark stitches and press. (18.6) Turn out the facings to the right side so the canvas is sandwiched between the facing and forepart. Using a needle, tease out the corner of the lapel. (18.7) Starting at the top of the lapel, with the less dominant hand, roll the seam so that the stitching is rotated towards the jacket front and won't be visible when the lapel is folded back into its finished position. Baste ⅜" stitches close to the edge. This will hold the seam in place until the finishing stage. Continue basting along the lapel, still rolling, and stop at the top button. (18.8) From the top button mark, roll the front edge seam in the other direction so that it's rotated towards the facing. Again, this is so the seam is not visible when the jacket is worn. Continue basting along the bottom curve to the hem and finish at the lining. (18.9) Starting 1" inside the first line, with slightly bigger stitches, baste a second line. From above the top button, add a small channel of ease between the rows. Below the button, push the ease back from the edge, and stitch slightly tighter to create shape. These two lines of basting will stay in the jacket until the finishing stage is complete. (18.10) Press out any fullness from the back of the lapel. At the bottom, press the front edge from the facing side.

(18.11) Turn back the lapel along the break line to allow the lapel to roll without tension. Stitch 1" back from the break line, through the lapel and down the centre of the facing. Then baste along the edge of the lining on the facing. (18.12) Turn back the lining, exposing the seams. With cotton, fell the raw edge of the lining to the canvas. Cross stitch the pocket bag to the canvas and continue to fell to the hem. (18.13) Turn the lining back so the right sides face up. From the front edge of the lining next to the shoulder pleat, baste to down around the armhole, past the underarm pleat, down the side body and stop around 4" above the hem. Then stitch back towards the front, finishing where the lining meets the facing. Ease the lining ¼" from the edges of the armhole, side seam and hem. (18.14) Trim the excess lining, leaving the following inlay: 0"/net across the shoulder, ¾" around the armhole, 1" at the top of the side body, 1½" at the side seam and 1" at the hem. (18.15) Fell the raw edge of hem. •

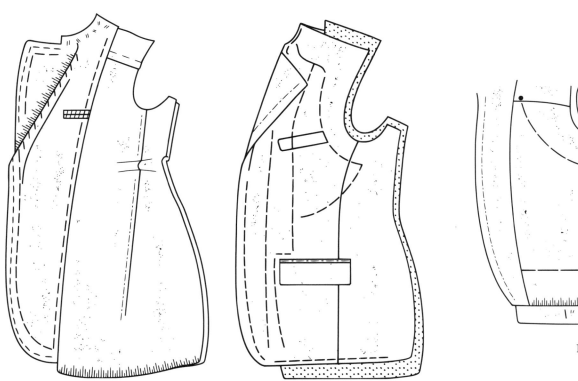

FIGS. 18.11

FIG. 18.13

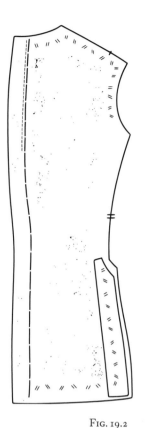

FIG. 19.2

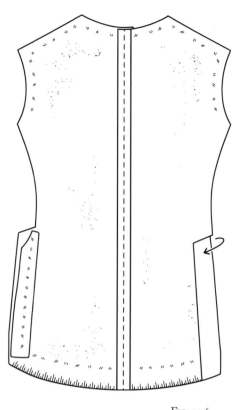

FIG. 19.6

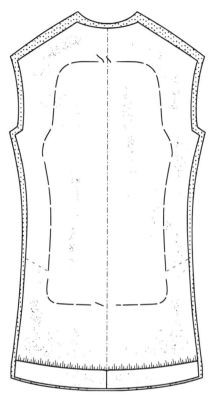

FIG. 19.10

19   MAKING UP THE BACK

(19.1) Lay the back coat pieces with the right sides together.
(19.2) Machine stitch the centre back seam along the baste stitches
made during the mark stitching stage. Back stitch at the neck point
and continue the stitches into the inlay at the hem. (19.3) Take the
back lining piece with right sides together and machine stitch
the small rectangle at the bottom of the centre back, marked earlier. Fold the lining over so the right side is facing up, and press
down the centre back pleat, using the machine stitches at the hem
as a guide. (19.4) Cut 2 pieces of fusible interfacing 1¼" wide, by the
length of the vent plus 1". (19.5) Open up the back coat piece and
lay it with the wrong side facing up. Place the fusible interfacing
strips over the vent inlay, ½" past the top and bottom of the vent,
with the mark stitches running through the centre. Using an iron,
press the fusible into place. (19.6) Turn the vent inlay back along the
mark stitches and press into place. (19.7) Lay the back lining with
the right side down. Place the back piece with the wrong side down,
aligning the machine stitches at the centre back of the coat piece,
with the pleat at the centre back of the lining pieces. (19.8) Starting
3" up from the bottom, sew a long running baste stitch up the centre back to hold the lining in place. Stop 2" down from the neck
line mark stitches. (19.9) Pull away the back side of the back coat
piece at the top and bottom to remove the suppression, so the front
half of the back is lying smooth and flat. (19.10) Baste through both
layers, attaching the back piece to the back lining, making sure to
ease the lining a good ½" in length and width. Starting from the
centre back, around 4" up from the hem, baste two long stitches.
Continue to baste up the side seams around 3" from the edge, and
begin to curve the stitches at the top of the side seam back towards
the centre back, making sure to leave enough room for the shoulder pads. (19.11) With the right side facing up, trim away the excess
lining: ½" down the side seams, 1½" through the shoulders, 1" at
the back neck collar, and 0"/net with the inlay at the bottom. •

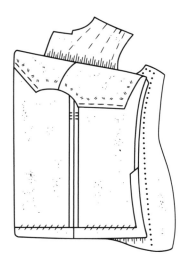

(20.1) Lay the forepart with the right side facing up and the lining facing down. On the wrong side, fold the lining away from the side seam, to clear it for stitching. (20.2) Lay the constructed back on top of the forepart with the right sides together, aligning the raw edge of the back side seam, with the mark stitches on the side body. Match the notches at the waist and chest for accuracy. (20.3) Baste a ⅜" seam from the top of the vent to the top of the side body. Machine stitch along the basted line, back stitching at both ends. Remove the basting. Press the seam open, stopping around 1¼" above the vent. (20.4) Place the half-assembled coat with the right sides facing down. Turn back the lining on the forepart and back to access the side seam. At this stage both vent allowances should be pressed open, in opposing directions. On the back, fold the lining back along the vent, ½" from the edge. Baste into place ¼" in from the edge of the lining. (20.5) Align the mark stitches on the side body vent allowance with the edge of the back vent. Fold the side body vent allowance towards the back piece, covering the back vent, and press into place at the top of the vent. The seam should only be pressed to one side at the top of the vent; the rest of the side seam should remain pressed open. (20.6) Starting ½" down from the top of the vent, prick stitch across the vent, through all layers, to fix it into place. (20.7) Turn the forepart lining back towards the side

seam. Fold the lining back along the vent allowance, ¼" from the edge. Baste it into place ¼" in from the folded edge of the lining. Continue to fold the forepart lining along the side seam, laying it on top of the back lining. Baste the linings together. From the waist up, only stitch through the lining fabric and do not catch the cloth. (20.8) Starting at the front scye, baste the lining 2" down from the armhole, around the armhole and through to the back scye, securing it in place for the insertion of the sleeves. (20.9) On the front (forepart and side body) turn back the bottom lining ½" away from the hem edge and baste it ¾" back from the edge of the lining. (20.10) Repeat steps 1–9 on the other side seam. (20.11) Turn the coat over so the lining is now facing down. The hem inlay on the back should still be loose and extend past the finished hem edge of the fronts. On the back hem inlay, on each side, mark the point at which the edge of the side body hem meets the back hem. Square across (this should be in line with the mark stitches). At the centre back, mark ¼" down from the square line, and draw in the shallow V-shape across the back hem. (20.12) Flip the coat back over so the lining is facing up. Turn up the back hem along the V-shaped line, and baste it into place around ½" down from the top of the inlay. With cotton, fell down the back hem inlay. (20.13) Turn back the bottom lining ½" away from the hem edge and baste it ¾" back from the edge of the lining. •

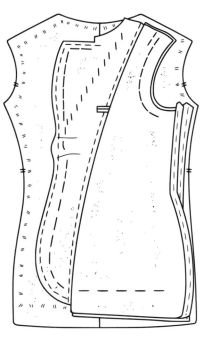

FIGS. 20.2

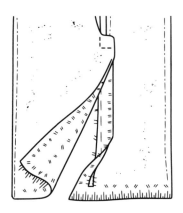

FIG. 20.5

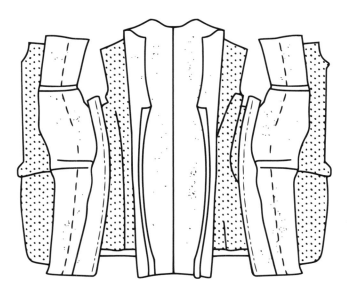

FIG. 20.7

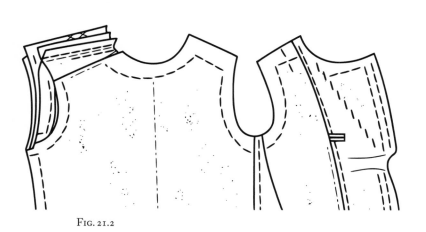

FIG. 21.2

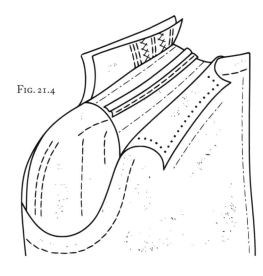

FIG. 21.4

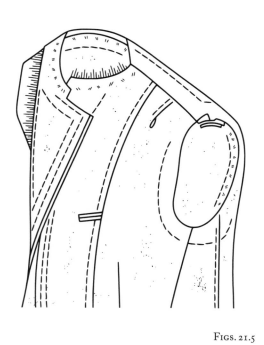

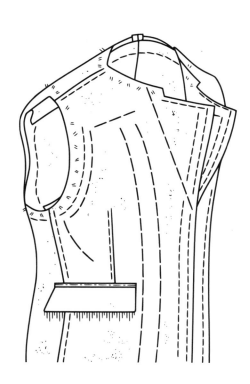

FIGS. 21.5

21   JOINING THE SHOULDERS

(21.1) Place the coat open and flat on a surface, with the right side facing down. Turn one of the foreparts under the back piece so the right sides are now together, and align the shoulder seam lines. The raw edge of the shoulder seam on the back piece should line up with the mark stitches across the front shoulder. (21.2) Catching only the cloth, tack the pieces in place at the neck point. Then baste along the shoulder seam ¼" down from the mark stitches. If the coat pattern commands ease through the back shoulder (around ½" is common) gently ease the seam with each stitch, creating a subtle ripple effect. Aim to put all of the fullness into the first third of the shoulder, as this is where the most movement occurs. (21.3) Press out the fullness and machine stitch a ⅜" seam across the shoulder line. Be careful to catch the cloth only and not the other layers. (21.4) Press the seam open. (21.5) Turn the coat right-side out and place the constructed shoulder around a sleeve board. Smooth the body canvas back up past the shoulder seam. Keep the lining clear. Baste through all layers except the lining: around the neck point, across the shoulder seam and down the front scye, 2" in from the armhole. (21.6) Repeat steps 1–5 on the other shoulder. •

(22.1) Fold one of the shoulder pads in half horizontally, leaving the back side 1" longer than the front. With the coat assembled, the right side facing out and the lining clear, slot the pad into the open armhole, aligning the fold with the shoulder seam. Make sure the thick, open edge of the shoulder pad is protruding ½" beyond the armhole sew line. (22.2) From the right side of the coat, starting at the front scye about 2" in from the armhole, pad stitch around the back edge of the shoulder pad, down to the back scye and back again to the front. Catch all layers except the lining, which should be folded out of the way. (22.3) Turn the coat inside out so the wrong side is facing out. Mirroring the pad stitches on the chest canvas, pad stitch the front of the shoulder pad to the canvas around the armhole and across the front shoulder. Catch only the canvas and not the cloth underneath. (22.4) Bring back the front lining and smooth it across the shoulder and armhole. Baste the lining down along the shoulder line and down the front scye, around 2" back from the armhole. (22.5) With the wrong side of the coat still facing out, position the sleeve board through the armhole so the shoulder seam and pad are lying flat. Fold the back shoulder lining back along the shoulder seam. Baste along the shoulder seam about ¼" back from the edge of the lining and around the back scye about 2" from the armhole. Make sure to leave a gap around the back neck to allow for the collar to be attached. (22.6) Repeat steps 1–5 for the other shoulder pad. •

(23.1) Place the coat, right side facing up, with the neck circle wrapped around a tailor's ham (a rolled-up towel will work just as well). On each side, measure around the neck circle from the centre back seam line to the shoulder line, then the break line, and onto the point at which the notch starts on the lapel. Make a note of the measurement to the shoulder (usually around 3½") and then the break line and notch, which will vary depending on the width of the lapel. The measurements should be the same on each side, but if one side happens to be larger than the other, work from the larger measurement as the smaller side can be adjusted later. (23.2) The collar is split and seamed at the centre back. From the collar canvas and melton, cut the collar shape, ensuring both are cut on the bias. The bottom edge of each side of the collar should equal the full measurement taken in step 1, plus at least ½" seam allowance at the top, 2" at the sides and a good ¼" at the back seam. At this stage the height should be at least 3¼" at the centre back and 2½" at the leaf edge. A lot of the allowances will be trimmed away later. (23.3) On both the canvas and melton, machine stitch the centre back seam and press it open. The collar shape should now be something like a large *moustache*. Place the canvas and the melton with the wrong sides together, aligning the open seams. ☞

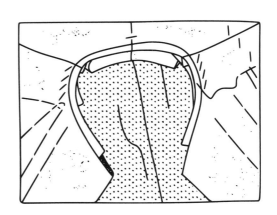

Fig. 23.1

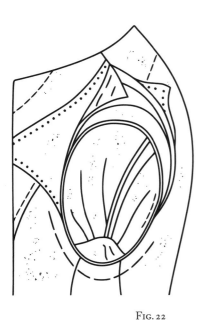

Fig. 22

Fig. 23.2

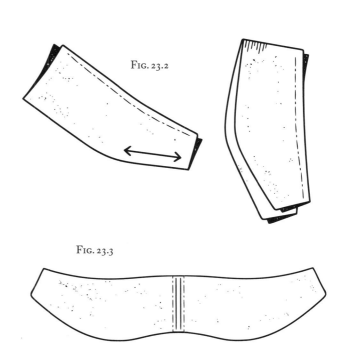

Fig. 23.3

(23.4) Using the first measurement from step 1, mark the shoulder point on the bottom edge of the collar, on the melton side. This should be measured back from the centre seam. Continue to measure around the bottom edge, and mark the break line point. (23.5) At the centre seam, measure up from the bottom edge 1⅜" and mark a point horizontally with chalk. Then measure up 1¼" from the shoulder point mark made in step 4, and mark that with chalk. Drawing a slightly curved line, connect the marks, finishing at the break line point. This is the collar stand. (23.6) Baste the canvas and melton together along the collar stand line. Then machine stitch along the line, making sure not to catch the basting. (23.7) On the canvas side, with chalk, draw in the collar shape. Leave ½" around the top, 1" at the sides and ¼" around the bottom. This will act as the padding guide. Starting from one end of the collar stand on the canvas side, directly below the machine stitch line, pad stitch across the length of the collar. Use light thread that matches the colour of the melton. The stitches should be short and tight, only just catching the melton underneath. With each stitch, roll the collar with the less dominant hand, working end-to-end from the machine stitch line to the bottom of the collar. Remember to stay inside the padding guide lines. (23.8) On the top of the collar (the fall), start the pad stitching from the same end, but begin at the notch point. Again, roll the collar with the less dominant hand, working end-to-end from the machine stitch line to the top of the collar. Remember to stay inside the padding guide lines. (23.9) Place the collar with the canvas side facing up and press it flat, ready for shaping. The shape is created initially by pressing the fall of the collar only, and not the stand, so do not cross the machine stitch line with the iron. Start by pressing along the top curve at the centre back, pulling the end of the collar down and taut to create a more rounded shape. Hold the iron in place for a few seconds to set the collar into place. Turn the collar around 180 degrees and press the other side in the same way. (23.10) Once the collar is pressed into a nicely curved semi-circular shape from the top, notice how the stand has become full and ruffled. It should naturally want to fold back on itself. At this point flip the collar over so the melton is facing up. (23.11) Press the stand down along the machine-stitched line, curving at the back neck. Pull the end of the collar upwards, straightening the curve from the neck point mark to the notch mark. Shrink away any fullness created around the top of the collar. Turn the collar 180 degrees and repeat on the other side. (23.12) At this stage the collar should no longer resemble a moustache, but now a *hump–backed bridge.* •

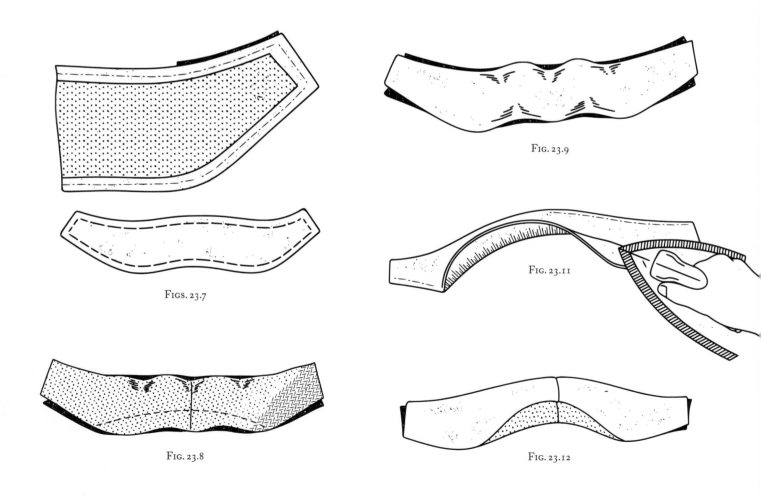

FIGS. 23.7

FIG. 23.8

FIG. 23.9

FIG. 23.11

FIG. 23.12

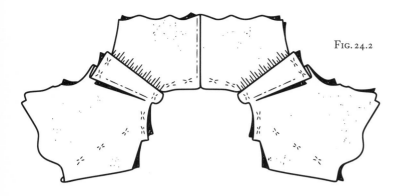

FIG. 24.2

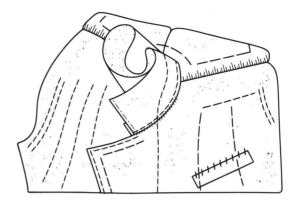

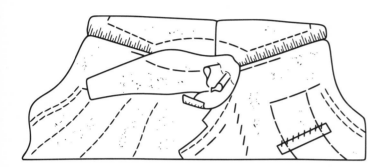

FIGS. 24.3

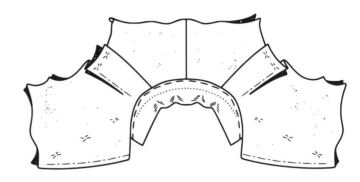

ATTACHING THE UNDERCOLLAR   24

(24.1) Trim the collar canvas back ⅛" along the bottom edge, making the stand 1¼". Leave the melton ⅛" longer to cover the raw edge. (24.2) Place the coat, right side facing up, with the neck circle draped flat around a tailor's ham and the lapels laying open. Starting at the centre back, place the bottom edge of the collar against the mark stitches, with the centre back collar seam and centre back coat seam aligned. Baste the collar into place at the centre back. (24.3) Using a pad stitch, baste the collar around the back neck line keeping the bottom edge aligned with the mark stitches. Stop at the neck point and back tack for strength. It is at this point the neck line really starts to curve, so make sure to hit the mark stitches. Ease the collar around and baste another ½" past the neck point then back tack again and stop. (24.4) Pull the collar back and straight, so it runs parallel with the lapel, and the collar stand machine stitch line runs smoothly into the break line. This will create a small bit of fullness in the collar stand, which will avoid tightness when the collar is sewn. Continue to baste the collar in place and stop around 1" past the top of the lapel. (24.5) Flip the lapel around the right way to trap the collar and ensure the break line runs smoothly into the collar. Pin the lapel into place. Flip it back open to expose the melton, and sew through the collar and lapel to secure it into place. (24.6) Working on the collar canvas side, pull the top of the back lining out of the way so that it doesn't get caught, then cross stitch around the neck line, gorge line seam allowance, across the top of the facing and around the back neck. •

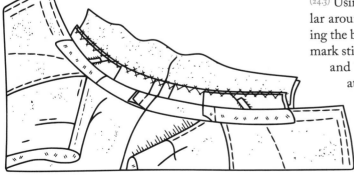

FIG. 24.6

25   TRIMMING THE COLLAR TO SHAPE

(25.1) Place the collar around a sleeve board and press the fullness out of the shoulders. (25.2) Lay the coat with the right side facing up and the collar canvas nearest the body. With a pencil, draw on the shape of the collar; measure 1½" down at the back neck and 1¾" at the shoulders. The notch at the collar end should be an equilateral triangle; each side should measure 1¼". Draw in a straight line from the top of the notch to the shoulder point, and then curve the line around to the back neck. Make sure both sides are cut symmetrically. (25.3) Trim the melton down ¼" across the top edge. •

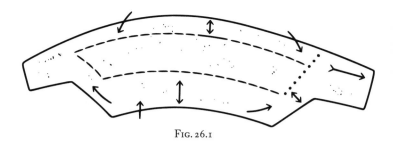

FIG. 26.1

26   SEWING THE TOP COLLAR

(26.1) With the coat facing right-side out and the canvas side of the collar facing up, smooth out the undercollar so it is lying flat. Lay the piece of collar fit-up cloth, wrong-side up, over the collar, and trace around the shape. Add the inlays: 1" across the top, 1½" at the side, 1" at the notch point and 1½" at the bottom. Cut out the new shape. (26.2) Fold the top collar piece in half vertically and mark the centre line. Press the bottom centre and pull the sides upwards to stretch the back neck, creating lots of ease. Turn the piece around and repeat the action across the top edge, but do so more gently, as this requires less fullness. (26.3) Place the coat as per step 1. Lay the top collar fabric with the right side facing up, over the undercollar, with the inlay falling beyond the collar edge. Line up the centre line of the top collar piece with the centre of the undercollar. Starting from the centre back and working outwards, about ½" from the top edge of the undercollar, baste the top collar into place. Gently ease the cloth with each stitch, not creating fullness, but making sure the top collar is smooth and not tight. Stop ½" from the undercollar edge, and stitch a new row of bastes below the first row, about ¼" from the folded edge, back towards the centre back. Repeat the process on the other side of the collar. (26.4) Flip the coat over so the melton side of the collar is now facing up. Starting from just past the neck point, ¼" below the collar stand machine line, stitch through all layers, catching the top collar underneath. Finish just past the other neck point. Use the non-stitching hand to hold the top collar into place, making sure it's lying flat and happy.

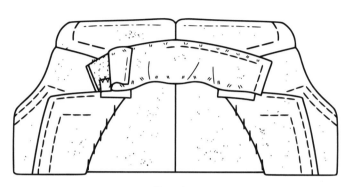

FIG. 26.3

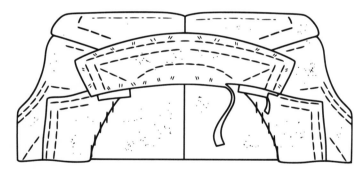

FIG. 26.5

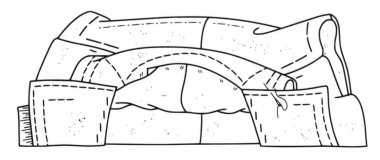

FIG. 26.6

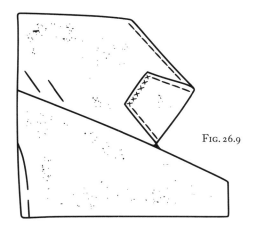

FIG. 26.9

(26.5) Flip the coat back so the top of the collar is showing. Focus on the top of the lapel and gorge line. Make sure the coat is lying flat and smooth. With chalk, mark from the notch, across the gorge line and top of the facing, stopping at the neck point. Trim away the excess inlay, leaving a seam around the chalk marks you just made. Make sure to leave the inlay around the back neck and the end of the collar to turn back. (26.6) Turn in the seam allowance at the gorge line and check that the top collar is sitting well with no tightness or fullness. Starting right in the corner of the lapel notch, stitch down the edge of the gorge line, making sure it's smooth and straight. Flip the coat around and continue the stitch on the inside, turning in the seam allowance perfectly against the facing with each stitch. From the neck point to the centre back, baste the inlay to the undercollar. (26.7) Repeat steps 5 and 6 on the other side of the collar. (26.8) Flip the coat over so the melton side of the collar is now facing up. At the centre back, trim the edge of the melton seams into a point to create less bulk when it's sewn down. Trim away the inlay across the top edge of the top collar to ½". Starting at the centre back, sandwich the top collar inlay in between the collar canvas and melton, and baste along the edge about ¼" down, fixing it into place. Use the needle to poke the cloth into position, ensuring it's nice and even, before each stitch. Stop at the end of the collar. (26.9) To finish the collar, fold back the end of the top collar towards the melton and baste into place. Trim away any excess inlay beforehand. The fold should measure about 1", with the side edges turned in to look clean. The back edge stays raw and is cross stitched at the finishing stage. (26.10) Repeat steps 8 and 9 on the other side of the collar. (26.11) Press gently around a ham to remove any extra fullness. (26.12) Sew down the bottom edge of the top collar to the canvas with small cross stitches. Then, baste the back neck lining into place, covering the cross stitches by at least ½". •

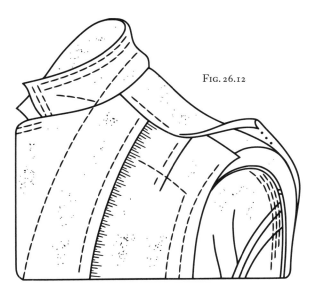

FIG. 26.12

LACING THE ARMHOLE   27

With basting cotton doubled up, baste around the front scye from the underarm seam to the shoulder. Back stitch from the shoulder to the underarm seam at the back scye, drawing the armhole in slightly with each stitch. Only sew through the fabric, not all layers. •

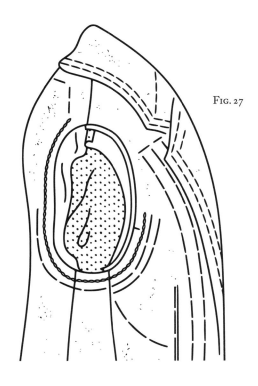

FIG. 27

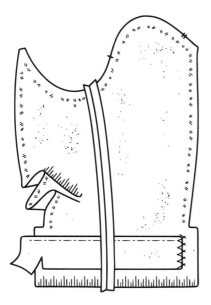

FIG. 28.2

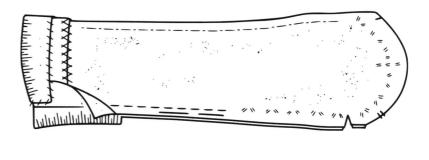

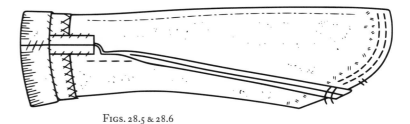

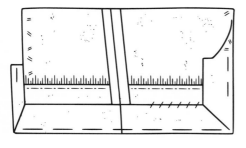

FIG. 28.3

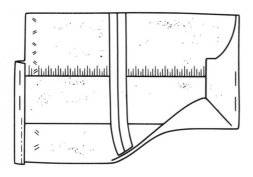

FIG. 28.4

28   MAKING UP THE SLEEVES

(28.1) Lay the top sleeve and undersleeve pieces with the right sides together. Baste the forearm seams into position and machine stitch a ⅜" seam. Press the seam open. (28.2) Lay the half-made sleeve with the wrong side facing up. Cut a piece of fusible interfacing 3" wide and the length of the finished cuff. Place it ⅜" below the cuff finish line and press it into place. (28.3) Turn back the edge of the button stand on the undersleeve ⅜" and baste down to the cuff finish line. Turn back the cuff vent on the top sleeve along the fold line and baste into place ¼" in from the edge of the fold wrap, stopping at the cuff finish line. (28.4) Turn up the cuff inlay along the cuff finish line. At the vent end, turn the inlay back at a 90-degree angle to create a mitred shape. On the button stand end of the undersleeve, turn back the seam and taper it in slightly. Baste everything into place and press. Fell the top of the cuff inlay, only catching the fusing, and down the button stand edge. Fell the corner of the vent about ½" up at the mitred edge, but leave it open so the buttonholes can be sewn. Fell the raw edge of the button stand and the vent to the fusible. (28.5) Fold the sleeve in half vertically with the right sides together, and place it with the top sleeve facing up. Align the hind arm seam on the top sleeve with the mark stitches on the undersleeve. Match the notches and make sure the cuff hems are level. (28.6) Baste along the hind arm with a ⅜" seam, stopping about ½" past the top of the vent. Turn back the top of the vent so that it doesn't get caught, and machine stitch along the baste line, stopping ½" below the top of the vent. Remove the basting. Press the seam open, stopping around 1¼" above the vent. At this point, turn the inlays towards the top sleeve and press them flat. Close the cuff in its natural finished position and baste it secure. This will make it easy to attach the lining. (28.7) Repeat steps 1–6 for the other sleeve. (28.8) Place the top sleeve lining piece and undersleeve lining piece with the right sides together. Align the forearm seams and baste a ⅜" seam. Machine stitch along the basted line and remove the basting. Press the seam open. (28.9) Align the hind arm seams, remembering that the undersleeve includes inlay (this should have been chalked when the linings were cut). Baste with a ⅜" seam, stopping ½" below the top of the vent position. Machine stitch along the baste line. Remove the basting and press the seam open. (28.10) Repeat steps 8–9 for the other sleeve lining. (28.11) Place the constructed sleeve with the wrong side facing out and the undersleeve facing up. Fold it along the forearm seam, but with both sides of the open seam showing. Lay the sleeve lining on top of the constructed sleeve in a mirrored fashion, with the undersleeve facing down and the top

sleeve facing up. Align the forearm seams and baste through the outer seam allowance from the armhole point to the top of the fusing. (28.12) Bag out the sleeve by pulling the lining downward, inside itself from the armhole edge, through the hem edge, until the sleeve is completely inside the lining. (28.13) Turn the undersleeve lining back and baste it around ⅛" from the edge of the vent. Then turn the top sleeve lining back and baste it ⅛" from the edge of the vent. Turn the edge at the top of the vent at an angle and baste into place. (28.14) Turn under the cuff lining inlay so it sits ¾" from the edge, and baste it in place ½" above the folded edge. Press the hem and vent. The hand stitching will be completed during the finishing section. (28.15) With 2 or 3 large basting stitches, fix the lining to the top sleeve a few inches down from the crown. (28.16) Repeat steps 11–15 to finish constructing the other sleeve. •

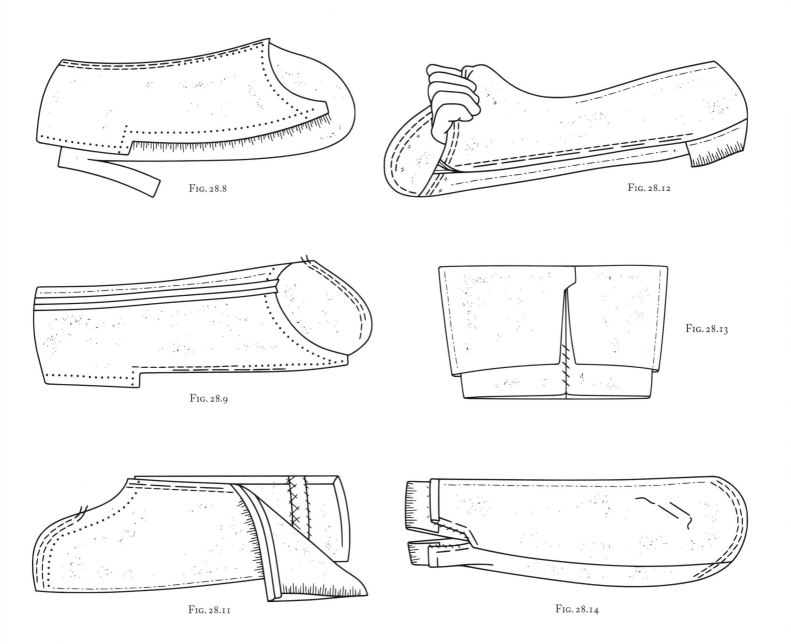

FIG. 28.8

FIG. 28.12

FIG. 28.9

FIG. 28.13

FIG. 28.11

FIG. 28.14

(29.1) Always start with the LEFT sleeve. Match the top of the fore-arm seam to the sleeve pitch mark at the bottom of the armhole (usually around ¾"–1¼" forward of the underarm seam). Baste a ⅜" seam clockwise around the armhole, through the cloth only, not the canvas. (29.2) Gently ease the seam backwards with each stitch, creating fullness around the sleeve head. Different sleeve patterns will have varying ease and tolerance, but most sleeves will include around 2"–2½" of fullness. (29.3) As a guide, aim for: no fullness in the first 2"–3"; a light amount through the front scye; maximum fullness (around ⅛" per stitch) spread evenly through the crown to the back pitch; and then whatever is left spread even-ly around the back scye, to the front pitch. (29.4) Turn the coat the right way round and check that the sleeve is hanging nicely with no puckers or drags. When the sleeve is pitched correctly, the fore-arm should land in the centre of the side pocket. (29.5) If the sleeve is not lying happily, repeat steps 1–3, spreading the fullness more evenly. Once the sleeve *is* pitched correctly, double baste around the armhole and press out the fullness from the inside. (29.6) For the RIGHT sleeve, repeat steps 1–5, but match the front pitch and work anti-clockwise around the armhole. •

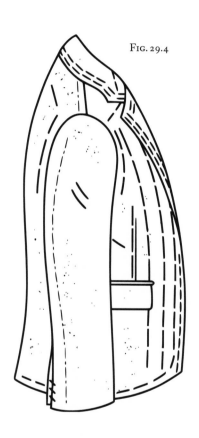

FIG. 29.4

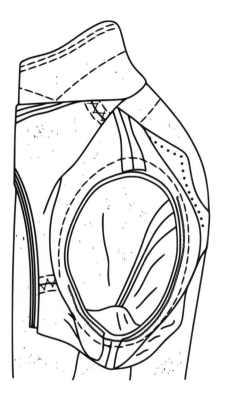

FIG. 30

30   MACHINE STITCHING THE SLEEVES

(30.1) Turn the coat wrong-side out, but leave the sleeve right-side out inside the body, ex-posing the armhole seam. Stitching only the cloth, from the sleeve side, machine stitch around the armhole seam line. Sew gradually, making sure the stitch line is smooth and continuous, and no puckers are created when sewing through the ease. (30.2) Take out the basting and do not press the seam. •

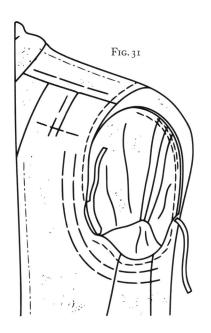

FIG. 31

(32.1) Still working on the armhole seam from the inside of the coat, turn the crown and shoulder pad back so the armhole seam pops out. Place the sleeve head wadding with the seamed side facing up around the crown. Line up the folded edge of the sleeve head wadding with the armhole seam, so the rest of the wadding extends into the top of the sleeve. (32.2) Starting ¾" round from the pitch point, sew the folded edge of the sleeve head wadding to the top sleeve seam allowance, as close to the armhole seam as possible. Finish about 1" past the back pitch. (32.3) Turn the coat the right way out, and check that the sleeve head wadding is sitting comfortably within the sleeve. If it is too bulky or causing tightness, trim the wadding back from the loose end. •

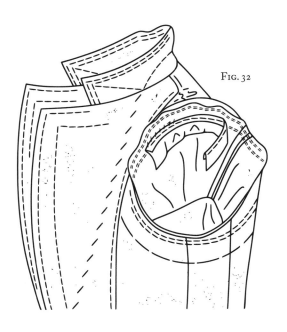

FIG. 32

SETTING THE SLEEVE 31

(31.1) With the right side facing out, place the armhole around the end of a sleeve board, with the shoulder and front scye lying flat. Smooth out the fabric and baste around the armhole, fixing the fabric into place so the front scye looks clean. Now working on the armhole seam from the inside of the coat, use double basting thread to baste along the machine stitch line with a small back stitch, trapping all layers. (31.2) Trim the shoulder pad back to ½". Trim the canvas back to ⅛". The armhole should look compact and neat. •

BASTING THE 33
SLEEVE LINING

(33.1) With the coat fully assembled and the wrong side facing out, reach into the sleeve and pull out the lining. Match the pitch points on the front and the back to ensure that the lining is not twisted and that it is lying smooth. (33.2) Turn back the raw edge of the lining a good ⅜" so it will be hidden inside the sleeve. Baste the lining around the armhole, spreading the fullness with each stitch (the fullness should be around the same amount as basting in the sleeve), and covering all of the stitches and raw edges inside the armhole. (33.3) Repeat steps 1–2 on the other sleeve. •

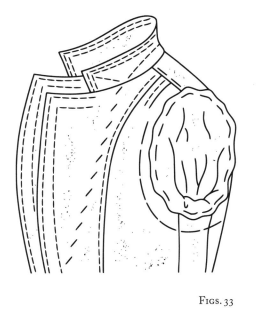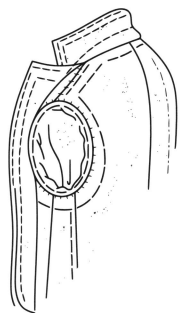

FIGS. 33

FINISHING THE COAT

1   MARKING THE BUTTONHOLES

On a men's coat, the front buttonholes should be sewn on the LEFT forepart. On a women's coat, the front buttonholes should be sewn on the RIGHT forepart.

(1.1) Mark the buttonholes with chalk, on the right side of the cloth. (1.2) Starting with the cuff; this example is based on a traditional coat, where there are four buttonholes on the cuff, spaced evenly apart. However, the number of holes does not really offer a practical function, so it is essentially just a style choice. The buttonholes may also be spaced closer together, making the buttons overlap when they are fastened. These are known as kissing buttons. Each hole should measure ⅝" long and be spaced ⅝" apart. The first hole should be marked on the top sleeve, 1¼" up from the hem and ½" in from the vent edge. Work upward towards the crown, adding as many holes as required at ⅝" intervals. (1.3) The front buttonholes should still be indicated by the mark stitches sewn at the beginning of the job. The top buttonhole is usually positioned at the waistline and the lower button 4"–4½" below that. The hole should measure ⅞" long and start ⅝" back from the front edge. (1.4) The lapel hole should run parallel to the gorge line, 1½" down, starting ⅝" from the edge of the lapel, and should measure ⅞" long. •

2   MAKING THE HANGER

On the wrong side of a small piece of lining fabric, sew a channel 3¾" long and ¼" wide. Trim away the seam as close to the stitching as possible and turn through so the right side is facing out. Press flat. Turn back the raw ends ⅜" and press into place, leaving a 3" by ¼" strip of lining ready to sew. •

3   CUFF LINING

(3.1) Fell the bottom of the sleeve lining to the cuff inlay, just below the baste stitches. Remember to leave a good ⅜" pleat around the bottom edge, for movement and to make sure the lining isn't tight. (3.2) Fell the lining to the edge of the vent on the top sleeve and undersleeve – if this wasn't completed during the construction of the sleeves. (3.3) Repeat steps 1–2 on the other sleeve. •

4   GORGE LINE

(4.1) Starting at the notch and sewing around to the back neck lining, use a draw stitch to close the gorge line seam. Make sure the stitches are invisible and not tight. (4.2) Repeat on the other side. •

5   SHOULDERS AND BACK NECK

(5.1) Fell the back lining across the shoulder, catching the front lining and the top of the facing. (5.2) Fell all the way around the back neck, catching the undercollar. (5.3) Repeat step 1 on the other shoulder. •

6   SEWING ON THE HANGER

Place the hanger at the centre back neck, 1½" each side of the centre back seam, and ⅛" either side of the back neck lining and top collar. Fell around the sides, catching and hiding the ⅜" of lining turned underneath. Prick stitch ⅜" from the sides to make it strong. •

7   FRONT LINING

(7.1) Find the 2" opening next to the in-breast pocket made earlier. Carefully cut into the lining parallel to the middle of the in-breast pocket, stopping the cut at the back of the pocket. (7.2) Turn the lining back ½" from the in-breast jets, and fell into place. Take care to be accurate and create a nice round or mitred shape around the corners. (7.3) Repeat steps 1–2 on the other side. •

8   SIDE SEAMS AND VENTS

(8.1) Fell down the side seam lining catching the back lining. (8.2) Fell the lining to the edge of the vents. (8.3) Repeat steps 1–2 on the other side. •

9   HEMS

(9.1) Fell the bottom 4" of front lining to the facing. (9.2) Turn back the bottom of the front lining ½" and fell it to the hem inlay, just below the baste line. The ½" pleat around the bottom edge allows for movement and ensures the lining isn't tight. (9.3) Turn back the bottom of the back lining ½" and fell it to the hem inlay, just below the baste stitches. (9.4) Repeat steps 1–2 for the other side. •

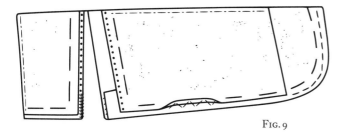

FIG. 9

10   ARMHOLES

(10.1) Fell the sleeve lining in place around the armhole. Keep the stitches small and firm, as this is an area of excessive tension and wear. (10.2) Repeat on the other sleeve. •

11   COLLAR AND MELTON

(11.1) Across the outer edge of the collar, fell the melton to the top collar. (11.2) Fell the sides of the 1" folded-back ends of the top collar, and cross stitch the raw edge. (11.3) Cross stitch the melton at the sides and bottom edge of the undercollar. •

12   FRONT EDGE

(12.1) Starting at the inner point of the notch, 1 mm in from the edge, prick stitch down the lapel and continue along the front of the coat. Finish at the back edge of the facing. These stitches hold the facing in place and stop the edges from rolling or separating. Be accurate and do not pull them tight, as they are the most visible. (12.2) Repeat on the other side. •

13   POCKETS AND FLAPS

(13.1) Starting with the out-breast welt, prick stitch each end of the welt a good ¼" in from the edge to trap the seam. Then prick stitch across the top of the welt 1 mm from the edge. (13.2) At the side pocket, prick stitch around the flap 1 mm in from the edge. Then D-tack at either end of the jets. (13.3) Repeat step 2 for the other side. •

14   SEWING THE BUTTONHOLES

Using the technique shown in the stitch guide (p. 160), sew the buttonholes previously marked in steps 1–4 of MARKING THE BUTTONHOLES. •

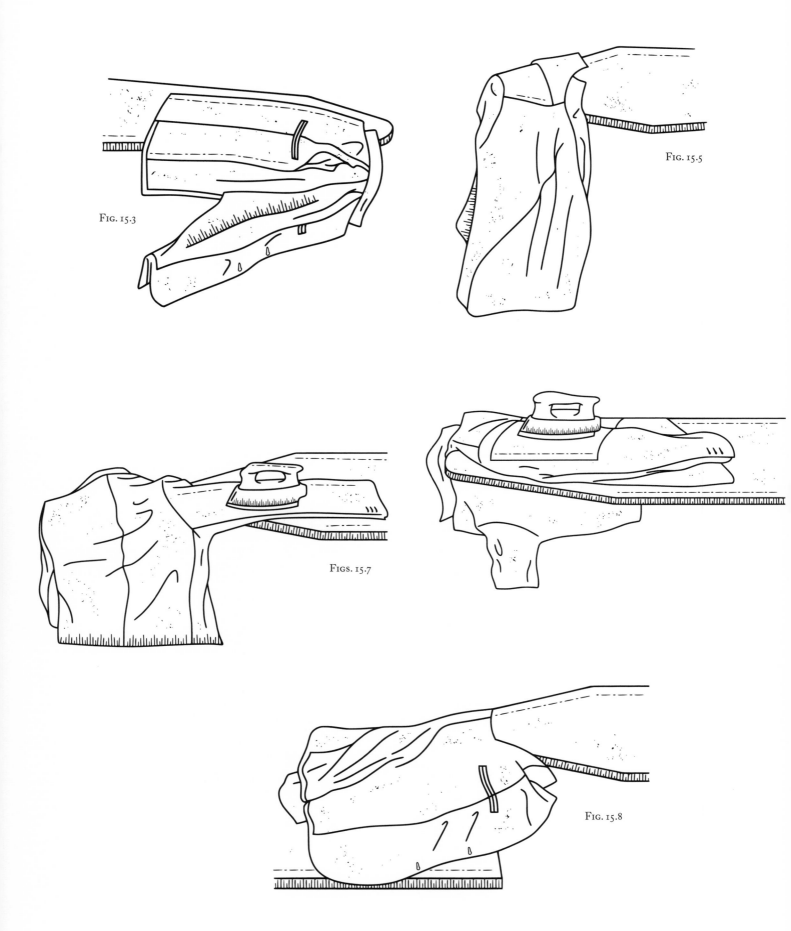

Fig. 15.3

Fig. 15.5

Figs. 15.7

Fig. 15.8

(15.1) Remove all remaining basting and mark stitches from the coat. (15.2) Place the coat so the lining is facing up, keeping it as flat as possible. Starting at the hem edge, press the facing and around the collar. Then press the hem inlay and the vents. When pressing on the lining, avoid using steam, as any water leaks will stain and damage the lining. (15.3) With the lining still facing up, drape the coat over an ironing board, with the forepart lying flat on the board. Again without steam, press the front lining flat, starting at the hem and working towards the shoulder. (15.4) Drape the rest of the coat around the ironing board with the lining facing up, pressing the areas that are flat: the side body, back lining and then the other forepart. When pressing the side body, make sure the vents are lying even and smooth on the underside. (15.5) With the lining still facing out, place the shoulder around the narrow end of the ironing board. (A sleeve board might be easier at this stage.) Press the front lining across the shoulder and then the back lining in the same way. Repeat on the other shoulder. (15.6) Turn the coat so the right side is facing out. In the same order as steps 2–5, press the outer body of the coat. (15.7) Lay the sleeve flat, with the top sleeve facing up and the armhole end towards the narrow end of the ironing board. Reach into the cuff and smooth the lining so everything is lying evenly. (Alternatively, insert a sleeve board into the sleeve, with the wide end at the armhole and narrow end at the cuff). Press the sleeve flat on both sides, but avoid the sleeve head. Only press through the centre of the sleeves, not the edge, as this will leave a crease. (15.8) With the lining facing up, place the armhole around the narrow end of the ironing board or sleeve board. Press, without steam, the bottom edge of the armhole. (15.9) Place the top collar shaped around a ham or edge of the ironing board. Gently press into place, taking care not to stretch it out of shape. (15.10) Turn the coat so the right side is facing out and draped over the edge of the ironing board. Pull the collar around the narrow end of the board and lay the forepart flat on the board, with the lapel rolled into position. Starting at the gorge line, press the break line down around 6". Do not press further, as the bottom of the lapel should roll naturally to the first button. Press the rest of the lapel smooth and repeat on the other side. •

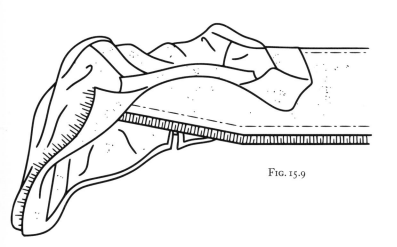

Fig. 15.9

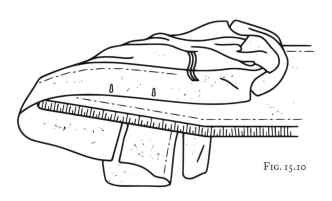

Fig. 15.10

16   SEW ON BUTTONS

(16.1) Lay the finished coat on a flat surface, with the front facing up. (16.2) Starting with the cuff, place the vent in its finished position so it lays flat and smooth. With chalk, mark through the buttonholes onto the button stand. Then sew the cuff buttons on the marks, through all layers, with double thread. (16.3) Repeat step 2 for the other cuff. (16.4) For the front buttons, turn the coat inside out so the right sides are together. Lay it on a flat surface with the left side facing up. This way, the back of the buttonholes will be exposed. (16.5) Align the front edges so the lapels and bottom curves run perfectly parallel. With chalk, mark through the back of the buttonhole, onto the right side of the cloth. Then sew the front buttons on the marks, through all layers, with double thread. Remember to leave at least a ⅛" shank on the button thread. •

PERFECTLY DRESSED:
A TIMELINE OF THE SUIT

The evolution of the classic men's suit, from the innovations of Charles II to present-day Savile Row silhouettes

ABOVE Suit styles may have changed over the years, but it remains the quintessential male garment.
OPPOSITE A present-day incarnation of the suit.

MEN'S TAILORING has gone through multiple iterations over the last 360 years, inspired in turns by society, sports, and style. More practical than might be appreciated, the suit – with its hardy cloth, practical cut, and clever features – has evolved and yet remains the quintessential male garment.

This timeline illustrates a progression of changing styles, instigated and popularised by influential designers, historical British figures – even the man on the street. Regency dandy Beau Brummell; Edward VII (Queen Victoria's son and one of the most photographed men of the day); and pop cultural icons like David Bowie all played a part in popularising the styles traced here. Partly it was their flair for dressing that ushered such styles to prominence. But more so was the singular blend of political, social and economic conditions of each individual era that helped bring a particular style to the fore. In this respect, the suit in all its iterations offers a portrait in three pieces of history at a given moment. •

CHARLES II

Late 17th century

SOMETIMES style evolves not for reasons of utility or even fashion for its own sake, but for reasons of business or politics. So it was that in 1666 the so-called 'Merry Monarch', Charles II, devised a way of boosting sales of English wool – and up-ending the dominance of French fashion – by introducing the waistcoat, albeit one cut to the knee. By layering this with a matching long, tailored jacket and breeches or knee-length trousers, Charles's new look became the progenitor of the three-piece suit. While some men still wore extravagantly embroidered waistcoats, certainly the new style was relatively sober compared with the flamboyance of European, and especially Louis XIV's, court fashion. In being so, it would also help direct menswear towards the dark, pared-back style dominant for centuries to come, not least because in Charles's time the court defined fashion at large. •

BEAU BRUMMELL

Late 18th century – Early 19th century

I
T MAY BE HARD to imagine that men – or at least the wealthy, upper-class variety – were once the peacocks, their clothing colourful, ornate, fanciful, and impractical. Arguably it was one English gentleman, George 'Beau' Brummell (1778–1840), who put paid to that notion, with his contrarian insistence on long trousers and a darker, more minimalistic and fitted tailoring – much closer to the body than ever before. In doing so he ushered in what became the template for the modern suit. Such was Brummell's command over perceptions of correct dress in fashionable society – not to mention the wide influence that came thanks to his on-off companionship with his 'fat friend', the Prince Regent, later George IV – that by 1824 Beethoven in Vienna was bemoaning his lack of a black coat to wear for the premiere of his Ninth Symphony. •

THE FROCK COAT

Early 19th century

THE FROCK COAT eventually came to be worn only by dignitaries and traditionalists. But at its peak in the 1850s, this hybrid of the greatcoat and more fitted jacket, buttoning at the front with skirts to the knee, was considered an essential component of fashionable everyday dress, especially for sportier, equestrian types. Worn in dark cloth with contrasting waistcoat, breeches, and boots, 'the frock', as it was more simply called, became the ideal template for experimentation: roll collar or lapels; larger buttons or tighter sleeves; single- or double-breasted; a shorter or longer skirt or something more like tails – the style went through multiple innovations and revivals until the late 19th century. •

THE DINNER SUIT

Late 19th century

T HE IDEA of dressing for dinner may be long gone, but the dinner suit lives on. With its black cloth, distinctive silk-lapelled jacket (borrowed from the arcane smoking jacket), and trousers with a braided seam, it is the epitome of stylish men's formal attire, especially when worn traditionally with white shirt and bow tie. It was Edward VII who ensured the dinner suit had widespread social acceptance and who popularised the idea that it should be made in 'blacker than black' midnight blue. But it was one of his dinner guests, American coffee broker James Brown Potter, who took the look back to the Tuxedo Park country club north of New York City, thus providing the dinner suit with its Americanised name. •

THE MORNING SUIT

Late 19th century

A LATE 19th-century evolution of the frock coat, morning dress came to be regarded as arguably the ultimate manifestation of men's formal dress, worn for royal occasions, state events, memorial services, weddings and, as James Bond demonstrates in *A View to a Kill*, upscale horse racing meetings. The black wool tailed coat, contrasting waistcoat, striped trousers (or less-formal matching trousers), and top hat became a symbol of Englishness, forever concerned with the rules of etiquette and expressions of class – and no wonder, given that a variation of it was adopted as school uniform for the children of the elite at Eton College. •

EDWARD VII

Late 19th century

THIS FASHION magpie, who would change many times a day, discovered Glen check (or plaid) while hunting in Scotland. It would soon be known as Prince of Wales check. His tailor, the story goes, ironed his trousers incorrectly (for the times) with a centre rather than a side crease – Edward henceforth wore all his trousers that way. Rather than muddy the bottoms of his trousers in the countryside, he turned them up – as cricket players did – and the trouser cuff was born. Blending sporting and city style, it was Edward who championed the blazer, too. Men still wear waistcoats with the bottom button undone because Edward did so, admittedly to make room for his expanding waistline. Tired of wearing white tie and tails for formal occasions, he helped drive the modern concept of dinner attire altogether: matching bow-tie and waistcoat, with a cutaway silk-lapelled jacket – as might be worn for riding – and trousers with a braided seam, similar to military uniforms of the day. •

THE LOUNGE SUIT

Late 19th century

I T MAY HAVE first appeared as an informal style in the late 19th century – worn for sports or in the country – but the end of World War One ushered in the era for which the lounge suit seemed newly appropriate. In came a push towards greater democracy, the first signs of a breakdown of class divides and of formal/informal distinctions. Capped with greater labour power, an easier, more Everyman style of dress was required to go with the spirit of the age. If the Victorian frock coat signified one's gentlemanly station in life, the lounge suit would define the fundamental tailoring style that's as familiar now as then. A hip-length coat with short lapels, waisted but with no waist seam, and worn with narrow, matching trousers (these perhaps with cricket-inspired turn-ups and later with pleats), this was tailoring's first multi-purpose garment. •

THE SPORTS JACKET

The 1930s

IN THE 1930s, to be sporting didn't necessarily mean having a fondness for football or tennis. 'Sport' often referred to country pursuits such as hunting, fishing, shooting, riding, and rambling. For these one still wore tailoring, albeit with some modifications, not least the use of hardy fabrics such as tweed or corduroy. The Norfolk jacket – arguably the first 'sports' jacket – came with large bellows pockets; front or rear box pleats for ease of movement; elbow and maybe shoulder patches; and a belt. It was, in a sense, one of the first instances of utility clothing for civilian wear. Over time the details would change, but what lasted was the idea that a man could wear separates; that his tailored jacket and trousers need not be in a matching fabric. A jacket for sport, then, ushered in the notion of a jacket for leisure. It was the beginning of casualwear. •

THE POST-WAR SUIT

The 1940s – 1950s

I N THE UNITED STATES, men's tailoring in the forties and fifties saw a boom-time of creativity: big, bold, colourful, wide-shouldered, double-breasted – the look of the era embodied the confident exuberance of excess. Not so in the UK, where rationing was still in force and suits were sober and single-breasted. Many men made do with the shapeless, low-quality 'demob' suit issued to them on leaving the Army for their return to Civvy Street. If the 'Man in the Gray Flannel Suit' was an American invention – suggesting the anonymous salaryman – the minimalism of the style, with its narrow lapels and trim, and turn-up-free trousers – was more likely the standard across war-ravaged Europe. The late forties and fifties offered some positivity, with the pioneering of dependable and affordable made-to-measure and later off-the-rack tailoring from Sir Montague Burton. •

THE PEACOCK REVOLUTION

The 1960s

IN THE SIXTIES, London was the epicentre of a pop cultural revolution. Nutter's, as Edward Sexton and the Kilgour-trained Tommy Nutter's business was called, cut suits with a modern if slightly thirties Hollywood flair: subtly exaggerated proportions, strong lines, narrow waists, parallel-legged trousers, wide peak lapels, and mixed-and-matched fabrics. The celebrities came in their droves, including Mick Jagger, Eric Clapton, Elton John, and The Beatles. Meanwhile, Douglas Hayward's fresh, streamlined approach brought other faces of the era to his door – Terence Stamp, David Bailey, and Michael Caine. The adventurous spirit of influential retailers also contributed to flamboyant experimentation in menswear: designer Rupert Lycett Green, for example, reimagined Edwardian style through his Mayfair boutique, Blades, whereas shirt maker Michael Fish introduced very wide 'kipper' ties, polo necks, and even dresses for men at his Mayfair shop, Mr Fish. •

THE NEW ROMANTICS

The 1970s–1980s

Retaining the fundamental idea of matching top and bottom, the 'leisure suit' of the seventies did away with padding and shaping, encouraging experimentation. Designers such as Antony Price – who made men's tailoring from softer, more vibrant fabrics that were traditionally the preserve of womenswear – pioneered a blend of retro and sci-fi influences for his band-muses Roxy Music and later Duran Duran. The early eighties New Romantic movement saw menswear embrace an anything-goes theatricality, with influential performers such as Spandau Ballet and Steve Strange of Visage exploring vivid suiting. Arguably more lasting was the influence of Giorgio Armani who, from the late seventies onwards, softened the silhouette of the tailored two-piece suit, introducing a cardigan-like ease while also prepping the new corporate workforce to wear the big-shouldered power suits of the eighties. •

THE POST-CORPORATE SUIT

The 2020s

The EXPANSION of remote working during the Covid-19 pandemic dealt yet another blow to men's formal tailoring. This did not mean the end of the suit, however; instead, we saw its reinvention, both in terms of when it was worn and how, with younger designers embracing the essential two-piece matching garment as a blueprint for bolder experimentation with colour, cloth, and cut – all historically rather restrained qualities in menswear. Designers now cherry-picked from the historic outliers of suit design – from the drape cut to the zoot suit to the oversized – to devise a more 21st-century incarnation. With this exploration came a new comfort and ease of wear, too, with a greater use of woven blends to provide more natural stretch and shape retention; a much more lightweight construction; and everything from Velcro fastenings to raglan sleeves and avant-garde flourishes to please the wearer. •

BESPOKE HAND-STITCHING TECHNIQUES

Stitching by hand is fundamental to bespoke tailoring – in fact, most of the garment is made by hand, particularly at the finishing stages. The most important stitching techniques referred to throughout this book are outlined below, in the approximate order for constructing a bespoke piece.

A   **USING A THIMBLE**

Made from durable metal, a thimble enables the tailor to push a needle through heavy fabric and interlinings while hand sewing. A tailor's thimble differs from the closed-top kind found at home or at haberdashers. The fingertip is left exposed for comfort and control, and allows the tailor to feel the fabric as they stitch.

Tailors wear their thimble on the middle finger of the hand that holds the needle. It should cover the finger up to the first joint, leaving about ⅛–¼" of the fingertip visible. When stitching, insert the needle into the fabric using the index finger and thumb, with the thimble finger (middle finger) closed towards the palm. Catch the back of the needle in one of the thimble ridges and push it through the fabric. Use the front part of the thimble that covers the fingernail, not the side, as this works against the natural joints and can cause pain after repetition. As the needle emerges, catch it with the forefinger and thumb of the sewing hand and pull the thread through. The art of using a thimble well is to complete these steps in one fluid motion. A good way to practise is by stitching through a single layer of fabric with no thread attached to the needle. •

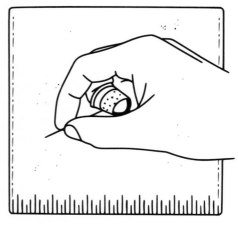

Fig. A

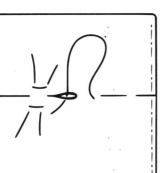

FIG. B

B   BASTING

*A long, loose stitch designed to join fabric, canvas, and linings
together temporarily and then be removed.*

(B.1) With the less dominant hand, hold the fabric ¼–½" in front of the area for the first stitch. With basting cotton, knotted at the end, insert the needle through all the layers to be stitched and out through the back just in front of the index finger holding the fabric in place. Push the needle all the way through the fabric with the front of the thimble (the part covering the nail) and pull the thread through. (B.2) Repeat the process, making stitches at least ⅜" long and ¼" apart. Pull the thread firmly, but not tight, so the fabric does not pucker. •

C   MARK STITCHING

*Also known as 'tailor's tacks' or 'thread marking',
this technique is used for transferring pattern markings to both sides of pieces of fabric.*

(C.1) Thread a needle with a long piece of basting cotton and pull it through to make a double strand without knotting the ends. With ½" stitches, baste through both layers of fabric at the start of the line that is being marked. (C.2) Leave 2" of thread loose at the first stitch. With each stitch, do not pull the thread tight, but leave a loop on top of the fabric to be cut later. Continue mark stitching along the line, and at the end leave another 2" of thread loose, so the thread does not pull out when the layers are separated. (C.3) Repeat the process on all of the pattern markings. Do not stitch around corners – always start and finish on the points. (C.4) Snip the loops of thread between the stitches on the top layer of fabric. Then, carefully turn back the top layer of fabric and snip through the exposed threads with the tip of a pair of sharp scissors or snips. The pattern markings will now be transferred to each side of the cloth. •

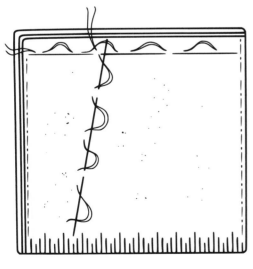

FIG. C.1

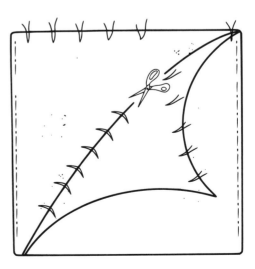

FIG. C.4

D	PAD STITCHING	E	BAR TACKS

These diagonal stitches secure two or more layers of fabric together to make the layers firm. The smaller the stitches, the firmer the fabric. Pad stitches are also used to create a fixed shape and add curvature to the layers, for example on the chest or for the collar and lapel.

^(D.1) Thread a needle with basting cotton and knot the end. Hold the section to be padded in the less dominant hand. With the sewing hand, insert the needle at the start of the section to be padded, push through all the layers, and pull the needle out the other side. (Bring the needle down at least ¼". The distance should be equal to the desired size of the diagonal padding stitch, for example, smaller on the collar and lapel than on the domette.) ^(D.2) Make a horizontal stitch from right to left, so that the needle appears directly below the point where the stitch above started. The stitch should be equal to half the length of the diagonal stitch. Push the needle all the way through the fabric with the front of the thimble (the part covering the nail) and pull the thread through. ^(D.3) Bring the needle down the same distance as in step 2, and make another horizontal stitch from right to left, directly below the previous stitch. ^(D.4) After making the last stitch at the end of the row, insert the needle back to where it last emerged. To begin the next row, make another stitch from right to left, setting the thread into position to work from the bottom to the top. ^(D.5) Bring the needle up halfway between the last diagonal stitch on the previous row, and make a stitch from right to left. Repeat the process. At the top of a row, repeat step 4, but sew downwards from top to bottom. •

A small area of dense stitches (around ¼"), used to reinforce points of high stress, such as the corners of pockets and buttonholes.

^(E.1) To make the 'bar' of the bar tack, use a machine cotton the same colour as the garment fabric, doubled up and knotted at the end. Insert the needle from the wrong side of the fabric, so it emerges in the position the bar tack will start. ^(E.2) Insert the needle back ¼" and pull it out where the thread first emerged. Repeat this stitch 2 or 3 times through the same points to complete the thread bar. ^(E.3) Do not cut the thread once the bar is complete, but continue the stitch with the same thread, inserting the needle under the thread bar and its left edge. Pull it through, tightening the stitch as close to the edge as possible. ^(E.4) Continue looping the thread around the bar, tightening the stitch as close to the previous stitch as possible. At the end of the row, insert the needle and pull it out from the wrong side, fixing it in place with a back tack. •

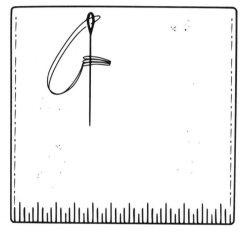

Fig. E

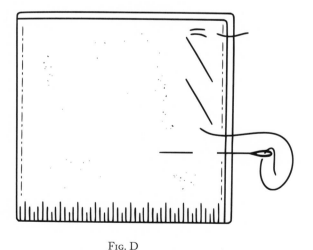

Fig. D

A small slit made to fasten buttons.

(F.1) Work on one buttonhole at a time with a fabric or leather hole punch. Punch an eyelet on the outer edge of the buttonhole mark at the point nearest the edge of the cuff or the front edge. With small scissors or snips, cut along the centre of the buttonhole line, starting at the punched hole. (F.2) To protect the edges of the buttonhole from fraying, sew around them with a felling stitch, catching all layers and making sure the body canvas is not visible. (F.3) Thread a needle with a long length of buttonhole twist (about 31.5" or 80 cm) in a colour matching the garment fabric and knot the end. Hold the cloth so the eyelet is away from the body. Starting at the back of the buttonhole (the opposite end to the eyelet), insert the needle between the top layer of cloth and the body canvas, on the left edge of the buttonhole. (F.4) Bring the needle out just beyond the edge, hiding the knot in between the layers of cloth and body canvas. Make a small buttonhole stitch (see below), but do not tighten it. (F.5) Cut

a piece of gimp (also known as guimp or guimpe) or buttonhole twist that is equal to twice the length of the buttonhole, plus 1½". Lay the gimp along the edge of the buttonhole, and slip ¾" through the loose buttonhole stitch. (F.6) To fix the stitch, pull the thread firmly back towards the body, then firmly forwards away from the body. Continue making buttonhole stitches along the edge of the buttonhole, being careful to start each stitch the same distance from the edge of the buttonhole and keeping the tension even with every stitch. (F.7) At the eyelet, fan the stitches around the buttonhole. Tighten by pulling upwards. Turn the fabric around so the eyelet is closest to the body. Continue making buttonhole stitches along the other edge of the buttonhole, keeping the tension even with each stitch. (F.8) At the back of the buttonhole, finish the edge with a bar tack (see section E) and cut away the loose ends of the gimp. (F.9) Repeat steps 1–8 for the other buttonholes. •

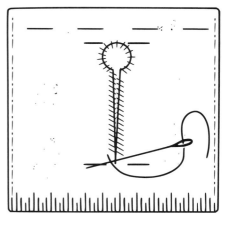

Fig. F.2 & F.3

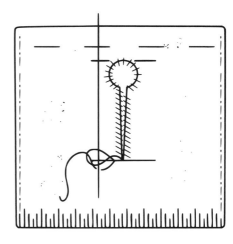

Fig. F.5 & F.6

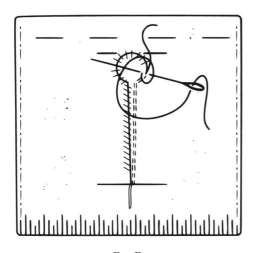

Fig. F.7

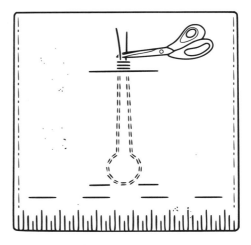

Fig. F.8

*The most common sewing stitch, this is a row of small, evenly
spaced stitches that run back and forth through the cloth without overlapping.
This stitch is predominantly used for basting.*

Thread a needle with basting cotton and knot
the end. Insert the needle through the right
side of the fabric and weave it in and out
of the fabric along the required stitch line
in evenly spaced stitches. Pull the thread
through, making the stitches firm but not
tight. End the stitches with a back tack. Use
longer stitches when basting. •

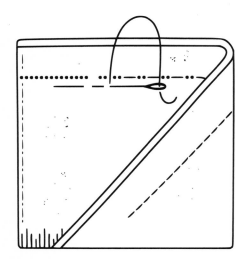

Fig. G

*A sewing technique that helps to secure the stitches in a seam,
and prevent them from coming undone.*

(H.1) Sometimes called a fastening stitch, the
back tack is used to end and secure a row of
stitches. At the end of the row, insert the
needle ¼" back from where the thread last
emerged, and bring it out at the exact point
the last thread emerged. Double the stitch
through the same points to make it extra
strong. (H.2) At times when a knot is too bulky,
it helps to start the row with a fastening stitch.
In this case, repeat the process in step one,
but leave a 2" loose thread at the start of the
stitches, so the thread does not pull through. •

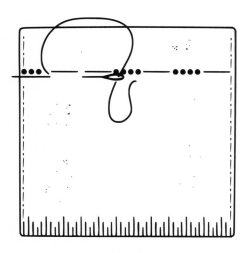

Fig. H

| I | **CROSS STITCHING** | K | **BACK STITCHING** |

Two rows of slanted, parallel stitches that cross each other near their ends. Used for neatly finishing a raw or cut edge.

A hand stitch strong enough to permanently attach two pieces of fabric. Back stitching most closely resembles the stitches made by a sewing machine.

Working from left to right, start the stitch ¼" down from the edge being sewn. Point the needle to the left and pick up a few threads from above the edge. Pull the thread through, then take a small stitch in the first layer of the fabric below the edge, ¼" down from the edge and ¼" to the right of the previous stitch. End with a back tack. •

Make a single stitch to the required length. Insert the needle just to the right of where the thread emerged from the first stitch and bring it out just to the left of the same point. Continue along the row, inserting the needle to the right, and pulling it out to the left of the point where the thread last emerged. •

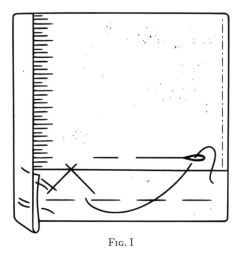

FIG. I

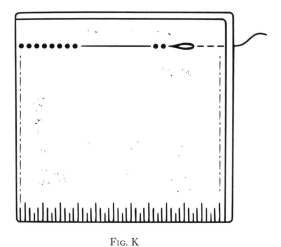

FIG. K

J **FELLING**

A finishing stitch used to join a folded edge of fabric to another piece of fabric, for example on closing linings, hems, and attaching bindings. It can also be used to quickly and neatly fix down a raw edge of fabric to another, when a cross stitch isn't required. In finishing, the stitch should not be visible on the edge on which it is being sewn.

Starting from the wrong side of the fabric, with a knotted thread, pull the thread right through to the very edge of the top edge. Insert the needle into the wrong side of the fabric ⅛–¼" to the left of the first stitch. Continue along the edge, making small, evenly spaced stitches that are almost invisible. •

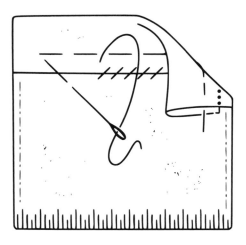

FIG. J

L PRICK STITCHING

An almost invisible back stitch that is predominantly used for top stitching or edge stitching. The stitches on the obverse side of the fabric are very small. It provides a neat finish along seamed edges such as facings, collars and pockets.

With knotted thread, draw the needle up from the wrong side of the fabric, and pull the thread through. Insert the needle directly behind (to the right of) the point that the thread emerged, and bring it back out around ¼" to the left of that point. Continue the process along the row and finish with a back tack. •

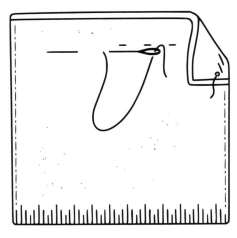

Fig. L

M BUTTONHOLE STITCHING

A knotted stitch used to secure the edges of buttonholes, as well as to reinforce buttonholes and prevent cut fabric from fraying.

Draw the needle up from the wrong side of the fabric, ⅛" from the top edge. Before the needle is fully out, loop the thread around the point of the needle in an anti-clockwise circle, then pull it out fully. Draw the needle up from the wrong side again, directly next to where the thread emerged from the first stitch, in whichever direction is being sewn. Loop the thread around the point of the needle again and pull the stitch upwards, creating a knot on top of the stitch. Continue to stitch the row with even spacing and tension. •

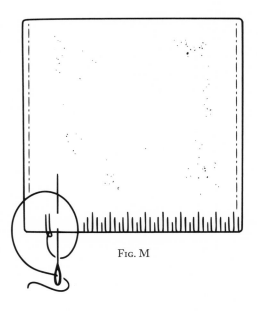

Fig. M

N DRAW STITCHING

A running stitch woven between two seamed edges, designed to draw them together securely and invisibly – most notably on the gorge line of a coat.

Working from the right side of the fabric, use a short running stitch ¹⁄₁₆–⅛" long, weaving the thread from one folded edge to the other. Draw the thread taut so that the two folded edges close together. Each stitch must be made separately, and the stitches must be close together, evenly spaced and parallel to one another so that no stitching is visible on the right side of the fabric. •

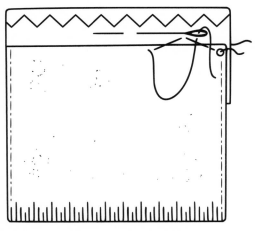

Fig. N

GLOSSARY

SAVILE ROW TAILORING TERMS AND PHRASES

The methods and language of the small community of tailors and cutters located in and around Savile Row have evolved through a bespoke tailoring lineage that stretches back some 700 years. Occasionally terms used in the tailoring or cloth-making world have entered everyday use – such as 'bespoke', 'codger', or 'to be on tenterhooks' – but most remain incomprehensible to anyone outside the trade.

What follows is a far-from-exhaustive list of the terms used in many workshops on Savile Row, and it should be noted that they even vary between workrooms, let alone different tailoring houses.

A

Alpaca
A smaller cousin of the llama, the alpaca provides a fine wool used for knitwear and cloth.

Armhole
The opening in a garment through which the wearer puts their arms.

Arris
Backside – from the Cockney rhyming slang, 'Aristotle', which rhymes with 'bottle', coming from the phrase 'bottle and glass', which rhymes with 'arse'. Some customers 'have a large arris'!

Astrakhan
A fabric with a curled pile that resembles the fleece of a young Astrakhan lamb. The effect is achieved by pretreating the pile yarn with heat and setting it in a helix shape.

B

Back straps
The pull strap extending into the back of a waistcoat, usually fastened with a buckle, with the aim of making the back tighter.

Bag out
Turning the garment piece right side out so all of the seams and stitching is hidden on the inside.

Balance
The hang of a coat. Its front edges should run straight up and down, while the bottom edges should be horizontal both side-to-side and front-to-back. If so, it is said to be 'in balance' – achieved by a delicate and highly skilled set of adjustments, which are particularly difficult to achieve on more irregularly shaped customers.

Balloon
A week without paid work.

Banger
A piece of wood used to weight down cloth during pressing.

Barathea
A soft-finish worsted cloth with a pebbled appearance that was traditionally used for evening wear, typically in midnight blue. It is usually composed of twilled hopsack or a broken-rib weave made of silk or worsted wool.

Barring
This means 'present company excepted', required to avoid being 'whistled' when saying anything derogatory (see Whistle and Bar, below).

Baste
A loosely tailored try-on garment for the early stages of fitting, basted together by hand rather than machine-sewn. Typically it has no top collar, facing, or pockets, and is made to be easily disassembled, allowing for a very significant degree of alterations following fittings.

Basting
Tacking together a job using white basting cotton (thread).

Basting up a snarl
Causing an argument.

Bearer button
A button at the closure of a pair of trousers, hidden on the inside of the waistband, intended to hold the trouser front flat.

Bedford cord
A fabric with rounded cords in the warp direction and pronounced sunken lines between them. The weave on the face of the cord is usually plain.

Beetling
Applying starch to linen that is then beaten with hammers for 140 hours.

Bemberg
See cupro, below.

Bias
The grain that runs at a 45 degree angle to the selvedge, giving the fabric more of an elastic stretch.

Birdseye
A fabric with a pattern of very small and uniform spots – the result of combining weave and colour.

BL
Bow legged, and VB is very bow legged.

Board
A tailor's workbench, typically 2 m wide by 1 m deep, set at waist height to make it easier to work when standing.

Bodge job
A bad piece of work.

Bodger
A poor quality tailor.

Botany
From Botany Bay – originally a cloth made from Australian wool, and now a famous bunch sold by Smith & Co.

Bouclé
A fabric with a rough or granulated surface produced by blending fancy yarns.

Box cloth
A heavy felted cloth, similar to melton, used in military overcoats and the famous Albert Thurston English braces (suspenders). It is made from spun wool with a surface that is completely covered so that no threads show. It comes in a variety of weaves and is very firm.

Braid
A narrow fabric produced on a loom or trimming machinery. It is made by interlacing three or more threads in such a way that they cross one another diagonally.

Break line
The line where the lapel and collar roll, usually ending just above the top button.

Bridle
A tape used to stabilise and stop the stretching of the break line of a coat or waistcoat, as it is cut on the bias.

Broadcloth
Fabric made from fine woollen yarns in a twill weave, which is heavily milled and given a dress-face finish. It is usually dyed in dark colours.

Brocade
This has a raised 'figured' or floral design that is made by floating the warp threads, weft threads, or both, and interlacing them in a more or less irregular order. The fabric usually has a single texture and the background is usually plain.

Buckram
A stiff, heavily sized linen or cotton plain-weave, open-set fabric used mainly for military or stand collars.

Buckskin
This fine merino wool is closely set, heavily milled, dressed and closely cut, with a texture that is similar to, but heavier than, a doeskin (see below).

Buggy label
A woven label sewn into the inside pocket of a coat, and typically onto the seat seam of a pair of trousers. The customer's name, the date of the garment's construction, the cloth number (usually), and in some houses the cutter and tailor's initials, are all indelibly typed or written on the label.

Bunce
A perk, typically a bit of mungo (see below), and sometimes a cash payment.

Bunch
A collection of cloths sold by a cloth house, bound in a hard cover with a cord handle, which is kept by the tailors. Typically the fabrics are of one particular weight and construction, and the bunch will be updated daily to ensure each cloth in the bunch is in stock. Stickers are put on cloths that are low or out of stock.

Bundle
The parcel given to a tailor, by the cutter, containing all of the cloth, fabric and trimmings to complete a job.

C

Cabbage
Scrap cloth.

Cable stripe
A stripe formed by creating very short sections of contrast in the twill, typically just three yarns wide, while pinstripe is created with a single pick of contrast yarn.

Calico
A plain cotton fabric, heavier than muslin.

Cambric
A light, closely woven plain fabric usually given a slight stiffening, and often used for handkerchiefs.

Camel hair
Bactrian (double-hump) and dromedary (single-hump) camels have strong, coarse outer hair and undercoats, which are often used in fabrics for overcoats.

Canvas
Typically linen, horsehair, or often a mix, used on the internal skeleton for bespoke clothes – one of several layers of interlining used in bespoke clothes between the outer cloth and the inner lining. Coats have separate chest, body, and collar canvases of different composition and stiffness; stand-collar coats have buckram (see the cloth section below) in the stand, whereas trousers have a waistband canvas.

Carthorse collar
A badly fitting coat where the collar sits way off the neck, like a carthorse's collar.

Cashmere
Hair from the downy undercoat of Asiatic goats.

Cat's face
A small shop, often off Savile Row, opened by a cutter from a large house starting out under his own name.

Cavalry twill
A firm warp-faced fabric in which the weave gives steep double-twill lines separated by pronounced grooves formed by the weft. The name originally applied to firm heavyweight fabrics for the cavalry's riding breeches, but later encompassed fabrics used for raincoats and other hard-wearing clothing.

Cellular fabric
Fabric constructed to have a close and orderly distribution of hollows or holes. In woven fabric this can be achieved by a honeycomb, a leno, or a mock-leno weave.

Chalk stripe
This is similar to a cable stripe (see above), but with a more diffuse stripe created by milling the fabric so it resembles a line of chalk.

Chest canvas
Typically made of horsehair, a sturdy, woven interfacing with a coarse texture, that adds body and spring to the chest of a coat.

Clapper
The same as a banger (see above).

Clobberer
Someone who repairs and removes stains from second-hand (or more) clothing; the origin of 'clobber', as in 'clothing'.

Coat
A tailored jacket.

Codger
Someone who repairs old clothes.

Collar Canvas
Used to interface the undercollar, this is made from extremely stiff linen which is malleable when steam-pressed but stiff when it cools.

Corduroy
From the French 'corde du roi' (the King's rope or cord), this cut-weft pile fabric is woven with weft yarns arranged in such a way that when the pile is cut, cords or ribs are formed in the direction of the warp.

Covert
A warp-faced fabric, usually of twill weave, with a characteristic mottled appearance achieved with a two-ply twist warp and a solid coloured weft.

Crown
Sometimes referred to as the sleeve head, it indicates the top section of the top sleeve, where it meets the armhole.

Cupro
Short for cuprammonium rayon, an early synthetic viscose made from cotton waste that was first developed in 1890. It is often called Bemberg (its original trade name) and is used as a lining fabric.

Curtain
A band of lining or silesia, stitched below the inside of a trouser waistband, to hide the seams and raw edges.

Cutter
A pattern cutter and fitter, typically responsible for the overall operation of the workshop.

D

Damask
A figured fabric made with one warp and one weft, in which warp satin and weft sateen weaves interchange.

Denim
A warp-faced twill fabric made from a yarn-dyed warp and undyed weft, typically in cotton.

Dobby
A mechanism for controlling a larger number of picks for creating complex patterns beyond the capacity of standard weaving.

Doeskin
A five-end satin or other warp-faced fabric with a dress-face finish.

Dogstooth
A small check that resembles sharp dogs' teeth. (See shepherd's check below.)

Domette
Imitation flannel made from a cotton warp and a wool or cotton wool weft, finished with a raised surface on both sides and used as an interlining – and in the past for pyjamas.

Drab
A dull olive colour used for military clothing.

Drag
To be running behind with work, or 'in the drag'.

Drape
The way a fabric or garment hangs.

Dress left/right
The side on which the customer's penis naturally falls – important information when cutting the fork of a pair of trousers, and more important with some customers than others.

Drill
A twill fabric similarly constructed to denim, with a clear twill appearance and usually piece-dyed, so the colour is flat. It is typically made from cotton, but some drills are made from five-end satin weave known as 'satin drills'.

D tack
A D-tack is sewn using prick stiches in a 'D' shape and typically used to reinforce the end of pocket jets.

E

Ease
Extra room in the pattern pieces beyond the measurements of the body.

Ermazine
Viscose Rayon Taffeta lining, still termed from its Germanic origins.

Extension band
An extension of the trouser waistband beyond the fly to help secure the trousers at the waist. Typically, only present with side adjusters, not belt loops.

F

Figuration
A customer's body shape, rather than measured size.

Finisher
A finishing tailor; a tailor, usually female, who sews the buttonholes, edge stitches, prick stitches the fly and fells the lining of the garment, all by hand.

Fitting
A try-on garment, either a baste or a forward, made in the final cloth.

Fit-up
Smaller pieces of cloth.

Flannel
An all-wool fabric with a plain or twill weave and soft handle. The cloth's surface is slightly milled and raised – it was originally woven using woollen spun yarn – making it fairly elastic. Today many cloth manufacturers offer a 'worsted flannel' – a worsted cloth with a heavily finished surface and a soft nap that resembles that of a woollen flannel.

Forward
A late-stage try-on garment with a top collar, facings, and pockets, but no buttonholes.

Fullness
The amount of extra fabric needed to create volume or gather in relation to the finished size.

Fusible Interfacing
Fabric interfacing with tiny glue dots on the back, which, when melted by the heat of an iron, bond with the material on which it is placed.

Fustian
This hard-wearing clothing fabric contains a large amount of weft yarns, typically made from natural fibres. Today fustian is used to describe a class of heavily wefted fabrics usually made from cotton, including moleskin, velveteen, and corduroy.

G

Gaberdine
A firmly woven, clear-finished, warp-faced fabric in which the end density considerably exceeds the pick density, so the twill line is produced at a steep angle. Largely used for raincoats and sportswear.

Gimp
A heavy viscose thread, placed underneath buttonhole stitches to reinforce and prevent the buttonhole from stretching out of shape.

Gingham
A lightweight, plain-weave cotton fabric, in which dyed yarns or white and dyed yarns form small checks.

Glenurquhart check
(also known as Glen plaid)
This twill cloth is woven with repeating sections of three types of check – a dogstooth check and two variations on a smaller scale. It is named after the Glen Urquhart Estate in Scotland, which originally commissioned the design. The Prince of Wales check is a variation of the Glen check, originally having a red or brown overcheck.

Gorge line
The connecting point between the collar and the lapel of the coat.

Grain
Also referred to as the 'grainline' or 'straight grain', this is the direction of the warp threads running up and down a length of cloth.

Guv'nor
The boss or owner of a tailoring house.

Grosgrain
A plain-weave fabric with a rib in the weft direction that is more pronounced than a taffeta rib. Often made from silk, grosgrain is used on the facings and button covers of dinner jackets.

H

Ham
The stuffed cloth pad on which a tailor shapes a job.

Hampton
A penis, from 'Hampton Wick', rhyming with 'dick'.

Hanger
A loop, usually made from lining, fixed to the inside centre back neck of a coat, to enable it to be hung without stretching the neck or shoulders.

HB
A 'hunchback' or very rounded back, requiring a much greater back length on a coat to ensure good balance.

Herringbone
A combination of twill weaves in which the direction of the twill is reversed to produce stripes resembling herring bones.

Hessian
Fabric made from single yarns of approximately the same density in warp and weft, usually made from bast fibres (made from plants) – particularly jute.

Hook and bar
A small metal closure used for closing overlapping edges, typically found on trouser fronts as an alternative to buttons.

Hopsack
A modification of plain woven cloth in which two or more ends and picks weave as one, giving a more pronounced texture.

Houndstooth
(see also Shepherd's check, below)
This small check is so named because it resembles a dog's sharp teeth.

Hunting Pink
A heavy scarlet twill worn by hunt staff. It is named after a tailor called Pink, who was famous for making such coats.

I

In-breast pocket
The inside chest pockets in the coat.

Interlining
Materials such as canvases and domette that are used within the construction of a tailored garment to provide structure and, in the case of domette, comfort.

J

Jacquard
A fabric in which a large number of warp threads, exceeding the capacity of a double loom, weave differently and produce an array of fine, detailed, woven fabrics in non-linear patterns.

Jet
The piped, outside edge of a pocket opening, usually found on the side pockets of a coat, or hip pocket of a trouser.

Job
A single piece of work or garment.

K

Kill
A spoiled job.

Kipper
A female finishing tailor. Workrooms in the past were male-dominated and at times highly misogynistic, so female finishers would travel in pairs to ward off unwelcome comments and attention.

L

Lacing
A stitch taken around the armhole, before the sleeve is inserted, to close all layers and draw the armhole in.

Lamé
Gleaming fabrics that contain a conspicuous amount of metallic threads.

Lapel notch
The triangular gap between the lapel and the collar at the gorge line.

Lawn
A fine, plain-woven fabric of linen or cotton made in a variety of finishes. It is sometimes known by the name of the finish applied, such as organdie.

Leno
A fabric in which warp threads are made to cross one another between picks for an open, cellular appearance.

Linen
Yarn and fabric spun entirely from flax fibres; used to reinforce pocket mouths.

Log
A weekly piecework invoice. Most tailors on Savile Row are self-employed and submit weekly logs for all the work they complete for their house.

Log rate
The fee agreed between houses and the tailors' union representatives for every type of job undertaken by the self-employed tailors working on the Row.

Lovat
A green-brown colour, designed as camouflage on the hills of Scotland and named after Lord Lovat, who originally commissioned the shade.

M

Madras
Commonly used to describe a brightly coloured, checked cotton fabric. Not to be confused with Madras muslin – a patterned gauze fabric with an extra weft that is bound into the figured parts and cut away elsewhere.

Marcella
A fancy or figured fabric with a piqué (geometric weave) structure, typically used for the collars, cuffs, and bibs of dress shirts; white tie waistcoats; and white bow ties.

Mark-up
To chalk any required alterations onto the cloth. These are made by the cutter during and after a fitting, and the marks are interpreted and followed by the tailor.

Melton
A heavyweight fabric that is all-wool or cotton warp and woollen weft, finished by heavy milling and cropping. The fibres in the fabric are tightly matted together by the milling process, giving it a felted appearance. It is used for lining the underside of coat collars.

Merino
Wool from merino sheep, noted for their fine coat. Originally from the arid mountain regions of Spain, merino sheep thrive in dry conditions and today are reared extensively in Australia, New Zealand, South Africa and the southern United States.

Mock-leno
A woven fabric with an open-mesh character.

Mohair
A fine, lustrous fibre from the angora goat.

Moiré
This ribbed or corded fabric, often made from silk, is subjected to heat and heavy pressure by rollers after weaving for a rippled appearance. The effect comes from differences in the reflection of the flattened and unflattened parts – hence it is often described as 'watered silk'.

Moleskin
A thick, heavy, cotton fabric that is heavily wefted and has a smooth face – used chiefly for outdoor clothing.

Mungo
Scrap cloth.

N

Neck Point
The shoulder seam intersection where the forepart meets the back at the collar.

Nett
No seam allowance included.

Notch
Sometimes referred to as 'balance marks', these are small snips made in the pattern and garment pieces, to help align the sections being sewn.

O

OBW
The 'out-breast welt' or chest pocket on a jacket.

On the cod
An extended drinking spree.

On the double
To fold fabric into two layers.

Overlocking
A stitch that sews over the raw-edge of cloth to stop it from fraying. Also referred to as serging, overedging or merrowing.

P

Pig
A garment rejected by a customer, or not collected for years after completion. Today these are often donated to charity for sale.

Pinstripe
A fine stripe in a cloth created from single-contrast yarns that form a row of small dots whose pattern resembles pinheads.

Piquet
A fabric with rounded cords in the weft direction with pronounced sunken lines between them.

Pitch
The correct position a sleeve should land in relation to the body.

Plaid
A shawl worn by a Scottish shepherd – although in America the term is interchangeable with tartan and other checks.

Pleat
A fold of fabric or cloth intended to create extra volume within the same measurement.

Pork
The same as a pig (see above).

Pressing point
A thin wooden block, with pointed ends, designed to help the pressing open of seams and darts.

Private
A job done by a cutter off the books – sometimes legitimately for friends and family, occasionally illegitimately. One notorious Savile Row cutter of the 2000s kept the money from orders paid in cash at one of the bigger houses over a period of many years and was eventually caught, having stolen more than £170,000. He was dismissed, but to avoid potential damage to their reputation, was not charged by the house in question. He went on to start up under his own name in a basement just a few doors down.

Prince of Wales check
See Glenurquhart check, above.

Prom
Short for 'prominent' and used when describing a customer's figure – 'prom blades' means prominent shoulder blades.

PTU
A trouser turn up, short for permanent turn up.

R

Raw edge
The cut edge of a piece of fabric or cloth that has not been bound or overlocked.

Right side
The side of the fabric or cloth that is meant to be visible from the outside of the garment.

Rock of eye
Using instinct or experience to cut or fit, rather than following a mathematical system.

S

Sateen
A weft-faced weave in which the binding places are arranged to produce a smooth fabric surface free from twill.

Satin
A warp-faced weave in which the binding places are arranged to produce a smooth fabric surface free from twill.

Scye
The side of the armhole at the chest or back.

Seat
The trousers' bottom (or 'arse').

Seersucker
A highly textured fabric, typically cotton, with alternate stripes of puckered and flat sections made from treated and untreated yarn. During weaving, the treated yarn shrinks more than the untreated yarn – to such an extent that the finished fabric has a puckered or crinkled appearance.

Selvedge
The 'self-edge' of fabric which keeps it from unravelling or fraying. Luxury fabrics are often woven with the composition or brand name incorporated.

Sett
This historic weaving term refers to the number of strands of warp yarn in an inch of cloth. This measurement determines the density of the fabric, the number of ends or picks in the fabric.

Shank
The neck or securing stitch of a button, that allows it to sit even with a buttonhole.

Shears
Scissors – there are specific shears for cutting pattern paper, for cutting cloth during striking, and for cutting work during tailoring.

Shepherd's check
Named after the plaids, or woollen shawls, worn by shepherds from the Scottish Borders, this cloth features a small colour-and-weave check effect developed in black and white or two similarly contrasting colours. These are generally in groups of four, six, or eight threads of the two colours, in alternating squares with twill sections.

Side adjusters
Also known as a 'strap and buckle', these are adjustable side straps sewn onto the outside waist of a pair of trousers to allow the waist to be cinched in. Two types of buckle are typically used, chosen by the house. Straps are typically mitred, but each trouser maker will have their own slight variation of shape.

Silesia
A lining fabric with a smooth face, originally a plain-weave fabric and typically piece-dyed. It is named after a region in Central Europe and used as a luxurious jacket pocketing.

Skirt
The section of the coat below the waist, which is typically slightly flared.

Sleeve board
A small ironing board, typically made of wood and covered in cloth, designed specifically to fit within and press a sleeve.

Sleeve head roll
A strip of cotton wadding used to create volume and shape in the crown of a sleeve.

Snips
Small sprung shears for snipping threads.

Stay tape
Made from linen or cotton, this is a narrow tape used to stop seams stretching.

Strike
To cut out a job. The pattern is chalked onto the cloth, and then cut out with cloth-cutting shears.

Super 100
The grades for wool range from 70 to 200. The 'Super' refers to wool cloth made entirely from a single natural animal fibre (sheep's wool, cashmere, vicuña); the number references the thickness of the original fibre from which the cloth is made – the higher the number, the finer the fibre. Super 100 fabric is made from 18.5 micron fibre: for every 100 the number increases, the diameter of the original fibre decreases by 0.5 micron. The number has no connection with the weight of the finished cloth – Super 100 cloth typically weighs 8 to 13 ounces. It is rare for finer, more expensive qualities to be in heavier fabrics.

Suppression
The shape of a garment as it narrows. For example: at the coat waist.

T

Tacking
See *Hand-Stitching Techniques* on p. 154.

Taffeta
A plain and closely woven, smooth, crisp fabric with a faint weft-direction rib. It is lustrous and lightweight and often used as a lining. Today it is typically made from viscose but originally was made from silk.

Tartan
Scotland's famous fabric, traditionally made from twill-woven woollen fabric, in checks of various colours and scales. Historically it was woven in the colours available to local weavers, and there were large regional variations that corresponded with the regions inhabited by different clans, hence later associations. Today, most Scottish clans have tartans, often several – a hunting and dress tartan being the most popular.

Teasle
The dried seed head of the 'fuller's thistle' (*Dipsacus fullonum*) used to 'full' a fabric – to raise a pile or nap – especially used in cashmere, for a distinctive ripple finish.

Thornproof tweed
Wool suiting produced from highly twisted yarns, closely set to give a firm, hard cloth that is resistant to thorns.

Top collar
The visible piece of cloth that covers the collar canvas.

Trotter
A workroom junior tasked with running, or 'trotting', work between cutting rooms and tailors' workrooms.

Tweed
A heavyweight fabric with a rough surface, woven in southern Scotland using wool-spun yarns in a variety of weave effects and originally used for outerwear. It got its name when a London cloth merchant misread an invoice, mistaking the word 'Tweel' (Scottish for twill) as 'Tweed' (the river on which the mill sat).

Tweed Merchant
Slang for a poorer-quality tailor who is only given easier, more forgiving jobs, such as working with tweeds.

Twist
A yarn comprising two single ends of different colours twisted together – the single ends are either solid colours or a mixture, also known as a 'marl yarn'.

Two-show-three
(also one-show-two and one-show-three)
When describing the closure of a double-breasted jacket, the first number stated is the number of working buttons used to close the jacket, and the second is the total number of buttons on each side – including the non-working 'show' buttons. A two-show-three has two working buttons and buttonholes, and a total of three buttons each side.

U

Undercollar
The combination of collar canvas and melton pad stitched together and pressed to create the overall shape of the collar.

V

Velour
Originally used for hats, this is a rabbit-fur felt with a top surface that is carded while wet to produce a long, soft pile.

Velvet
A cut warp-pile fabric, originally only made from silk, in which the cut ends of the fibres form the surface of the fabric. Today, most quality velvet is made from cotton, and silk velvet is very rare.

Vent
The slit at the rear of a coat. Savile Row coats trace their origins to riding attire and typically have two side vents (so the jacket does not rip at the sides), but the customer can choose one centre vent or no vents at all (more common on dinner and smoking jackets).

Vicuña
The finest, rarest, and most expensive textile fibre, combed from the undercoat of the Vicuña – the smallest of the llama family – which lives mainly in the high plains of Peru.

W

Wedge
The small triangle cut out of the side of the forepart, connecting to the dart, that becomes the pocket line. Intended to create shape over the abdomen.

Whistle and Bar
A workroom game. Any person saying anything derogatory, or anything which, while innocently intended, could be interpreted as derogatory, can be 'whistled' by anyone else in the workroom. If successfully whistled, the derogatory statement is turned upon the person who said it. To prevent a whistle, any person saying anything derogatory must 'bar' the statement by saying the word 'barring' either before or after they speak. Masters of the game manage to whistle the most benign statements. Everyone in the workroom must maintain a constant state of conversational vigilance.

Woollen spun
A spinning process in which the carded fibres are spun uncombed, giving the yarn a loftier, softer feel and more elasticity. Cloth made from woollen-spun yarns, such as traditional flannels and tweeds (especially lower quality ones), can bag a little at the knees and elbows over time.

Worsted fabric
A wool fabric made from worsted yarns, which are typically flat finished, resulting in inelastic cloth that does not bag.

Worsted spun
A spinning process in which the wool fibres are combed straight before spinning, for a flatter, inelastic yarn.

Worsted yarn
Yarn spun exclusively from combed wool that has reasonably parallel fibres.

Wrap over
The distance the front edges overlap at the top button.

Wrong side
The side of the fabric or cloth that will be hidden on the inside.

Z

Zig-Zag
A back-and-forth stitch typically used for seam finishing or appliqué.

DIRECTORY OF TEXTILE MILLS AND TRIMMINGS MERCHANTS

TEXTILE MILLS

Cashmere
Johnstons of Elgin, Elgin, Scotland (Est. 1797). Also known for its tweeds, below.
Joshua Ellis, Pudsey, Leeds (Est. 1767).

Flannel
Fox Brothers, Wellington, Somerset (Est. 1772). Specialist in organic west-of-England flannel.

Specialist cloths
HW Hainsworth, Pudsey, Leeds (Est. 1783). Specialist in wool melton.
Linton Tweeds, Shaddongate, Carlisle, Cumbria (Est. 1912). Specialist in bouclé tweed.
Lochcarron, Selkirk, Scotland (Est. 1892). Specialist in tartan.
Stephen Walters, Sudbury, Suffolk (Est. 1720). Specialist in jacquard weaving.

Tweed
Ardalanish Tweed, Bunessan, Isle of Mull, Scotland (Est. 1999). Specialist in organic undyed tweed.
Breanish Tweed, Ness, Isle of Lewis, Scotland.
Garynahine Harris Tweed, Garrynahine, Isle of Harris, Scotland.
Islay Woollen Mill, Bridgend, Isle of Islay, Scotland (Est. 1883).
Johnstons of Elgin, Elgin, Scotland (Est. 1797).
Kenneth MacLeod, Harris Tweed Hebrides, Shawbost, Isle of Lewis, Scotland (Est. 1920).
Kenneth McKenzie, Stornoway, Isle of Lewis, Scotland (Est. 1906).
Lovat Mill, Hawick, Scotland (Est. 1999). Specialist in estate tweed.
Luskentyre Harris Tweed, Luskentyre, Isle of Harris, Scotland.

Worsted
Bower Roebuck (including Savile Clifford), Huddersfield, West Yorkshire (Est. 1899). Specialist in fine worsted.
Pennine Weavers, Keighley, West Yorkshire (Est. 1969). Specialist in fine worsted.
Taylor & Lodge, Huddersfield, West Yorkshire (Est. 1883). Specialist in fine worsted.
William Halstead, Bradford, West Yorkshire (Est. 1877). Specialist in worsted mohair.

SHIRTING AND TRIMMINGS MERCHANTS

Acorn Fabrics, shirt fabrics
Bernstein & Banleys, trimmings
Button Queen, buttons and trimmings
John Lewis, trimmings
Kenton Trimmings, trimmings
Liberty, shirt fabric and trimmings
London Trimmings, trimmings
MacCulloch & Wallis, trimmings
Pongees, silks
Richard James Weldon, trimmings
Ringhart, shirt fabrics
Thomas Mason, shirt fabric
William Gee, trimmings

MEET THE MAKERS

The artisans of Savile Row

CHRIS KTORI
TROUSER MAKER

Chris Ktori came to London from Cyprus at age 16, having learned to make trousers from his father. On his arrival in the West End, he undertook a five-year apprenticeship with Savile Row trouser maker Louis Costandis before striking out on his own.

He moved into his compact workshop at the top of a steep flight of stairs on Kingly Street in Soho, just a few minutes' walk from Savile Row, in a lofty warren of workshops occupied by half a dozen other tailors. His workshop has 30 years of stories to tell through accumulated fit-ups and shelves filled with log slips. In the corner is a small fridge holding milk and oranges – no visit to Chris's workshop is complete without being given an orange to take away. Watching over him from a little shelf above his board is a photograph of his beloved daughter.

Chris has worked for many of the great names of Savile Row, including some 25 years for Norton & Sons, as well as H Huntsman & Sons; Anderson & Sheppard; Tommy Nutter, and later Chittleborough & Morgan; and Gieves & Hawkes. Over the years he has tailored trousers for rock stars such as David Bowie and Charlie Watts of the Rolling Stones; giants of Hollywood such as Burt Lancaster and Jack Nicholson; and Prince Philip, Duke of Edinburgh and King Charles III. He has made for countless other famous and infamous men, but modestly claims he can't recall them. Despite being one of the world's best trouser makers, Chris doesn't make his own. It takes five to six hours of his time to make a pair, and he has to pay his finisher £95, so he buys them instead.

Sharing Chris's workroom is Oscar, his latest apprentice. Chris has had many apprentices pass through his workroom over the 61 years he has worked on Savile Row but he's lost count of exactly how many. •

RACHEL ALICE SMITH
COAT MAKER

Rachel Alice Smith started sewing at age six, when her mother bought her a sewing machine for Christmas. Her great-great-grandmother had been a shirt maker; both her grandmother and mother were dress and pattern makers, and her mother even trained as a needlework teacher in the seventies, so making clothes is in the blood.

At 15, Rachel began teaching herself how to make clothes, creating a jacket for her older brother. A few years later she spent school holidays learning from Paul 'Griff' Griffiths, a former Anderson & Sheppard coat maker. Through his connections, on her 18th birthday Rachel began a formal apprenticeship on Savile Row at Dege & Skinner, working under the legendary Stefano Tornambe. Tornambe, who had been a tailor in Sicily since he was seven years old, was in his seventies by then and recognised Rachel's potential, admiring her beautiful hand sewing. After completing most of her training she moved to Norton & Sons, where she was mentored by Dennis Cooper, and formally completed her apprenticeship just before her 21st birthday.

Rachel is one of a fast-growing number of young female tailors slowly changing the gender balance and dynamic in the once very male and very white workshops of Savile Row. She has in turn passed on her skills to her apprentice, Kirsten McDove, one more in a growing lineage of exceptional female coat makers to have occupied the workrooms at Norton & Sons over the past 15 years.

During her career Rachel has worked on some unique and fascinating garments. She made Thom Yorke's suit coat for the video of his band Atoms for Peace's 2013 single, 'Ingenue'; worked with Norton & Sons Head Cutter, Nick Hammond, to create the world's first 'intelligent' coat as part of the Google Jacquard project in 2015; and made the coat Sam Smith wore to the 2016 Oscars to collect their award for best theme song for *James Bond: Spectre*. She was even asked to make a suit for a somewhat eccentric client's alien spaceship. She's made coats for Tommy Lee Jones, Jon Voight,

Bryan Adams, Michael Caine and Anne Hathaway.

Having taken a short time out to raise her daughter, Rachel is back working for Norton & Sons and Dege & Skinner, dividing her time between Savile Row and her home in Margate. •

FELICITY HAMACHER
WAISTCOAT MAKER

Felicity Hamacher was born and raised in Cologne, Germany, and taught herself to sew so that she could make herself costumes for the city's annual carnival. These were much admired by her friends, and after leaving school at 18 she decided to begin an apprenticeship at Roeben, a traditional bespoke tailors in the centre of the city. Here she trained for three years under Herr Roeben, and after finishing her studies she travelled to London where she walked into Anderson & Sheppard and asked if they needed any tailors. To her great delight, they did. Thanks to her slightly less-than-perfect English, she began as a finishing tailor and then moved on to alterations. One day they had many waistcoats to produce for a film and Anderson's one waistcoat maker was unable to finish them all. The foreman at the time, Mr Pitt, asked Felicity if she could help. Her waistcoats were so good that she has never made anything else since.

When she started a family a few years later, Felicity decided to work freelance, continuing to serve Anderson & Sheppard and also other clients, including Brian Russell, who had worked for Anderson's for 20 years before setting up his own firm in Hanover Square. Through Brian she picked up Meyer & Mortimer, one job led to another, and in her nearly 30 years working for Savile Row she has made for H Huntsman & Sons; Gieves & Hawkes; and Norton & Sons, where she has been the principal waistcoat maker for many years.

She is not one for worrying about who she makes for, but in her time she's made for film stars including Tom Cruise and Ralph Fiennes; musicians including Elton John, Robbie Williams and Charlie Watts; as well as King Charles III. No matter who they are, she sews all the waistcoats with the same dedication and care. •

LIZZIE WILLETT, KATH MUIR, & JACQUIE GRANT
SHIRT MAKERS

SAM WAKELY
HEAD OF CUTTING

Lizzie Willett is Head of Sewing at the Emma Willis workshop in Gloucester, where she was born and raised in a sewing household, taught by her grandmother and mother. She studied textiles at school all the way up to 'A' Level and then took an Art Foundation course at SGS College in Stroud, where she learned pattern cutting and full garment making. Through one of her tutors at Stroud she found out about and won the Emma Willis-Condé Nast Sewing Scholarship, a sponsored apprenticeship programme. Here she was taught shirt making by Kath Muir, who retired in March 2023 after many years as Head of Sewing at Emma Willis and Turnbull & Asser before that.

Kath Muir's career in sewing began in 1981 in Goole, Yorkshire, where she worked in the Meritina factory, making coats for Marks & Spencer. Six years later she moved to Gloucester and joined Turnbull & Asser, which had previously made all of its shirts in London and then acquired the Eagle Shirts factory to expand capacity. At the time it was making ready-to-wear shirts under the T & A name for upmarket department stores in the United States such as Bergdorf Goodman and Neiman Marcus, and for other brands including Burberry and Hawes & Curtis. Around 1994 they started to produce bespoke shirts, too, using the same method. Kath started with six months developing her skills on 'yoke to back'; six weeks on 'fronts'; a fortnight on sleeves; and then on to collars. Lizzie learned from Kath in the same way, section by section, learning and then working on each section to perfect her techniques over a year-long apprenticeship. On Kath's retirement, Lizzie took over her role as Head of Sewing after six years in the workroom. During her tenure at Emma Willis, Lizzie has made for King Charles III; for Benedict Cumberbatch at the Met Gala's 'Camp: Notes on Fashion'; and for Kenneth Branagh in his role as Hercule Poirot in *Murder on the Orient Express*.

Jacquie Grant is the 'collar hand' – a specialist within the shirt-making workroom who makes collars and cuffs. Jacquie left school in the early eighties and went straight to work at the Turnbull & Asser factory, where her talent for collars was quickly spotted.

Sam Wakely is Head of Cutting and began her shirt-making career in the sewing room before moving to patterns, where she cuts individual bespoke patterns for clients. She is responsible for cutting out the work as part of the workshop's three-person cutting team in the workshop. •

PATRICK GRANT is the co-owner of
Norton & Sons and the co-owner and
Director of Community Clothing.
He won Menswear Designer of the Year
at the 2010 British Fashion Awards and is
best known as a judge on the BBC One
show *The Great British Sewing Bee*.

Exclusive garment patterns
are available to download from
gestalten.com/savilerowpatterns

Regarding measurement: on the whole Savile Row
still works in imperial, but there are occasions
where metric units are also used. Readers will see
a combination of the two in the book.

THE SAVILE ROW SUIT
The Art of Bespoke Tailoring

This book was conceived by Patrick Grant
and gestalten.

Edited by Robert Klanten and Laura Allsop
Contributing Editor: Patrick Grant

Texts by Patrick Grant with support
of Riki Brockman for the manuals
Timeline text by Josh Sims (pp. 140–153)

Illustrations by Oriana Fenwick c/o
kombinatrotweiss.de
Technical Illustrations by Matthew Wood/
matthewwoodillustration.com

Editorial Management by
Anna Diekmann and Lars Pietzschmann

Cover, Layout and Design by Joana Sobral
Typeface: Adobe Caslon Pro by Carol Twombly

Cover illustration by Oriana Fenwick,
based on a photography by Nicholas Andrews,
Maximiliano Braun

Printed by Printer Trento s.r.l., Trento
Made in Europe

Published by gestalten, Berlin 2024
ISBN 978-3-96704-125-5

© Die Gestalten Verlag GmbH & Co. KG,
Berlin 2024

All rights reserved. No part of this publication may
be reproduced or transmitted in any form or by any means,
electronic or mechanical, including photocopy or any
storage and retrieval system, without permission in writing
from the publisher.

Respect copyrights, encourage creativity!

For more information, and to order books, please visit
www.gestalten.com

Bibliographic information published by the Deutsche Nationalbibliothek. The Deutsche Nationalbibliothek lists this
publication in the Deutsche Nationalbibliografie; detailed
bibliographic data is available online at www.dnb.de

None of the content in this book was published in exchange
for payment by commercial parties or designers; gestalten
selected all included work based solely on its artistic merit.